Disney

P9-CEJ-924

# KINGDOM HEARTS

**3**

Adapted by
## Shiro Amano

**TOKYOPOP**®

HAMBURG // LONDON // LOS ANGELES // TOKYO

### Kingdom Hearts Vol. 3
### Adapted by
### Shiro Amano

Associate Editor - Peter Ahlstrom
Retouch and Lettering - Jose Macasocol, Jr.
Production Artist - Fawn Lau
Cover Layout - Gary Shum


Editor - Zachary Rau
Digital Imaging Manager - Chris Buford
Production Manager - Jennifer Miller
Managing Editor - Lindsey Johnston
VP of Production - Ron Klamert
Publisher and E.I.C. - Mike Kiley
President and C.O.O. - John Parker
Chief Creative Officer and C.E.O. - Stuart Levy

A  Manga

TOKYOPOP Inc.
5900 Wilshire Blvd. Suite 2000
Los Angeles, CA 90036

E-mail: info@TOKYOPOP.com
Come visit us online at www.TOKYOPOP.com

ISBN: 1-59816-219-5

First TOKYOPOP printing: April 2006
10 9 8 7 6 5 4
Printed in the USA

DISNEY SQUARESOFT

KINGDOM HEARTS

# Our Story So Far...

After being swept away from his island home and his friends Kairi and Riku, Sora finds himself lost in a mysterious new land. Soon, he meets Court Wizard Donald and Captain Goofy, who are desperately trying to find their missing King. Now the trio must travel from world to world, find the keyhole to each planet's Heart and lock it with the magical Keyblade. Only this will be stop the Heartless from consuming every world in Darkness. Having already defeated Jafar in Agrabah and trained with the Satyr Phil on Olympus, the companions are ready to face the Heartless head-on, but someone from Sora's past threatens to stand in their way...

# KINGDOM HEARTS: VOLUME 3
## TABLE OF CONTENTS

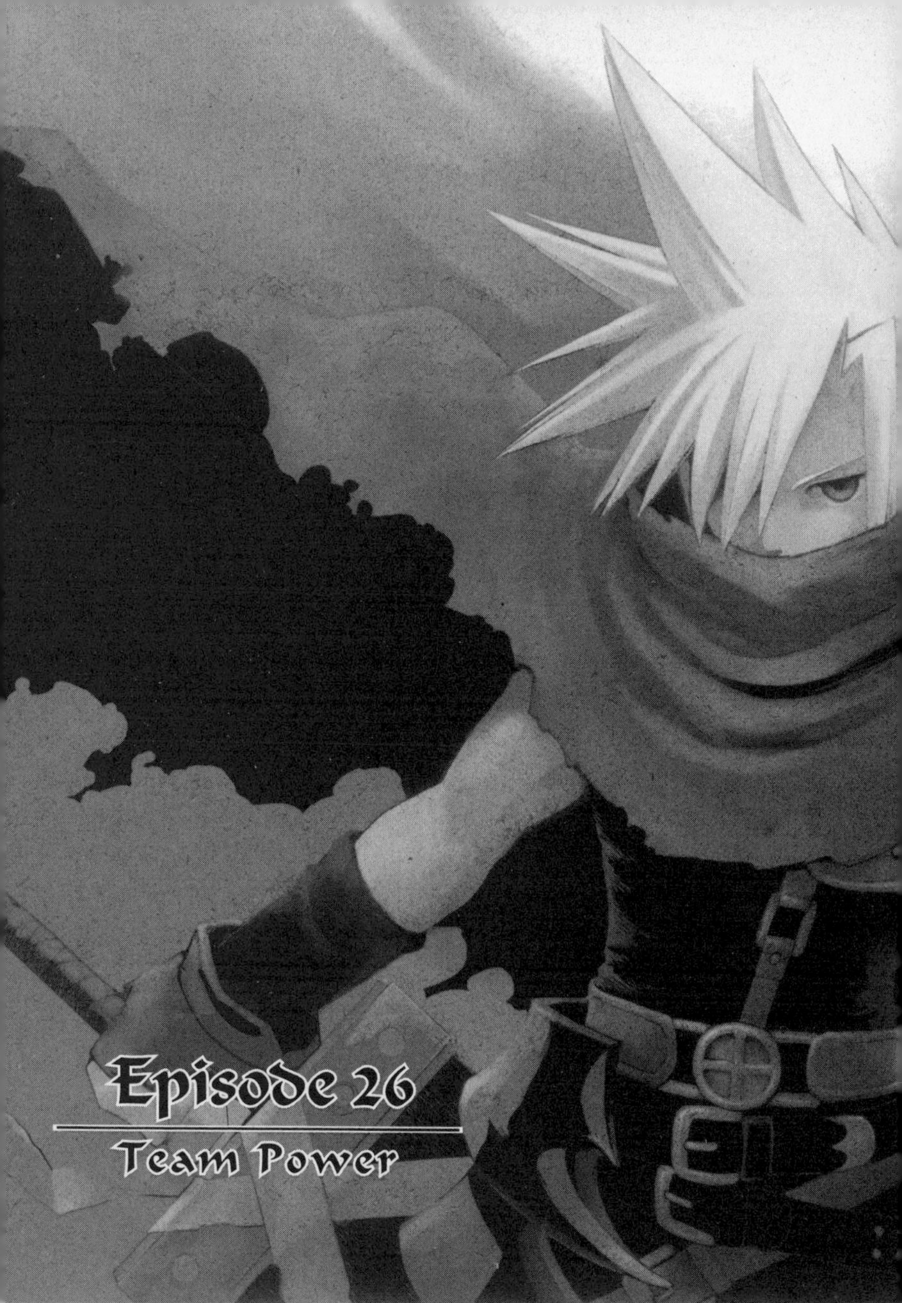

# Episode 26

## Team Power

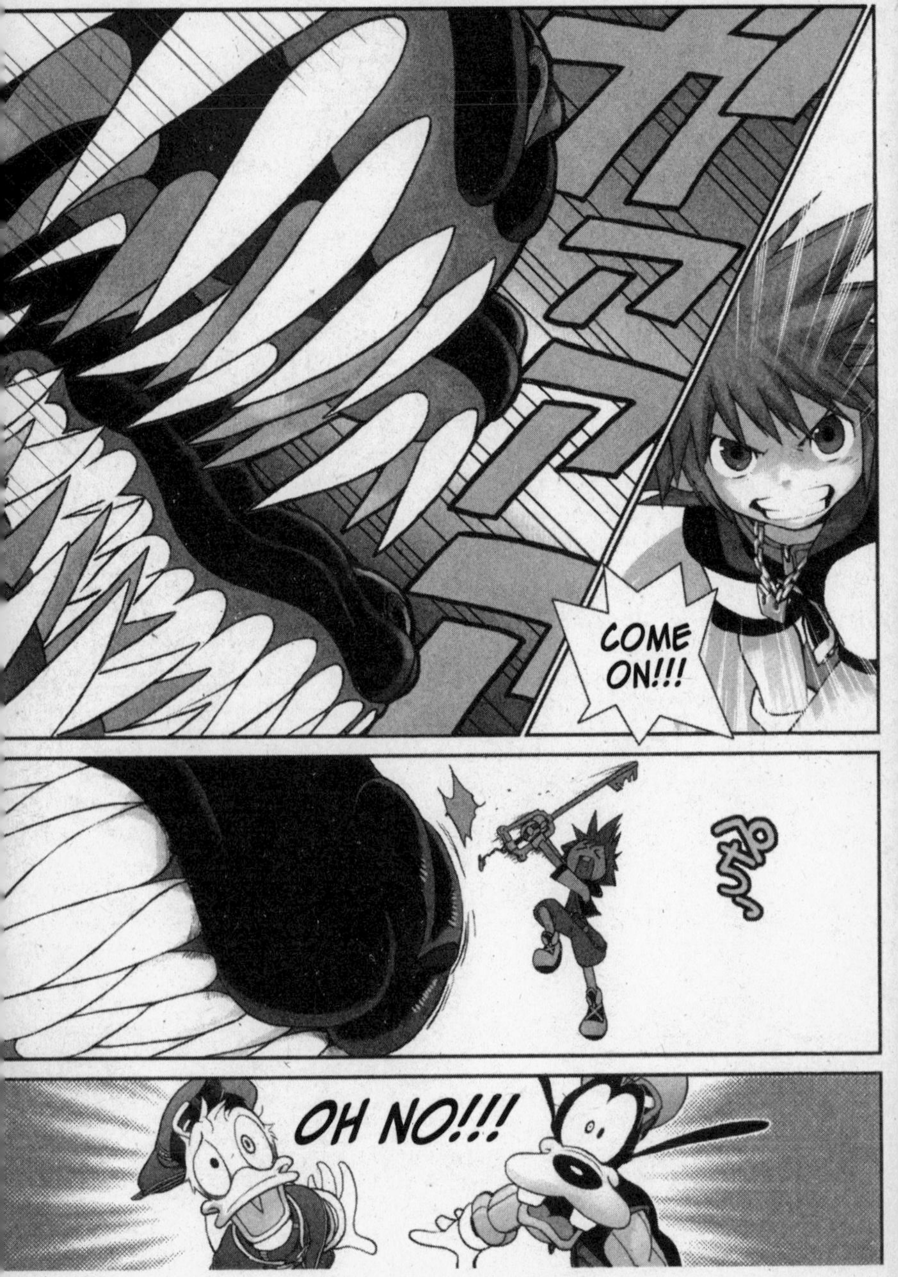
COME ON!!!
OH NO!!!

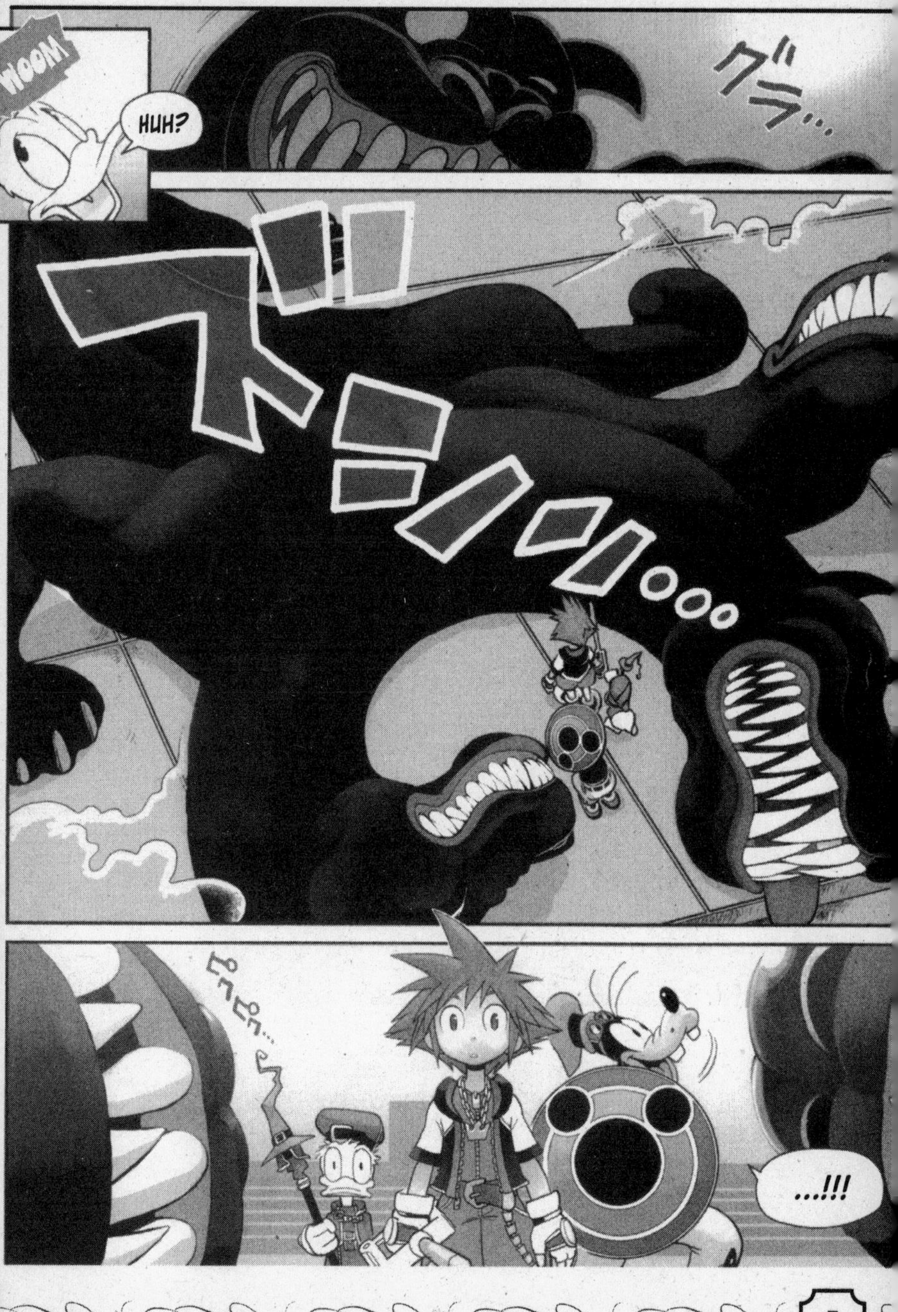
WOOM
HUH?
グラ…
ピクピク…
…!!!

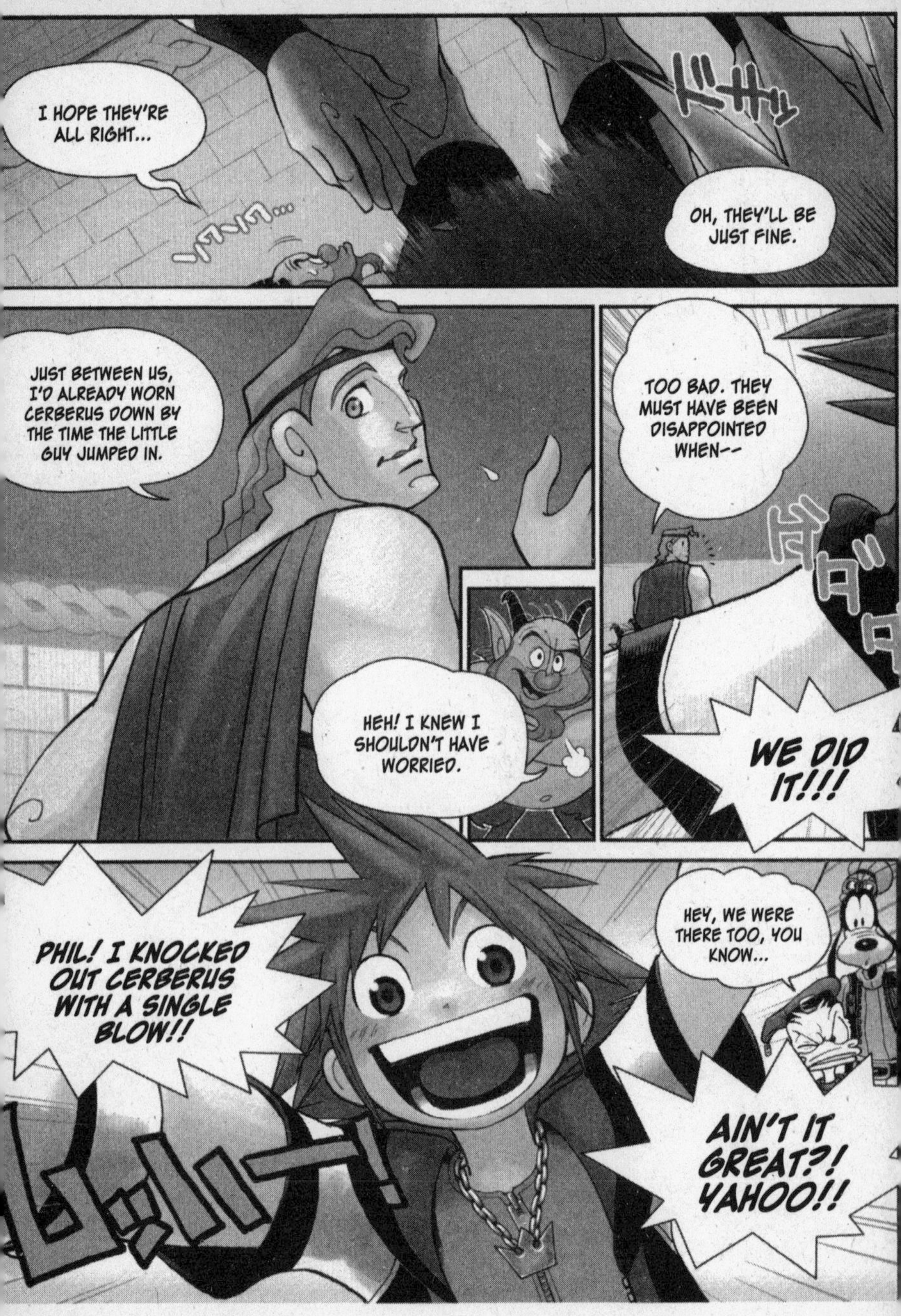
I HOPE THEY'RE ALL RIGHT...
OH, THEY'LL BE JUST FINE.
JUST BETWEEN US, I'D ALREADY WORN CERBERUS DOWN BY THE TIME THE LITTLE GUY JUMPED IN.
HEH! I KNEW I SHOULDN'T HAVE WORRIED.
TOO BAD. THEY MUST HAVE BEEN DISAPPOINTED WHEN--
WE DID IT!!!
PHIL! I KNOCKED OUT CERBERUS WITH A SINGLE BLOW!!
HEY, WE WERE THERE TOO, YOU KNOW...
AIN'T IT GREAT?! YAHOO!!

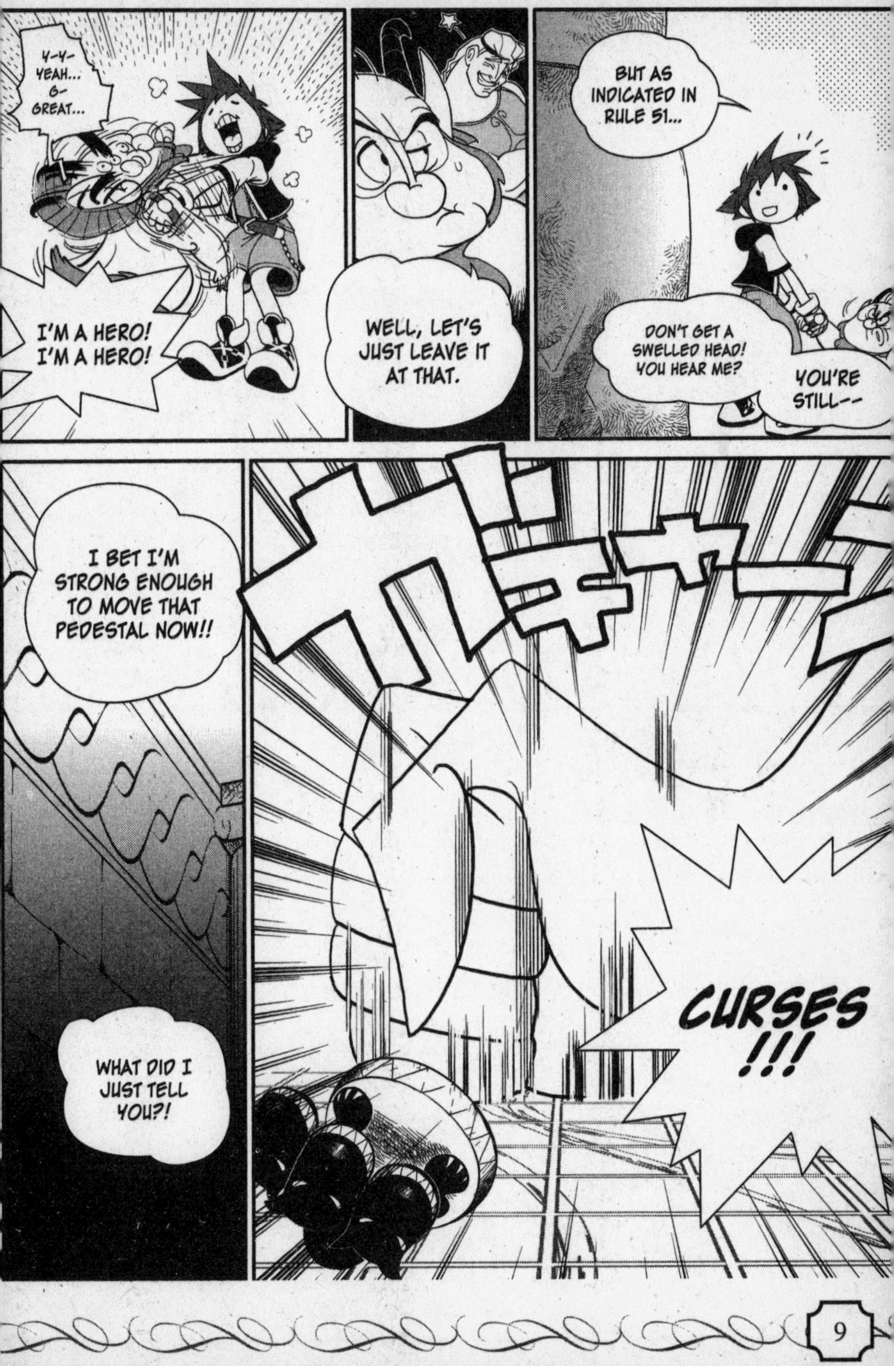
Y-Y-YEAH... G-GREAT...
I'M A HERO! I'M A HERO!
WELL, LET'S JUST LEAVE IT AT THAT.
BUT AS INDICATED IN RULE 51...
DON'T GET A SWELLED HEAD! YOU HEAR ME?
YOU'RE STILL--
I BET I'M STRONG ENOUGH TO MOVE THAT PEDESTAL NOW!!
WHAT DID I JUST TELL YOU?!
CURSES !!!

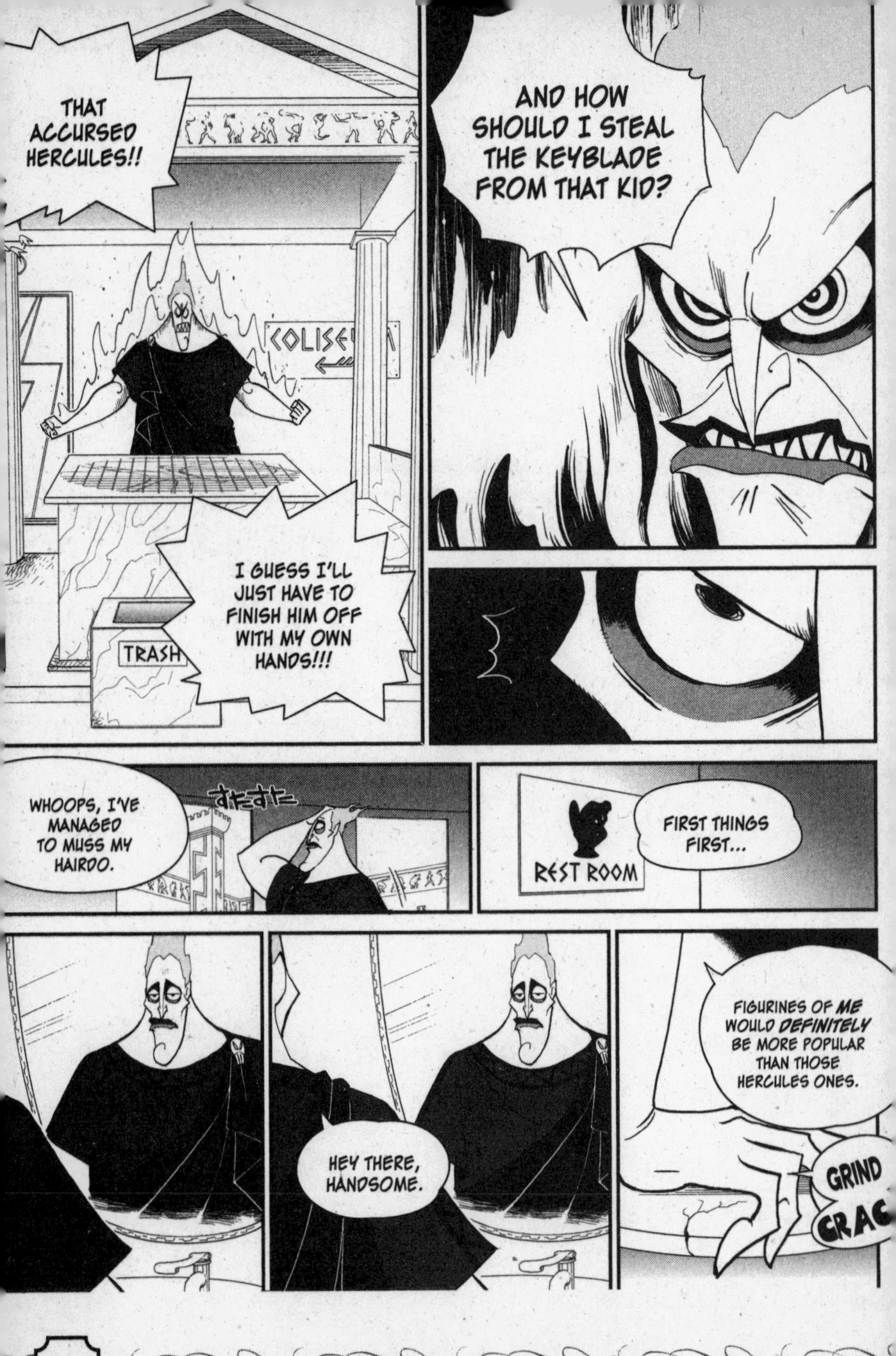
THAT ACCURSED HERCULES!!
COLISEUM
TRASH
I GUESS I'LL JUST HAVE TO FINISH HIM OFF WITH MY OWN HANDS!!!
AND HOW SHOULD I STEAL THE KEYBLADE FROM THAT KID?
WHOOPS, I'VE MANAGED TO MUSS MY HAIRDO.
すたすた
REST ROOM
FIRST THINGS FIRST...
HEY THERE, HANDSOME.
FIGURINES OF *ME* WOULD *DEFINITELY* BE MORE POPULAR THAN THOSE HERCULES ONES.
GRIND
CRAC

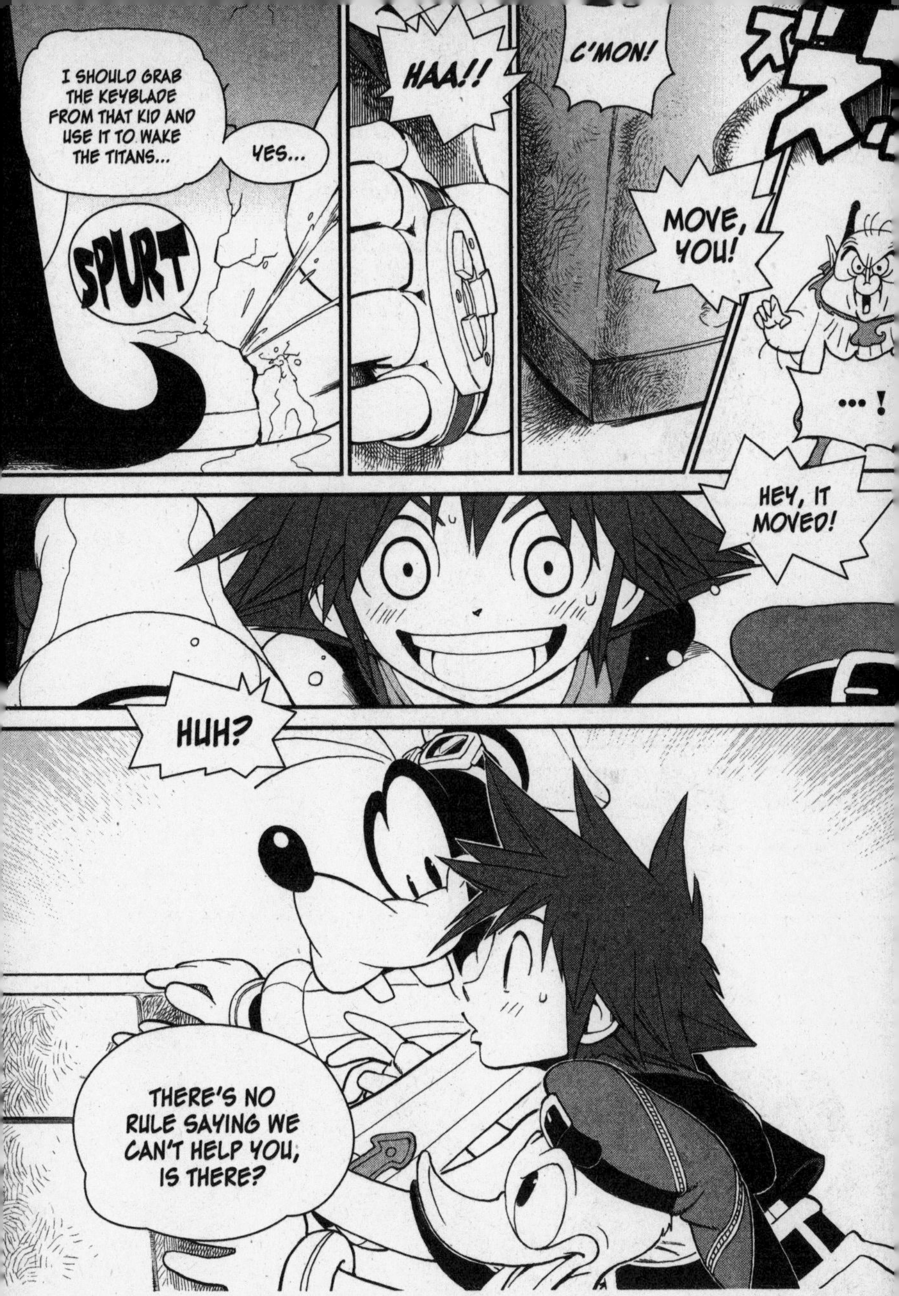
I SHOULD GRAB THE KEYBLADE FROM THAT KID AND USE IT TO WAKE THE TITANS...
YES...
SPURT
HAA!!
C'MON!
MOVE, YOU!
...!
HEY, IT MOVED!
HUH?
THERE'S NO RULE SAYING WE CAN'T HELP YOU, IS THERE?

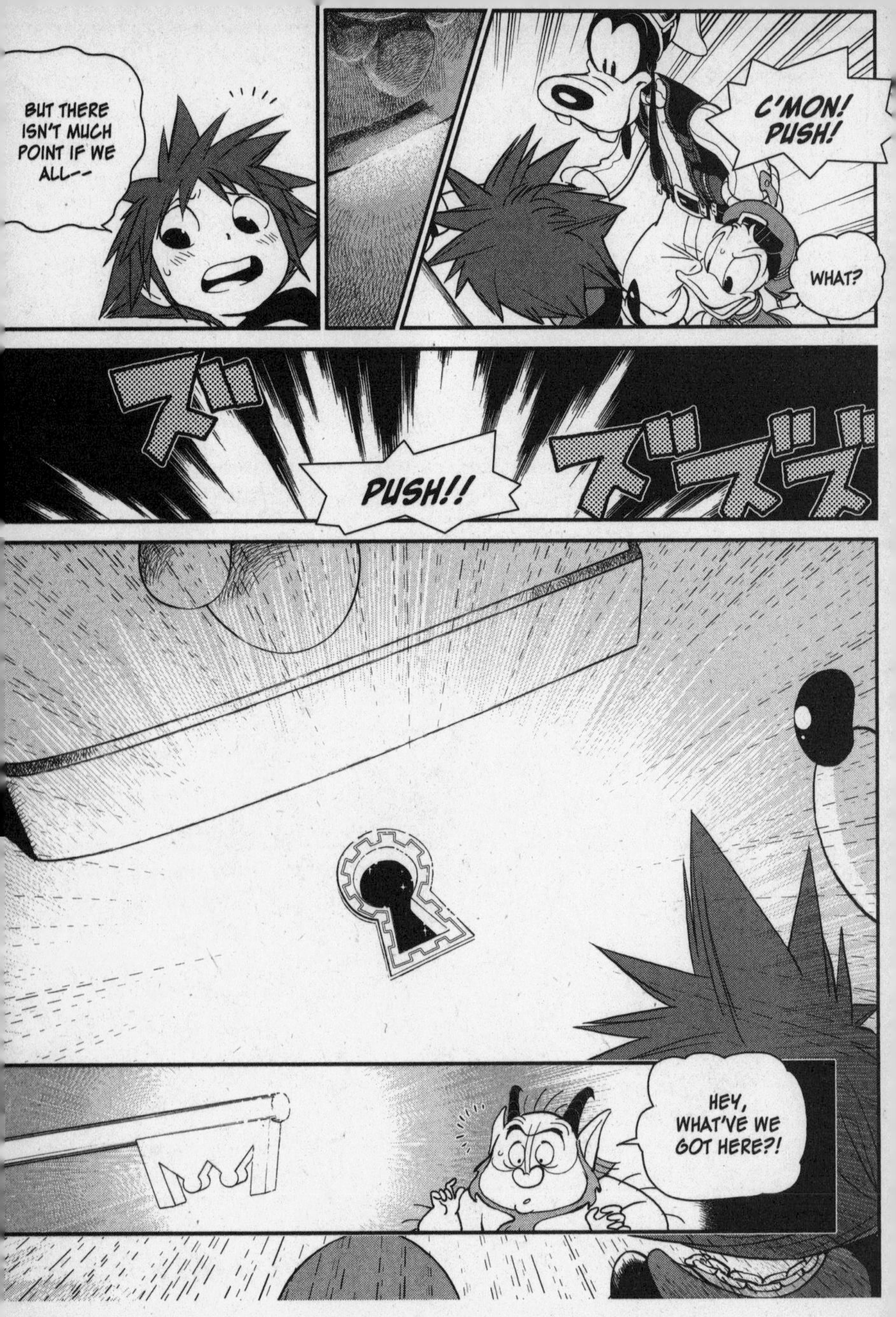
BUT THERE ISN'T MUCH POINT IF WE ALL--
C'MON! PUSH!
WHAT?
ズ
PUSH!!
ズズズ
HEY, WHAT'VE WE GOT HERE?!

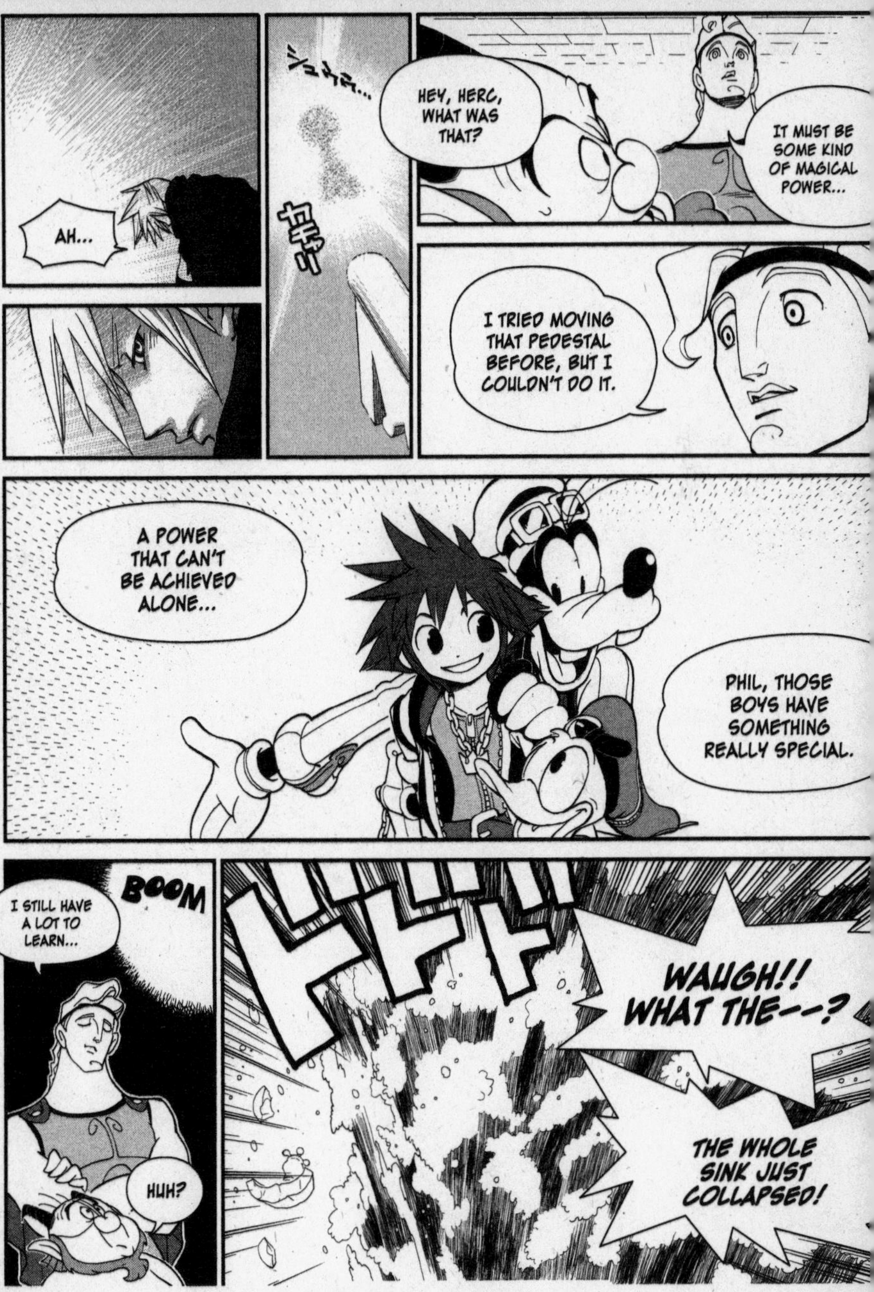
AH...
シュウウ...
カチャッ
HEY, HERC, WHAT WAS THAT?
IT MUST BE SOME KIND OF MAGICAL POWER...
I TRIED MOVING THAT PEDESTAL BEFORE, BUT I COULDN'T DO IT.
A POWER THAT CAN'T BE ACHIEVED ALONE...
PHIL, THOSE BOYS HAVE SOMETHING REALLY SPECIAL.
I STILL HAVE A LOT TO LEARN...
BOOM
HUH?
WAUGH!! WHAT THE--?
THE WHOLE SINK JUST COLLAPSED!

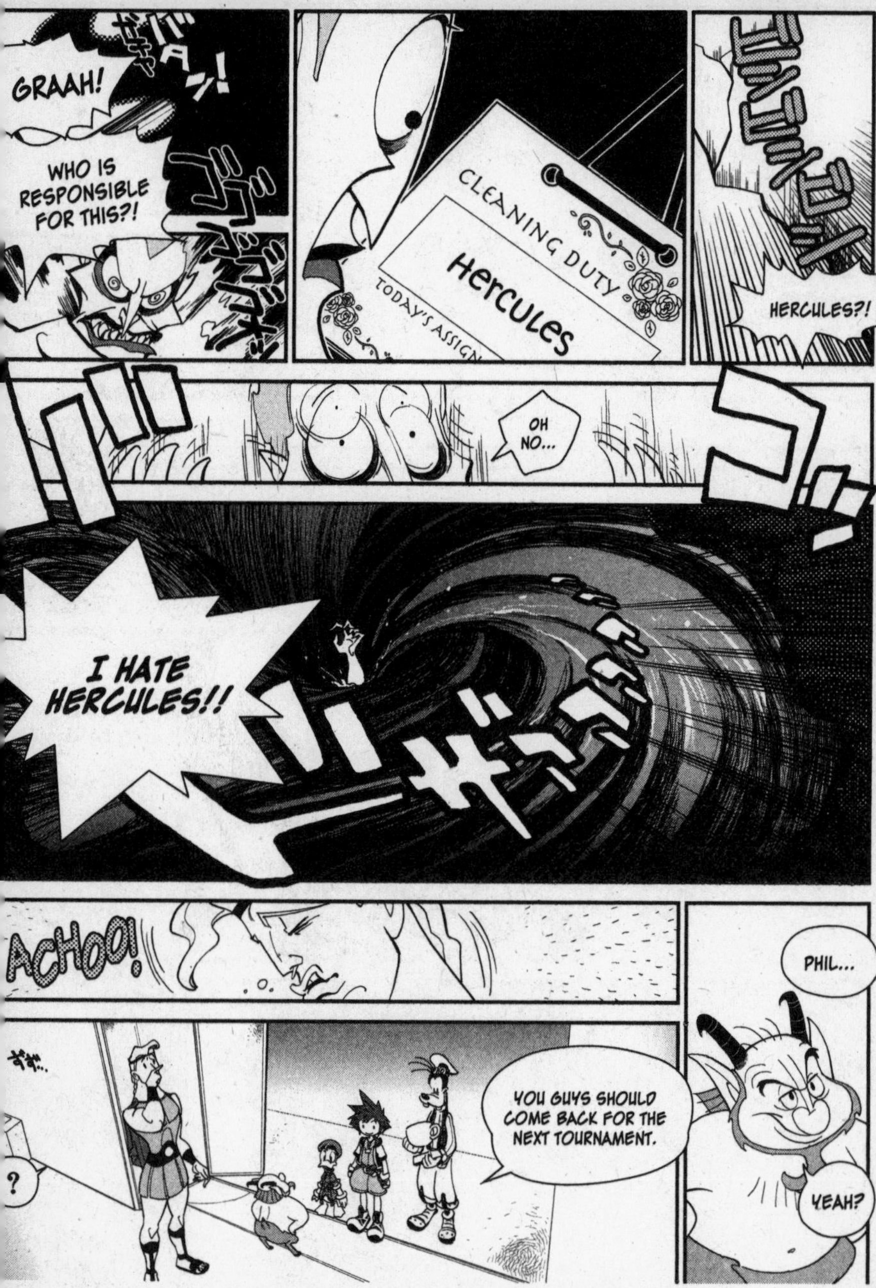
GRAAH!
WHO IS RESPONSIBLE FOR THIS?!
CLEANING DUTY
Hercules
TODAY'S ASSIGN
HERCULES?!
OH NO...
I HATE HERCULES!!
ACHOO!
PHIL...
?
YOU GUYS SHOULD COME BACK FOR THE NEXT TOURNAMENT.
YEAH?

NEXT TIME YOU SEE US, YOU'LL BE CALLING EVERY ONE OF US A HERO!

LOOKING FORWARD TO IT!

HEY...

HERE'S A FAREWELL GIFT.

......

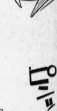

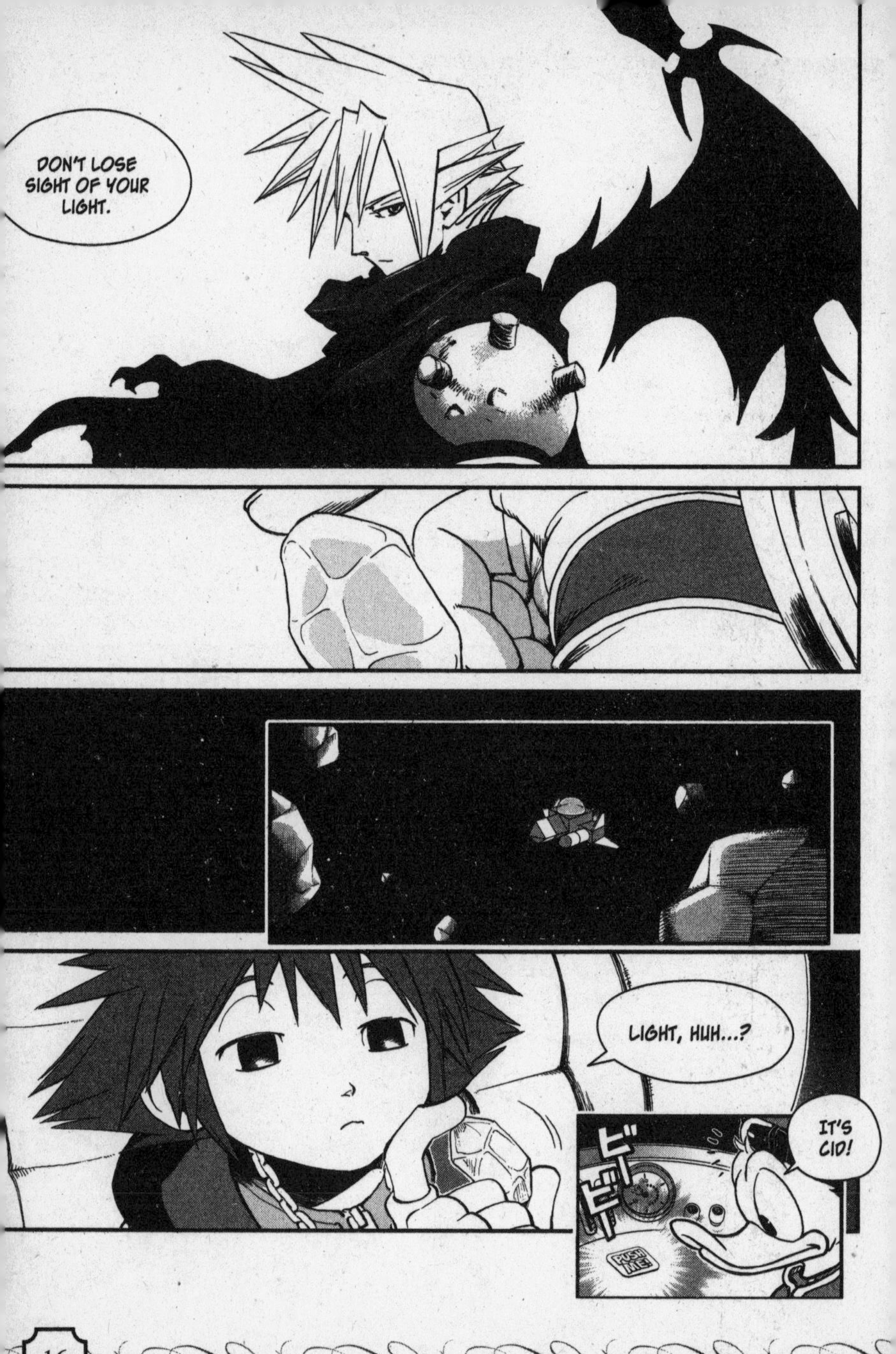
DON'T LOSE SIGHT OF YOUR LIGHT.
LIGHT, HUH...?
ビー ビー
IT'S CID!
PUSH ME!

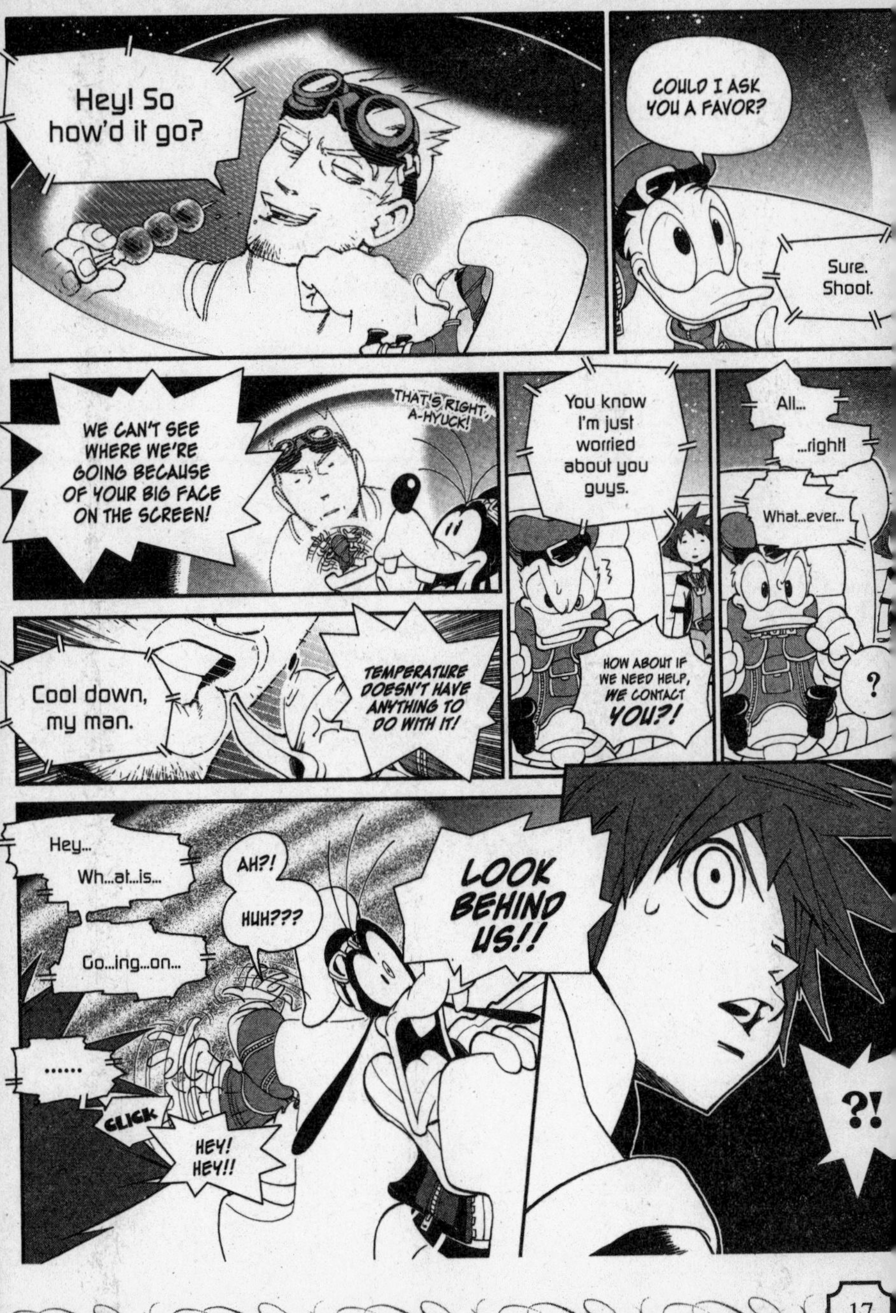
Hey! So how'd it go?
COULD I ASK YOU A FAVOR?
Sure. Shoot.
WE CAN'T SEE WHERE WE'RE GOING BECAUSE OF YOUR BIG FACE ON THE SCREEN!
THAT'S RIGHT, A-HYUCK!
You know I'm just worried about you guys.
All...
...right!
What...ever...
Cool down, my man.
TEMPERATURE DOESN'T HAVE ANYTHING TO DO WITH IT!
HOW ABOUT IF WE NEED HELP, WE CONTACT YOU?!
?
Hey...
Wh...at...is...
Go...ing...on...
......
CLICK
HEY! HEY!!
AH?!
HUH???
LOOK BEHIND US!!
?!

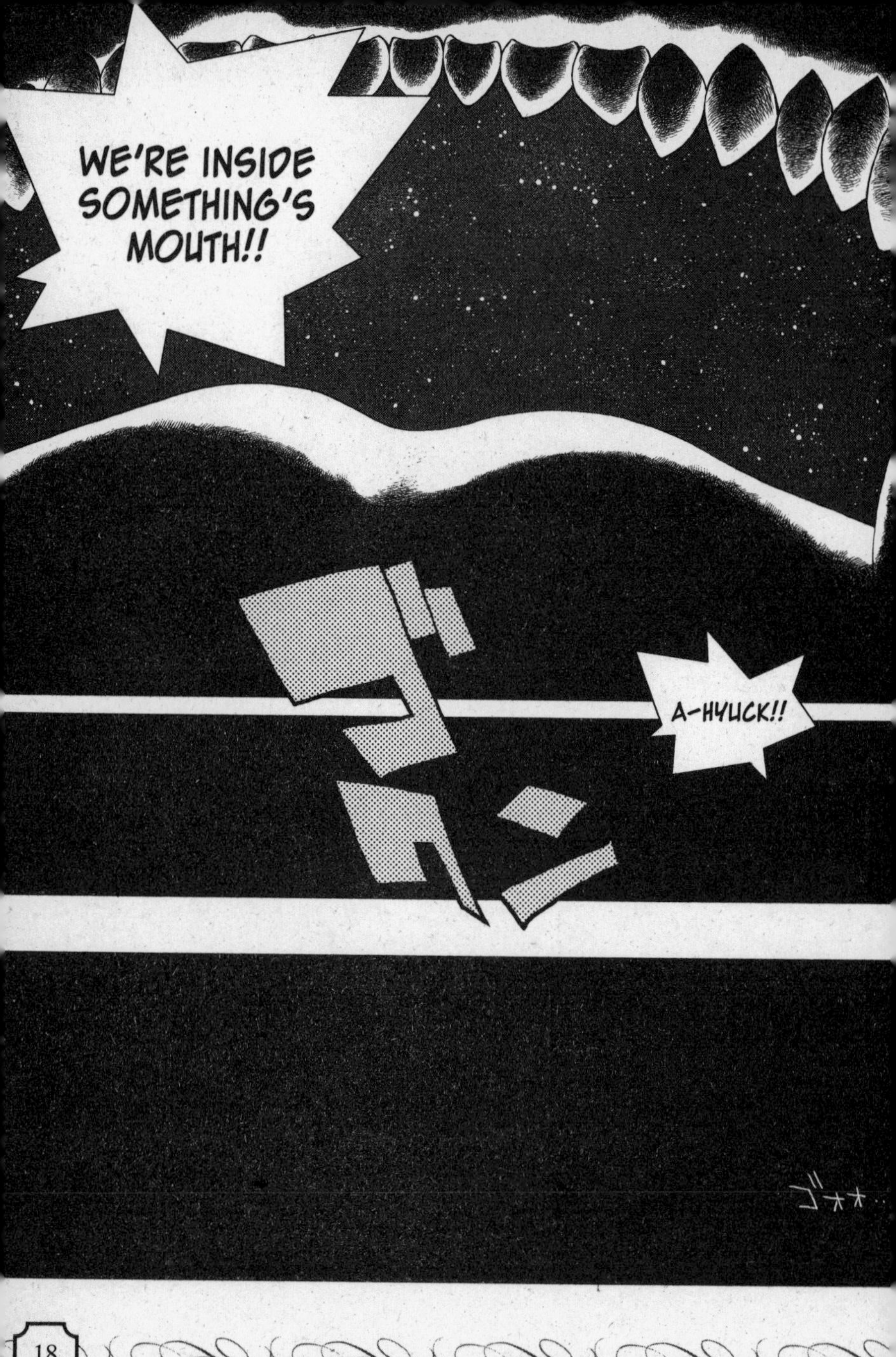
WE'RE INSIDE SOMETHING'S MOUTH!!
A-HYUCK!!

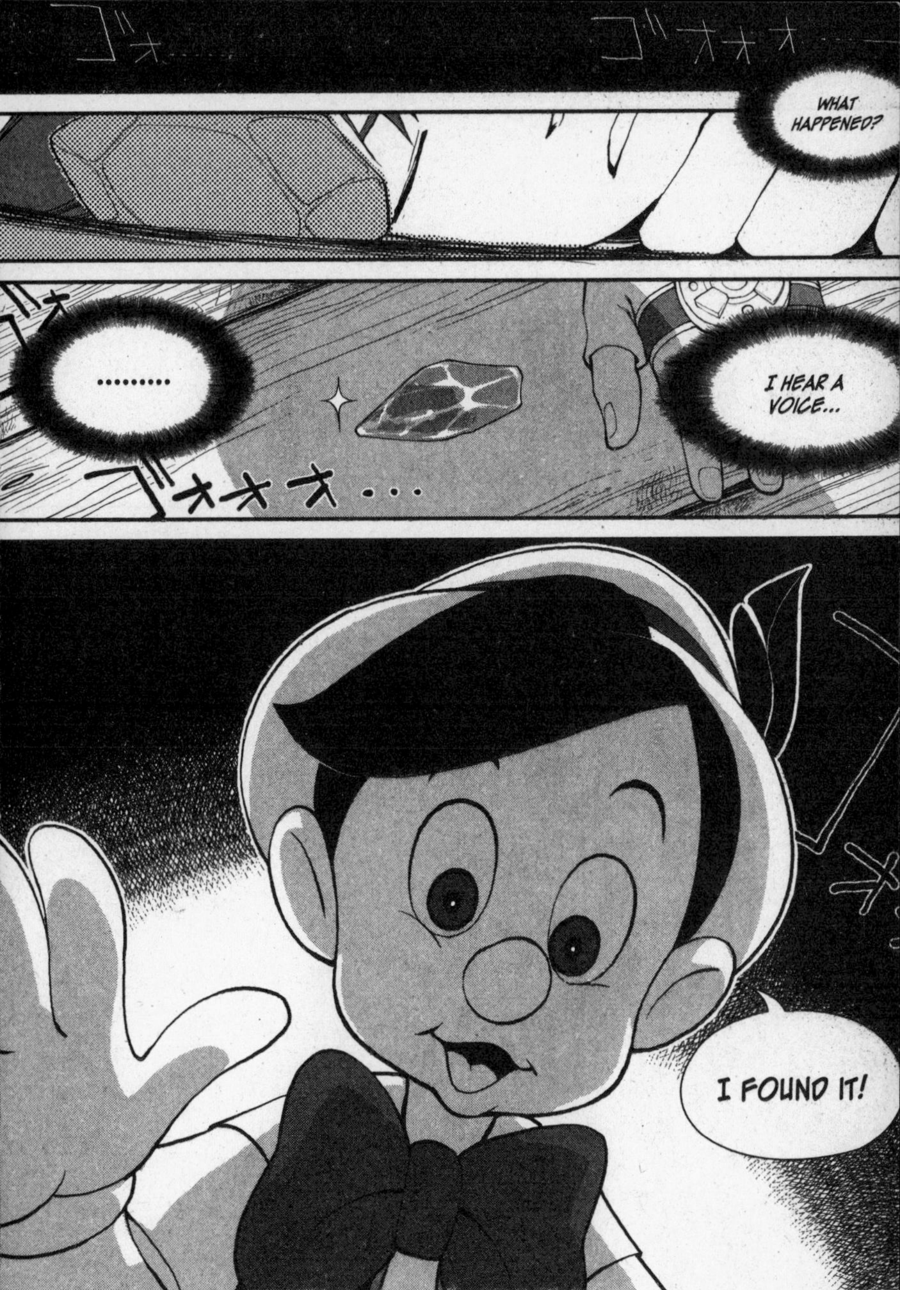
ゴオ……
ゴオオオ
WHAT HAPPENED?
I HEAR A VOICE...
.........
ゴオオオ…
I FOUND IT!

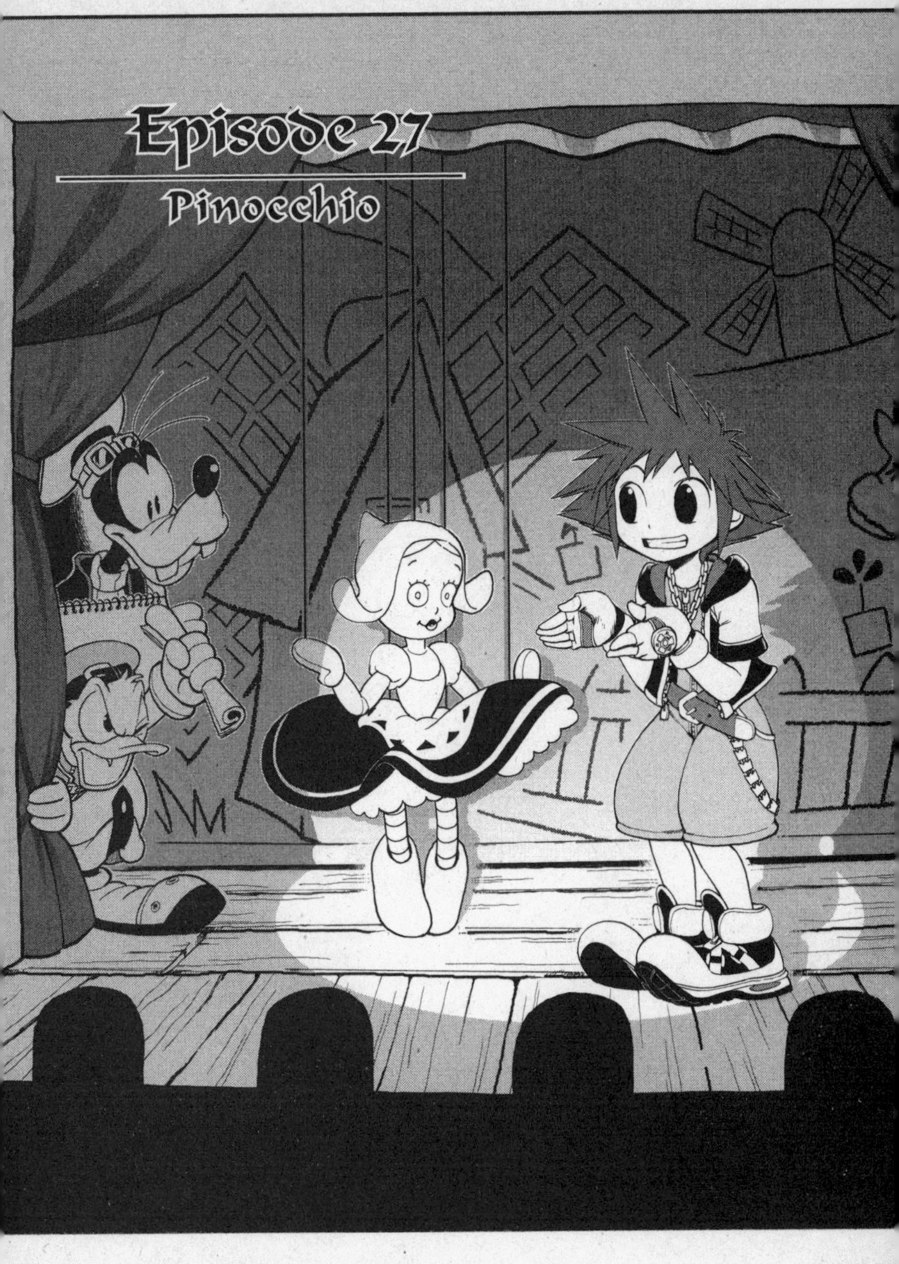
Episode 27
Pinocchio

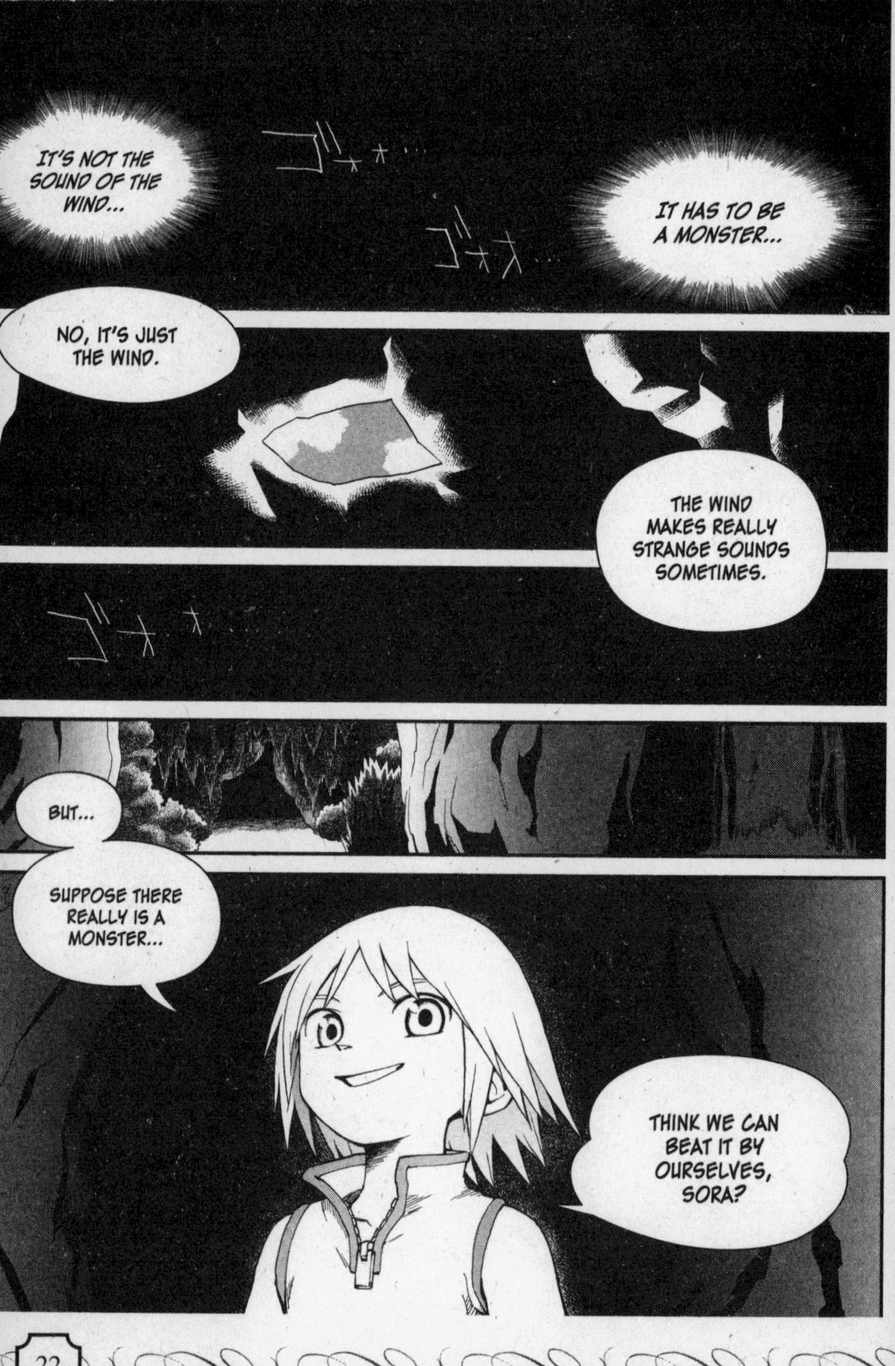
IT'S NOT THE SOUND OF THE WIND...
IT HAS TO BE A MONSTER...
NO, IT'S JUST THE WIND.
THE WIND MAKES REALLY STRANGE SOUNDS SOMETIMES.
BUT...
SUPPOSE THERE REALLY IS A MONSTER...
THINK WE CAN BEAT IT BY OURSELVES, SORA?

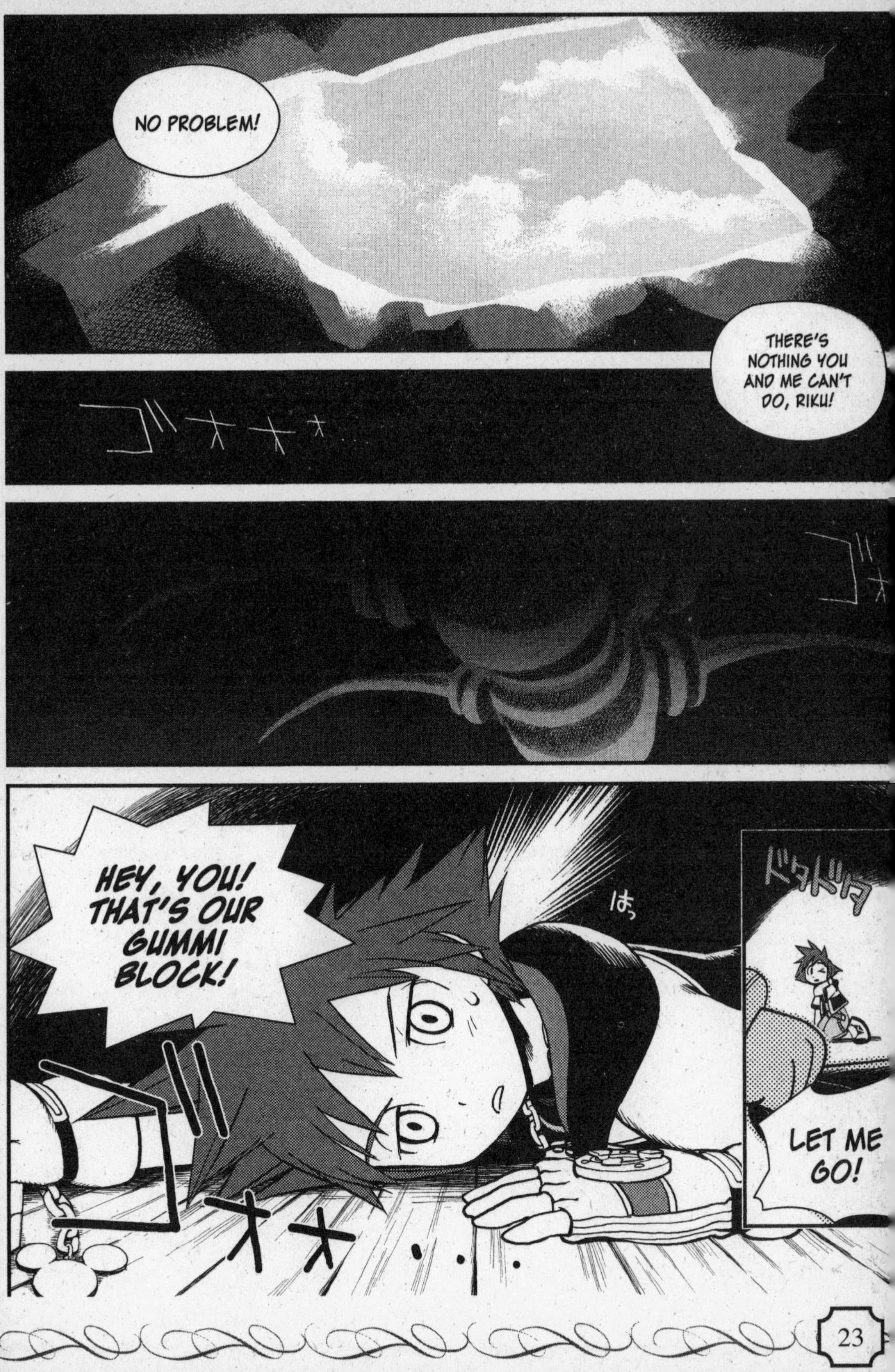
NO PROBLEM!
THERE'S NOTHING YOU AND ME CAN'T DO, RIKU!
ゴオオォ…
ゴオ
HEY, YOU! THAT'S OUR GUMMI BLOCK!
はっ
オオ…
ドタドタ
LET ME GO!

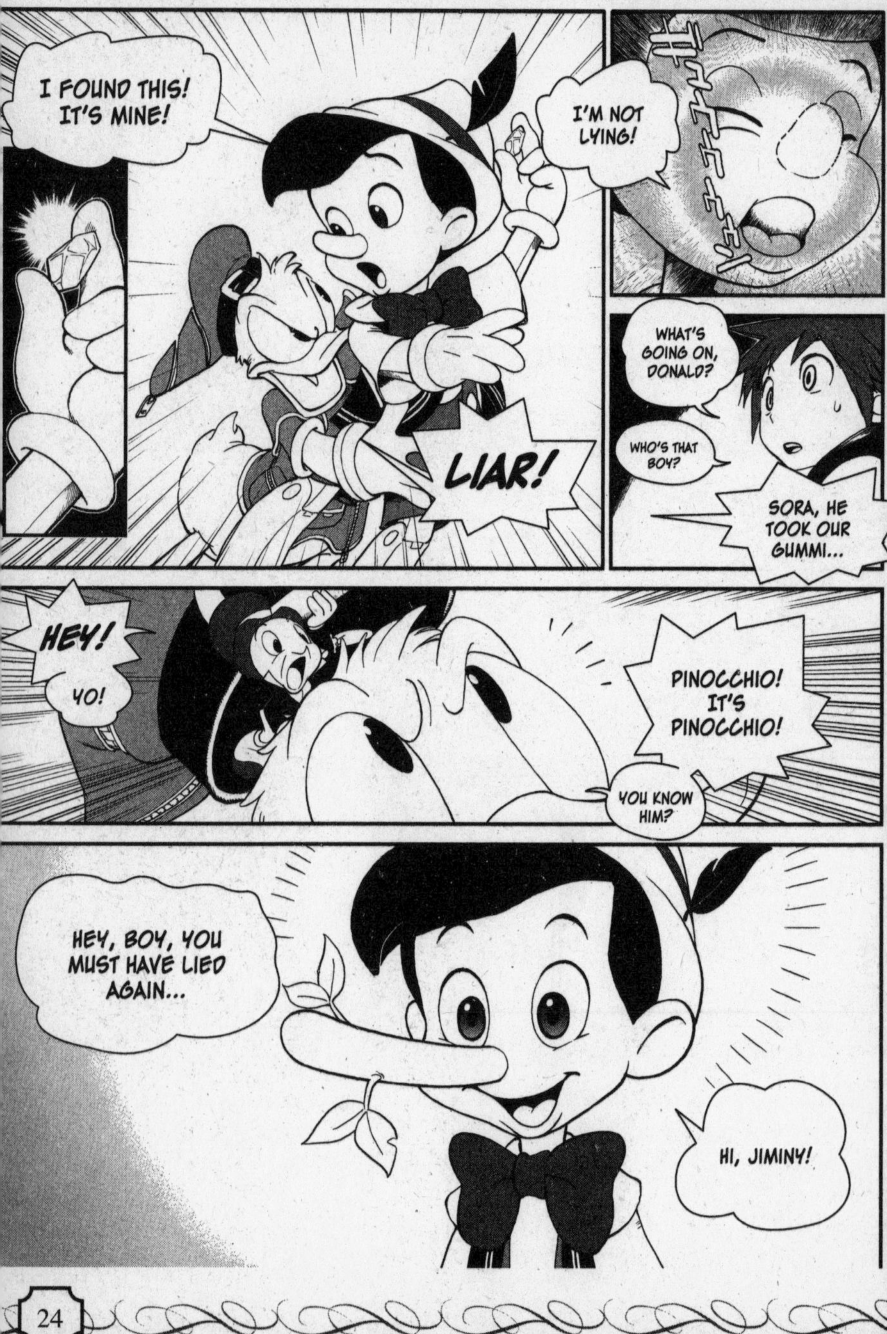

I FOUND THIS! IT'S MINE!
I'M NOT LYING!
LIAR!
WHAT'S GOING ON, DONALD?
WHO'S THAT BOY?
SORA, HE TOOK OUR GUMMI...
HEY!
YO!
PINOCCHIO! IT'S PINOCCHIO!
YOU KNOW HIM?
HEY, BOY, YOU MUST HAVE LIED AGAIN...
HI, JIMINY!

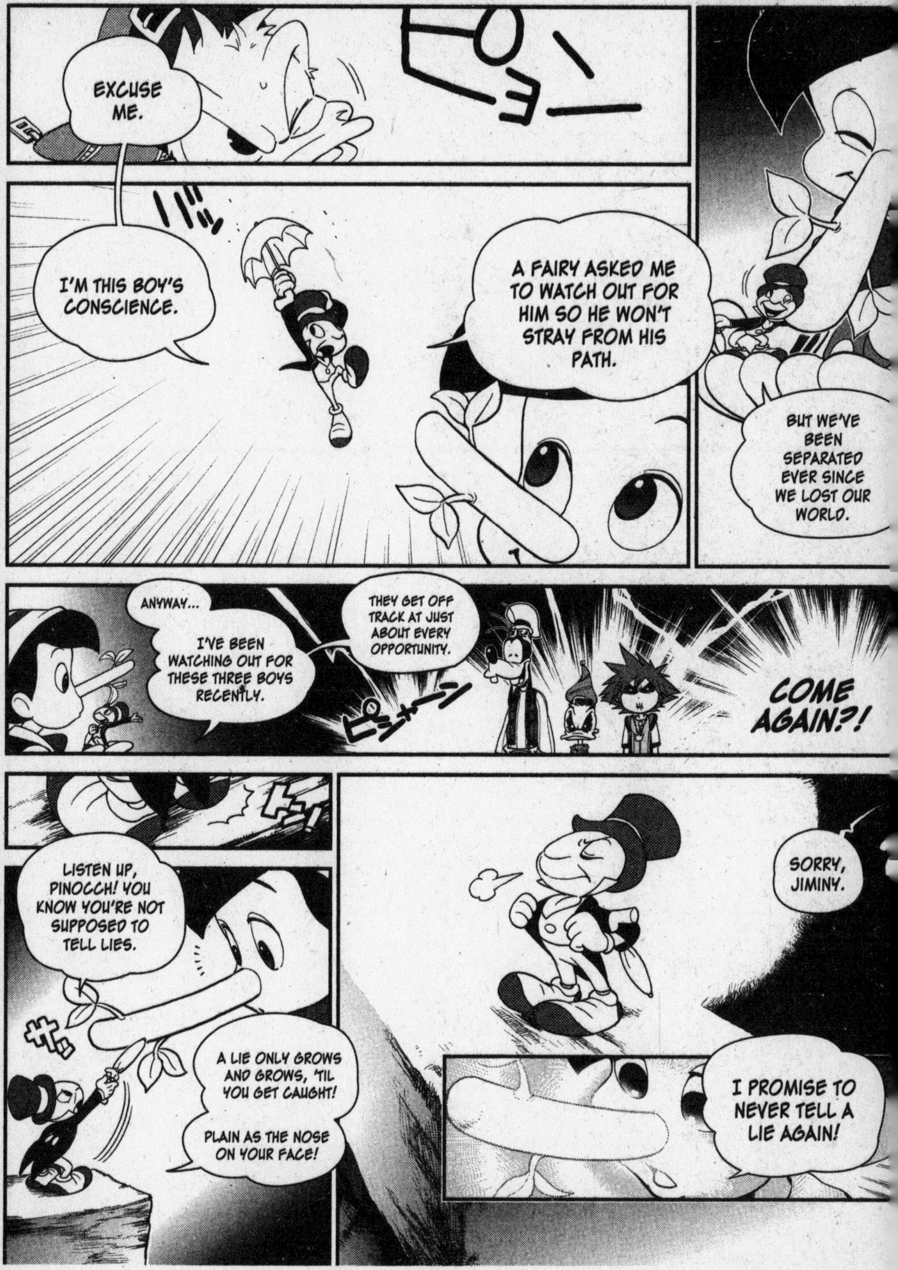
EXCUSE ME.
I'M THIS BOY'S CONSCIENCE.
A FAIRY ASKED ME TO WATCH OUT FOR HIM SO HE WON'T STRAY FROM HIS PATH.
BUT WE'VE BEEN SEPARATED EVER SINCE WE LOST OUR WORLD.
ANYWAY...
I'VE BEEN WATCHING OUT FOR THESE THREE BOYS RECENTLY.
THEY GET OFF TRACK AT JUST ABOUT EVERY OPPORTUNITY.
COME AGAIN?!
LISTEN UP, PINOCCH! YOU KNOW YOU'RE NOT SUPPOSED TO TELL LIES.
A LIE ONLY GROWS AND GROWS, 'TIL YOU GET CAUGHT!
PLAIN AS THE NOSE ON YOUR FACE!
SORRY, JIMINY.
I PROMISE TO NEVER TELL A LIE AGAIN!

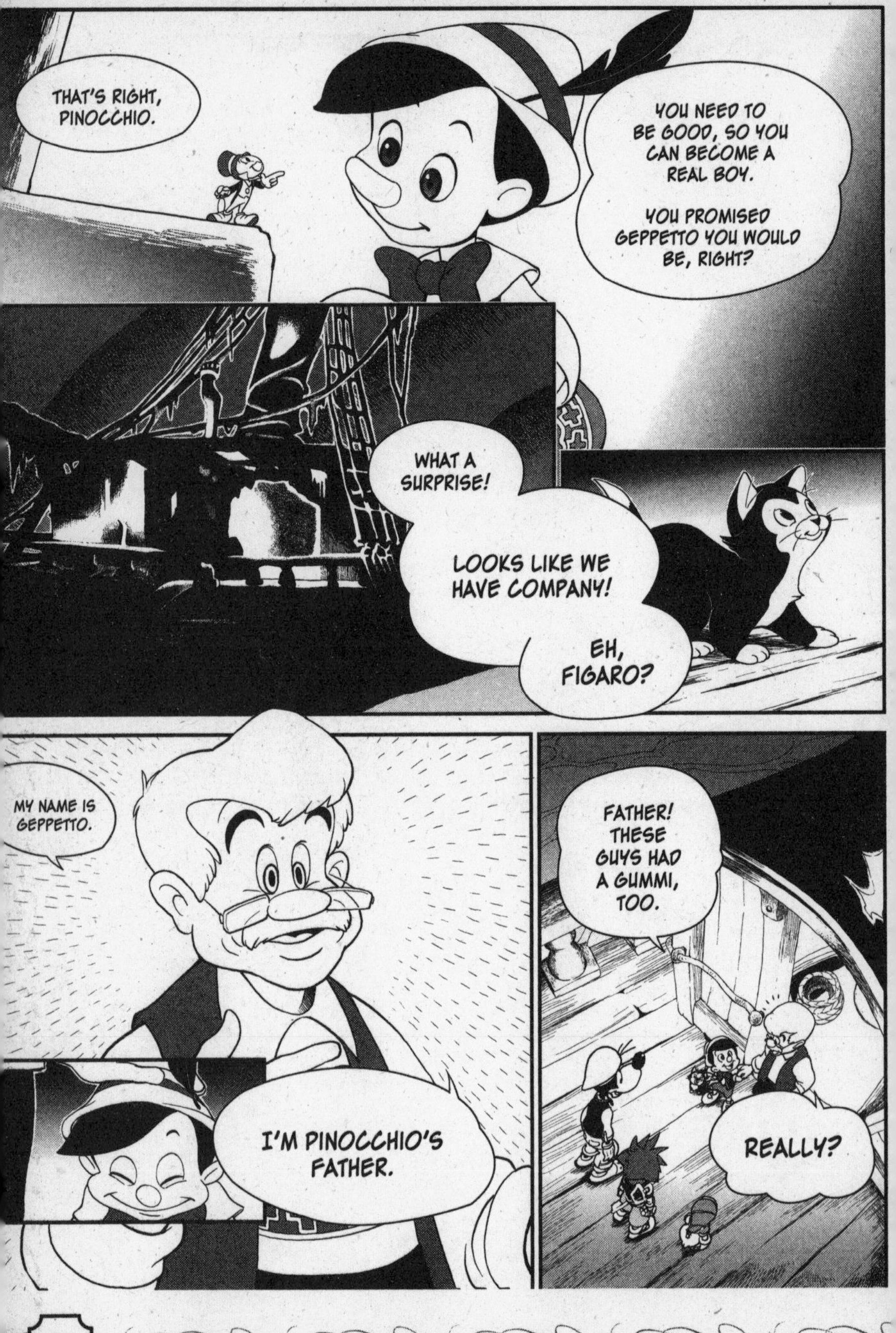
THAT'S RIGHT, PINOCCHIO.
YOU NEED TO BE GOOD, SO YOU CAN BECOME A REAL BOY.
YOU PROMISED GEPPETTO YOU WOULD BE, RIGHT?
WHAT A SURPRISE!
LOOKS LIKE WE HAVE COMPANY!
EH, FIGARO?
MY NAME IS GEPPETTO.
I'M PINOCCHIO'S FATHER.
FATHER! THESE GUYS HAD A GUMMI, TOO.
REALLY?

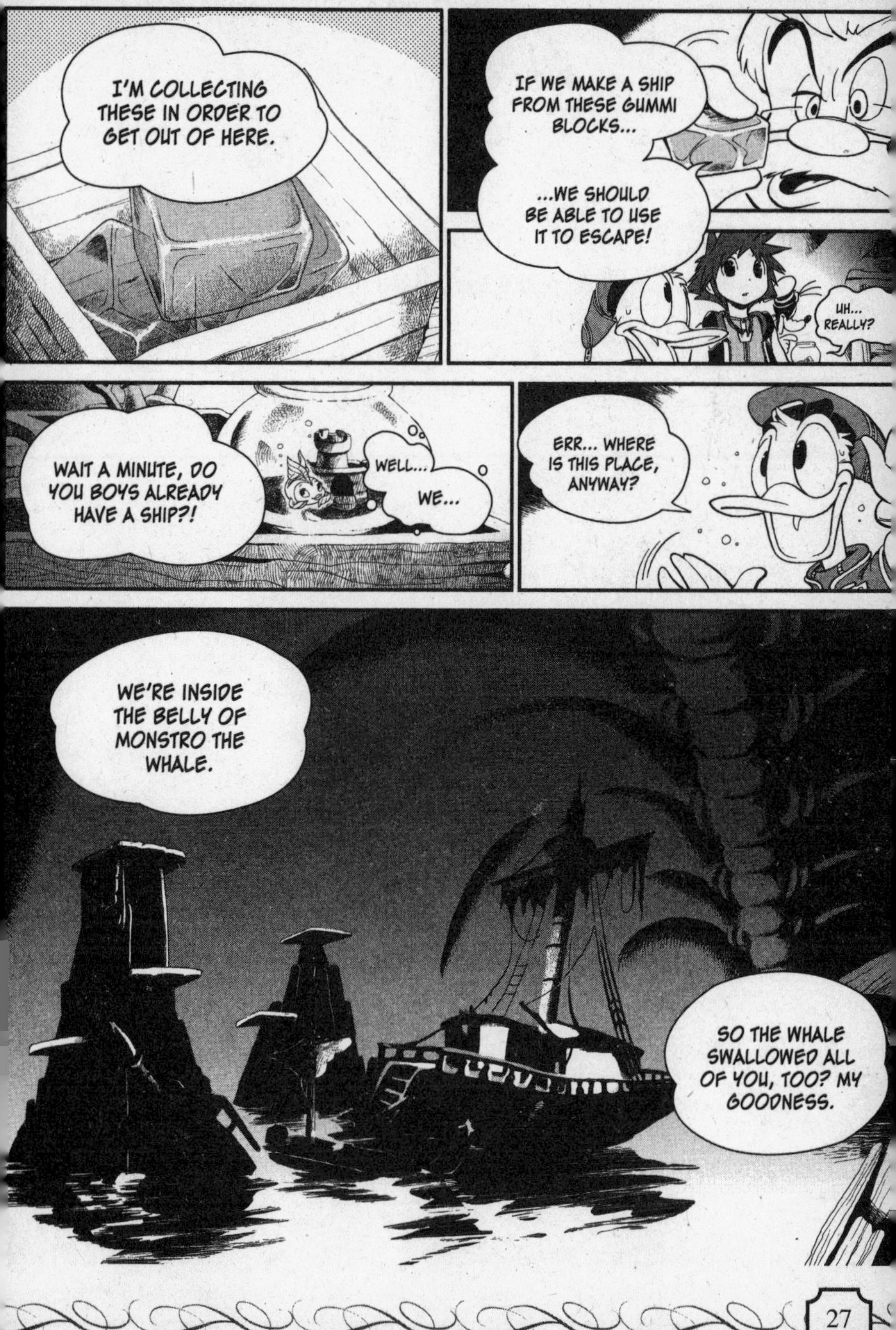
I'M COLLECTING THESE IN ORDER TO GET OUT OF HERE.
IF WE MAKE A SHIP FROM THESE GUMMI BLOCKS...
...WE SHOULD BE ABLE TO USE IT TO ESCAPE!
UH... REALLY?
WAIT A MINUTE, DO YOU BOYS ALREADY HAVE A SHIP?!
WELL...
WE...
ERR... WHERE IS THIS PLACE, ANYWAY?
WE'RE INSIDE THE BELLY OF MONSTRO THE WHALE.
SO THE WHALE SWALLOWED ALL OF YOU, TOO? MY GOODNESS.

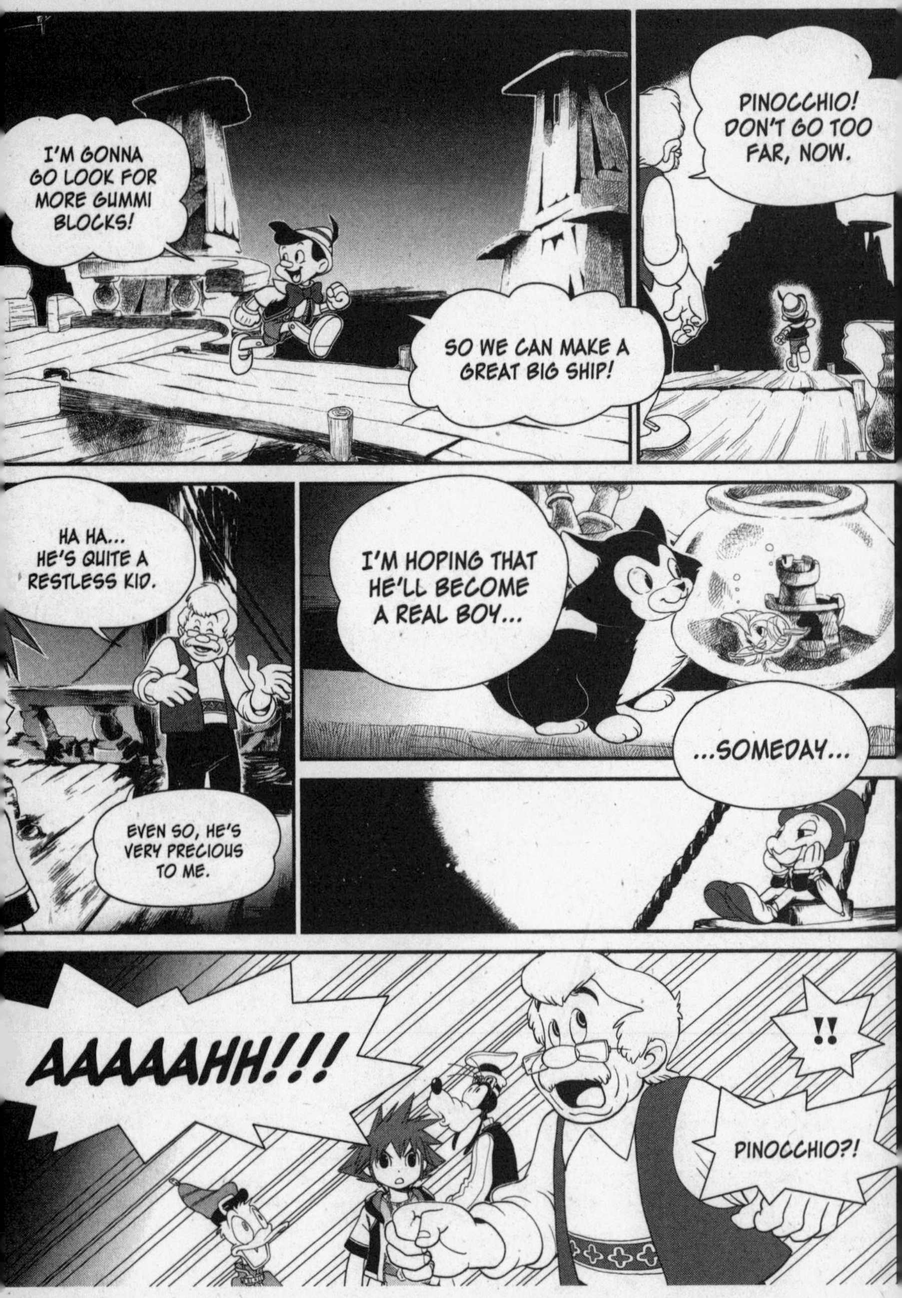
I'M GONNA GO LOOK FOR MORE GUMMI BLOCKS!
SO WE CAN MAKE A GREAT BIG SHIP!
PINOCCHIO! DON'T GO TOO FAR, NOW.
HA HA... HE'S QUITE A RESTLESS KID.
EVEN SO, HE'S VERY PRECIOUS TO ME.
I'M HOPING THAT HE'LL BECOME A REAL BOY...
...SOMEDAY...
AAAAAHH!!!
!!
PINOCCHIO?!

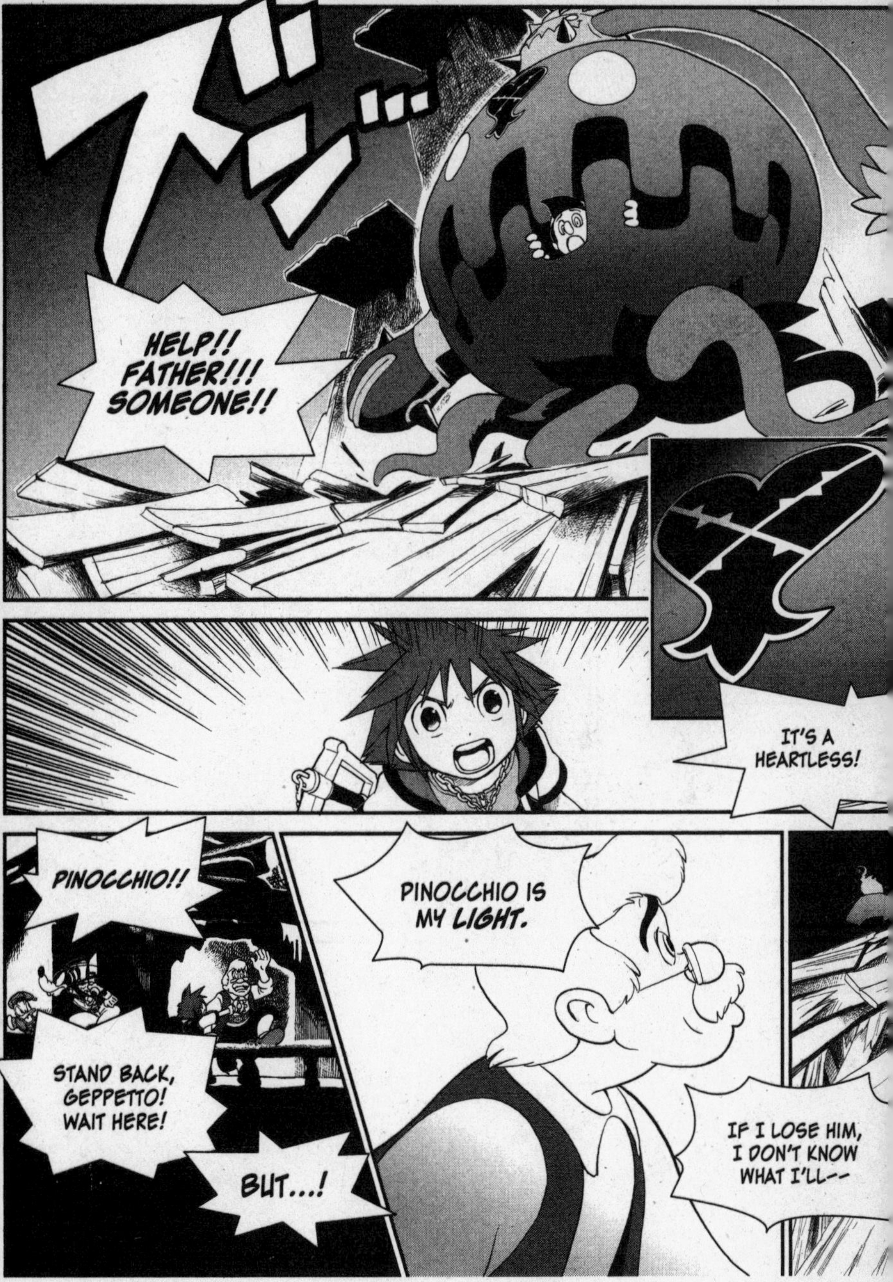
ズ...
HELP!! FATHER!!! SOMEONE!!
IT'S A HEARTLESS!
PINOCCHIO!!
STAND BACK, GEPPETTO! WAIT HERE!
BUT...!
PINOCCHIO IS MY LIGHT.
IF I LOSE HIM, I DON'T KNOW WHAT I'LL--

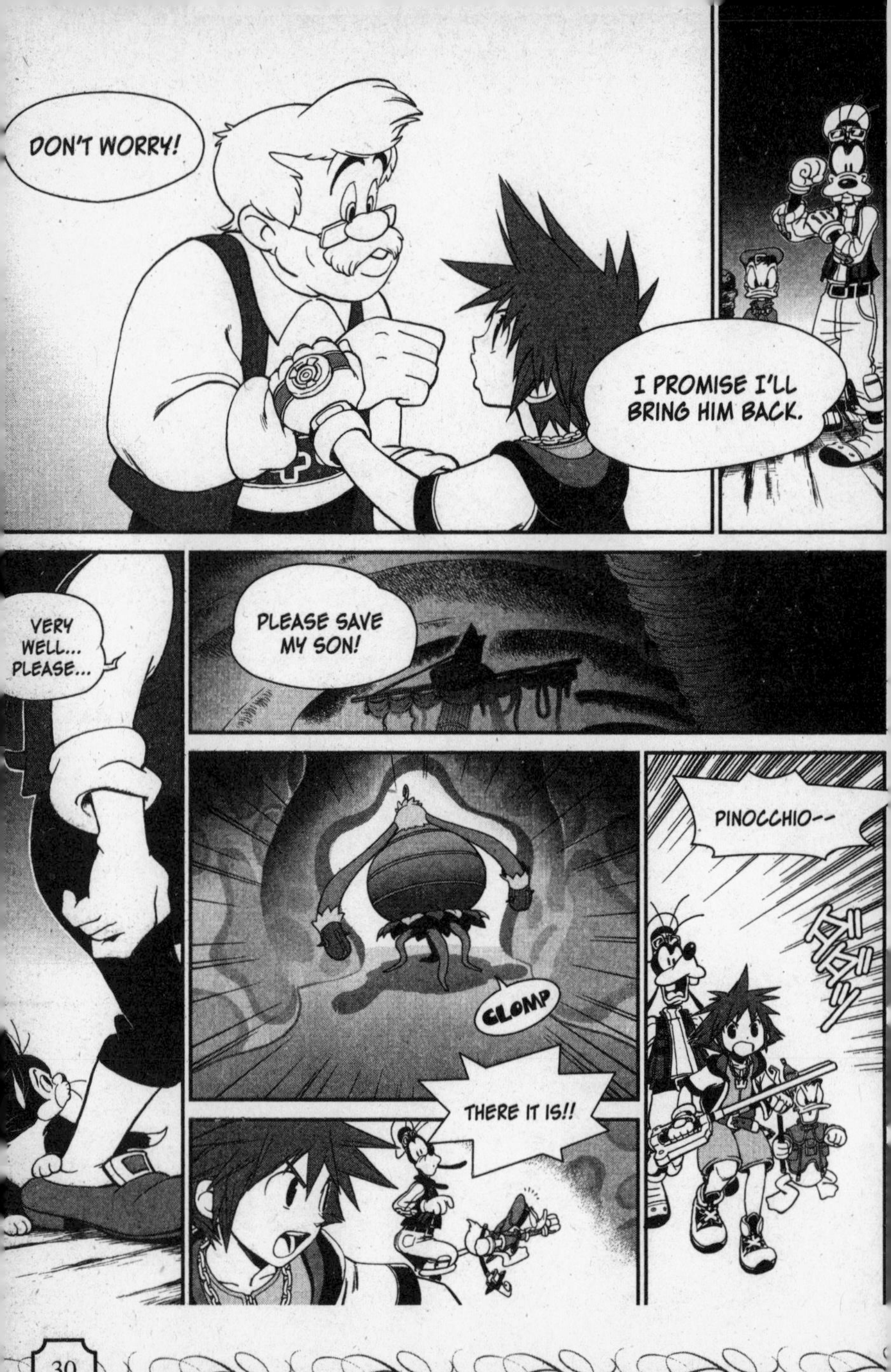
DON'T WORRY!
I PROMISE I'LL BRING HIM BACK.
VERY WELL... PLEASE...
PLEASE SAVE MY SON!
CLOMP
THERE IT IS!!
PINOCCHIO--

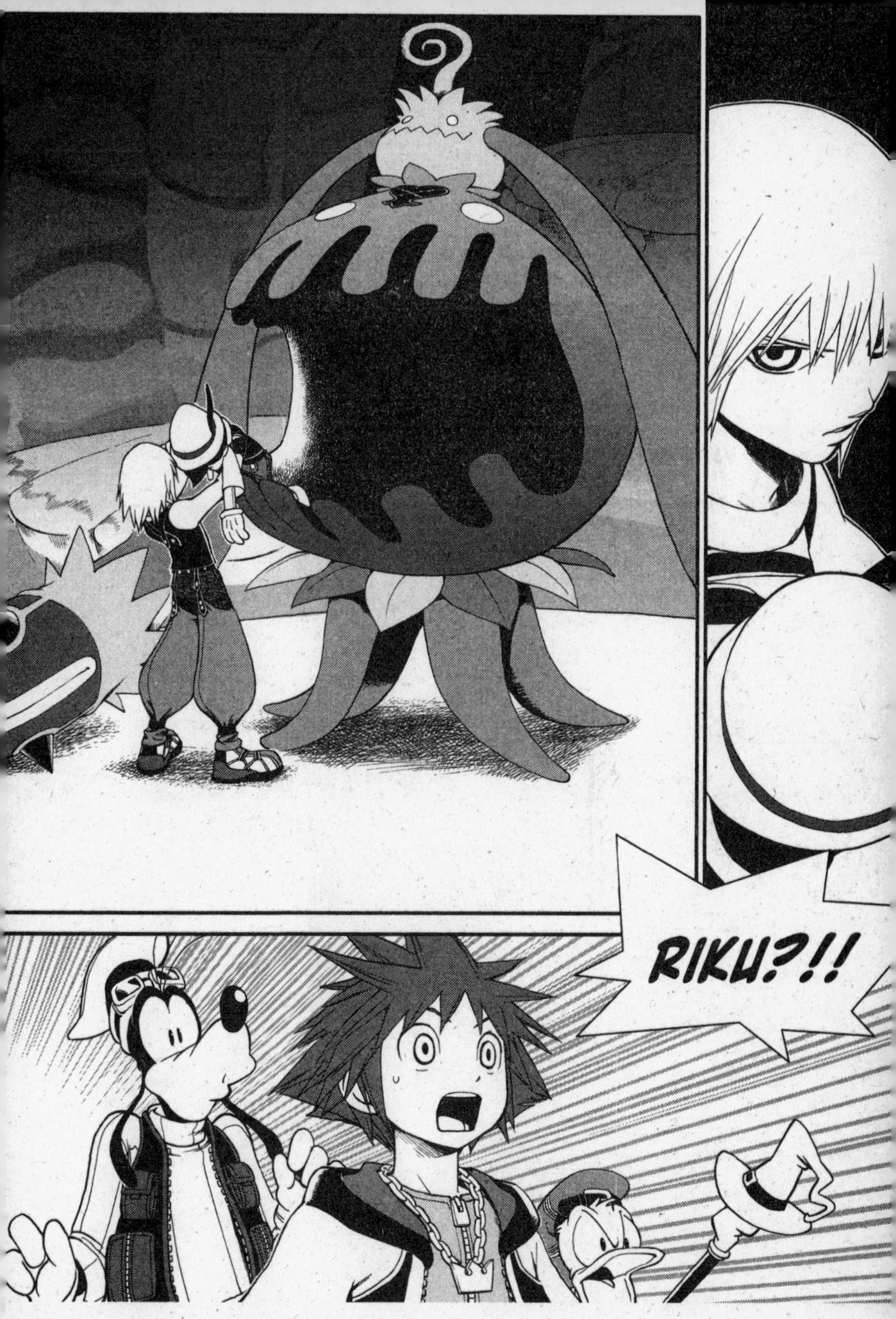
RIKU?!!

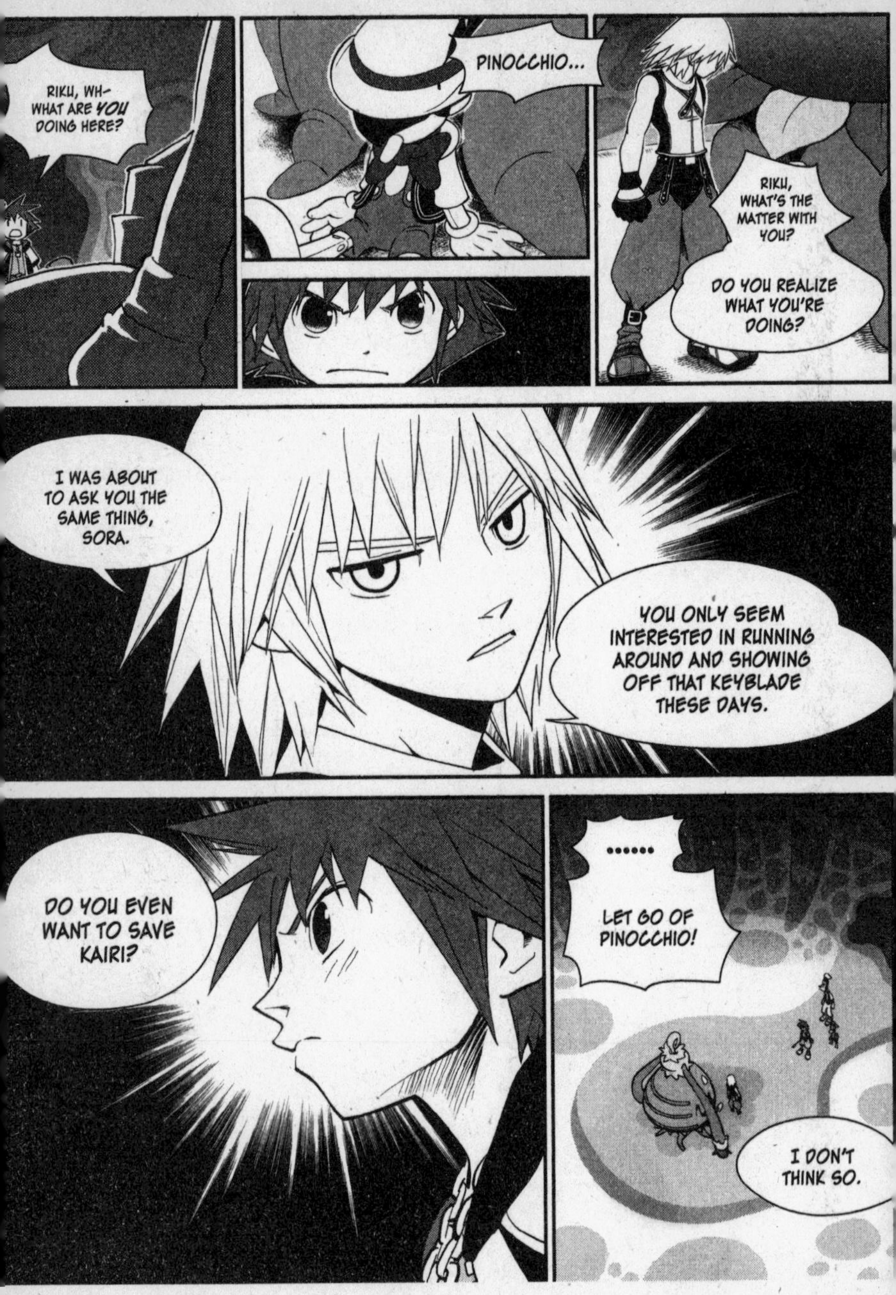
RIKU, WH- WHAT ARE YOU DOING HERE?
PINOCCHIO...
RIKU, WHAT'S THE MATTER WITH YOU?
DO YOU REALIZE WHAT YOU'RE DOING?
I WAS ABOUT TO ASK YOU THE SAME THING, SORA.
YOU ONLY SEEM INTERESTED IN RUNNING AROUND AND SHOWING OFF THAT KEYBLADE THESE DAYS.
DO YOU EVEN WANT TO SAVE KAIRI?
......
LET GO OF PINOCCHIO!
I DON'T THINK SO.

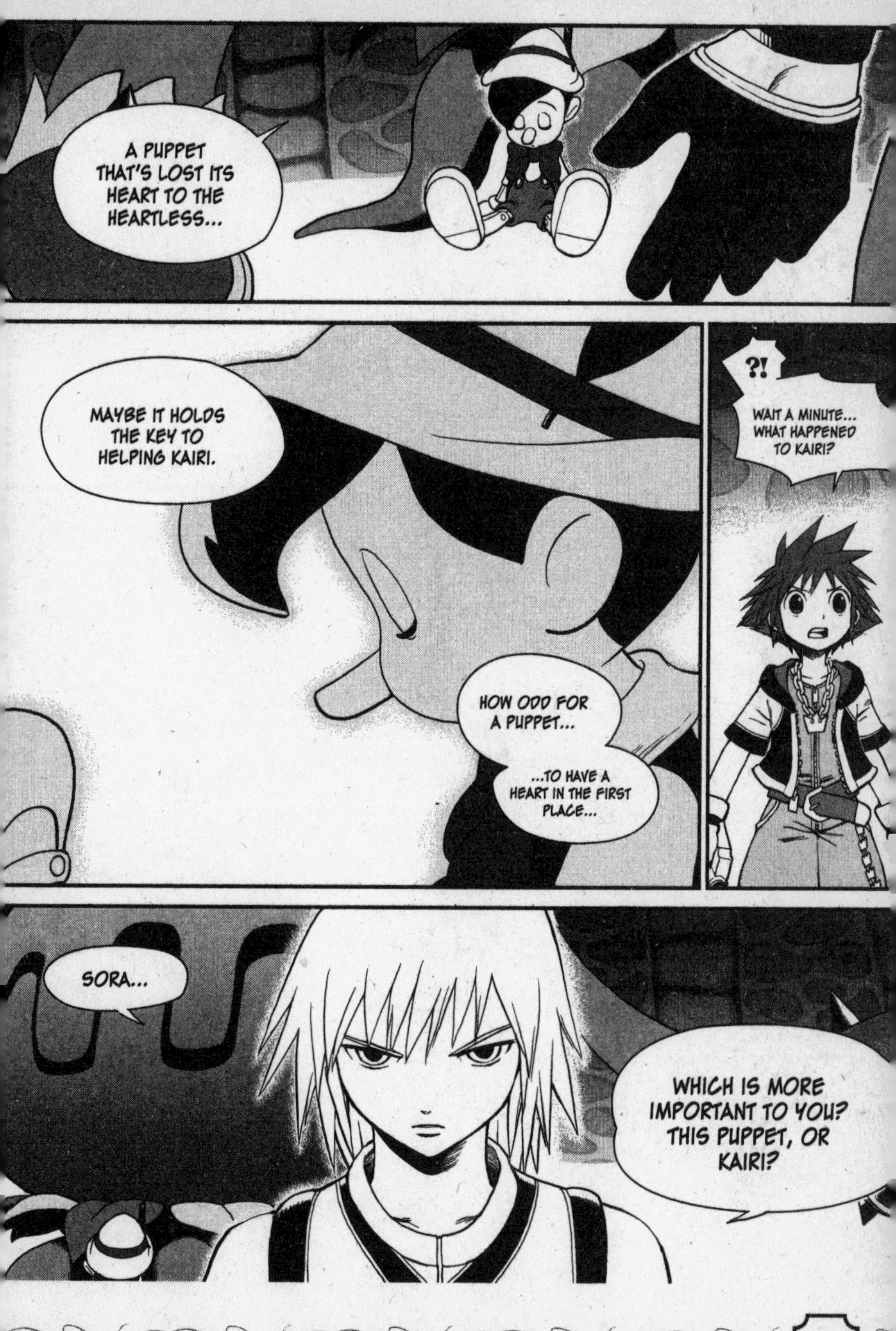
A PUPPET THAT'S LOST ITS HEART TO THE HEARTLESS...
MAYBE IT HOLDS THE KEY TO HELPING KAIRI.
HOW ODD FOR A PUPPET...
...TO HAVE A HEART IN THE FIRST PLACE...
?!
WAIT A MINUTE... WHAT HAPPENED TO KAIRI?
SORA...
WHICH IS MORE IMPORTANT TO YOU? THIS PUPPET, OR KAIRI?

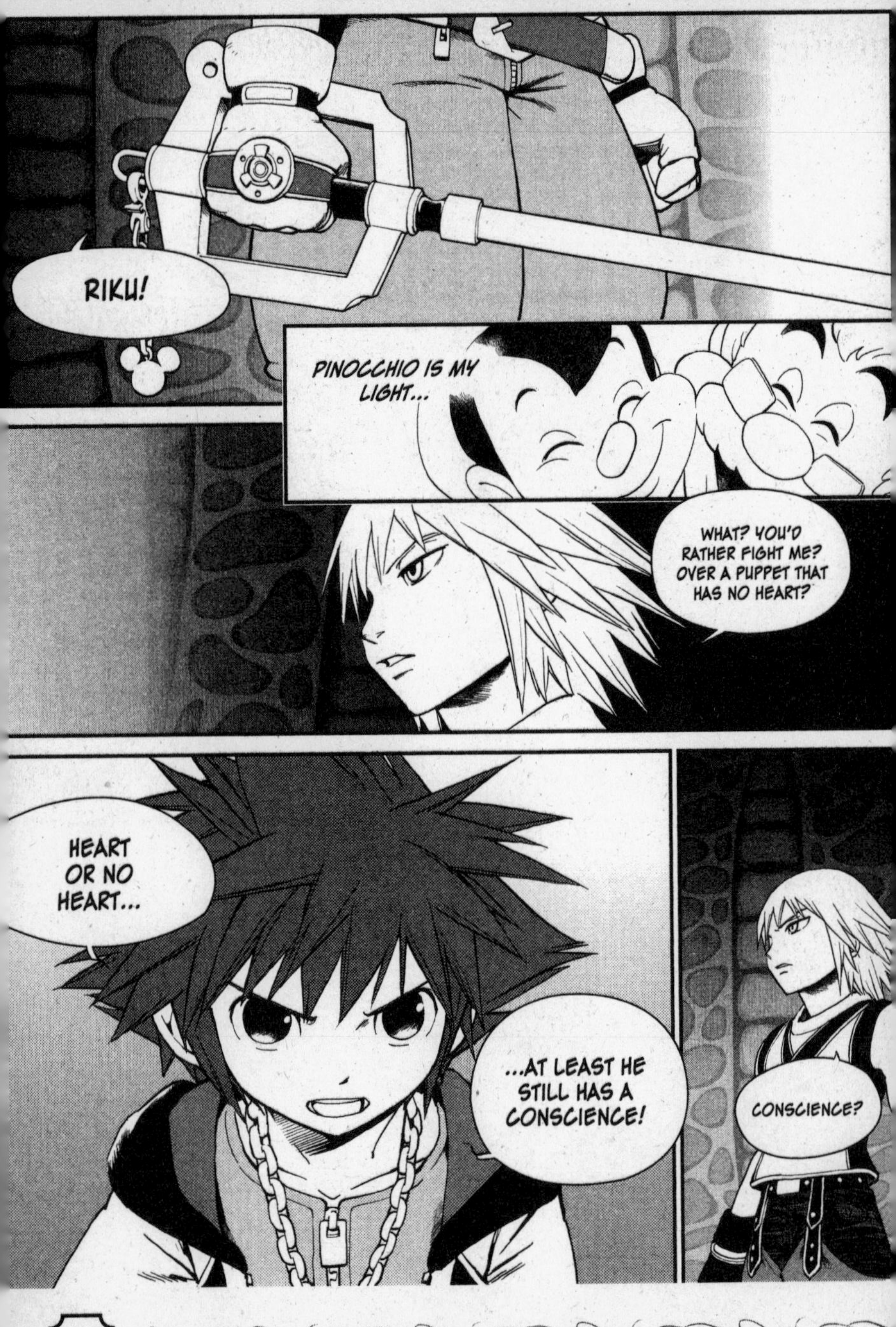
RIKU!
PINOCCHIO IS MY LIGHT...
WHAT? YOU'D RATHER FIGHT ME? OVER A PUPPET THAT HAS NO HEART?
HEART OR NO HEART...
...AT LEAST HE STILL HAS A CONSCIENCE!
CONSCIENCE?

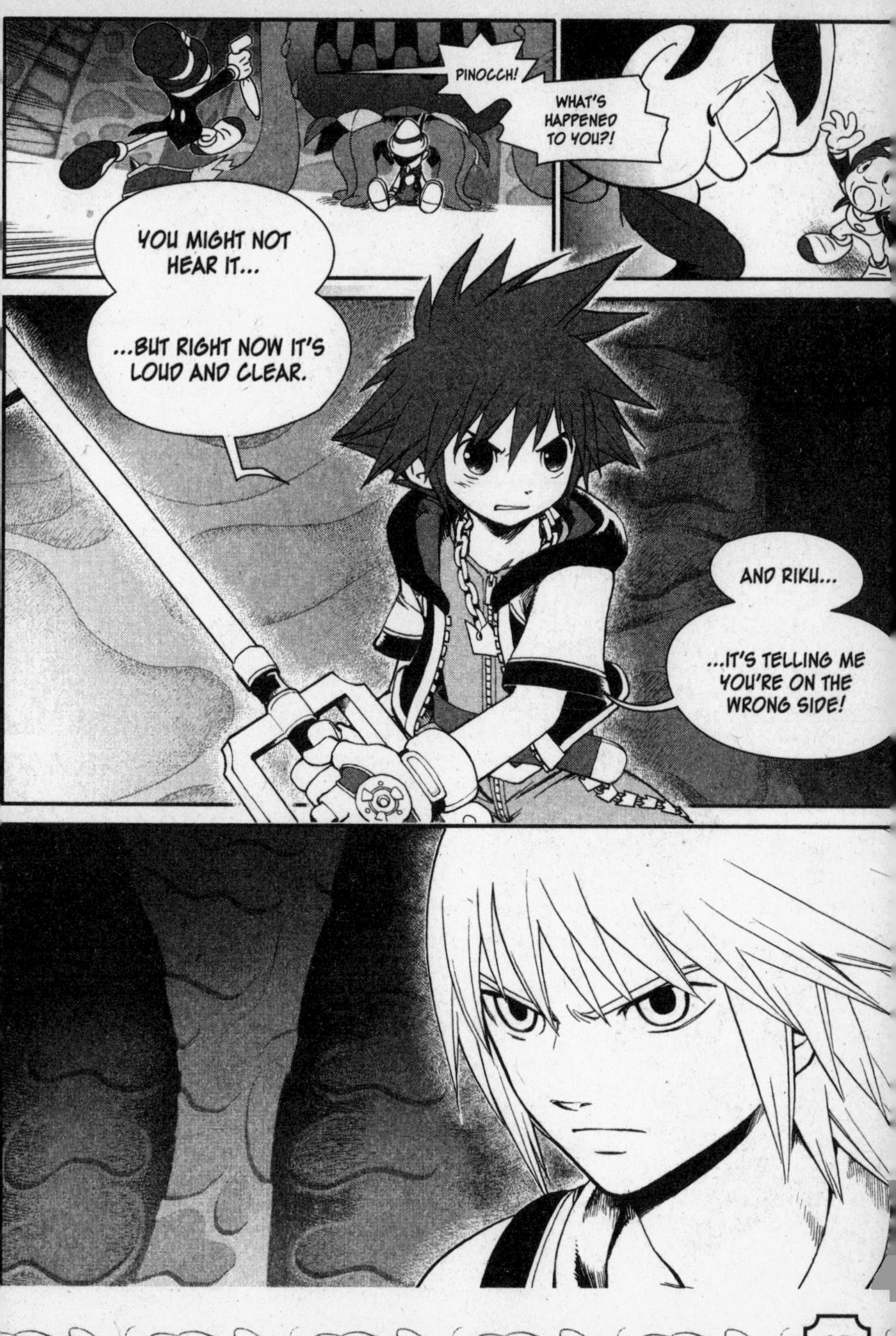
PINOCCH!
WHAT'S HAPPENED TO YOU?!
YOU MIGHT NOT HEAR IT...
...BUT RIGHT NOW IT'S LOUD AND CLEAR.
AND RIKU...
...IT'S TELLING ME YOU'RE ON THE WRONG SIDE!

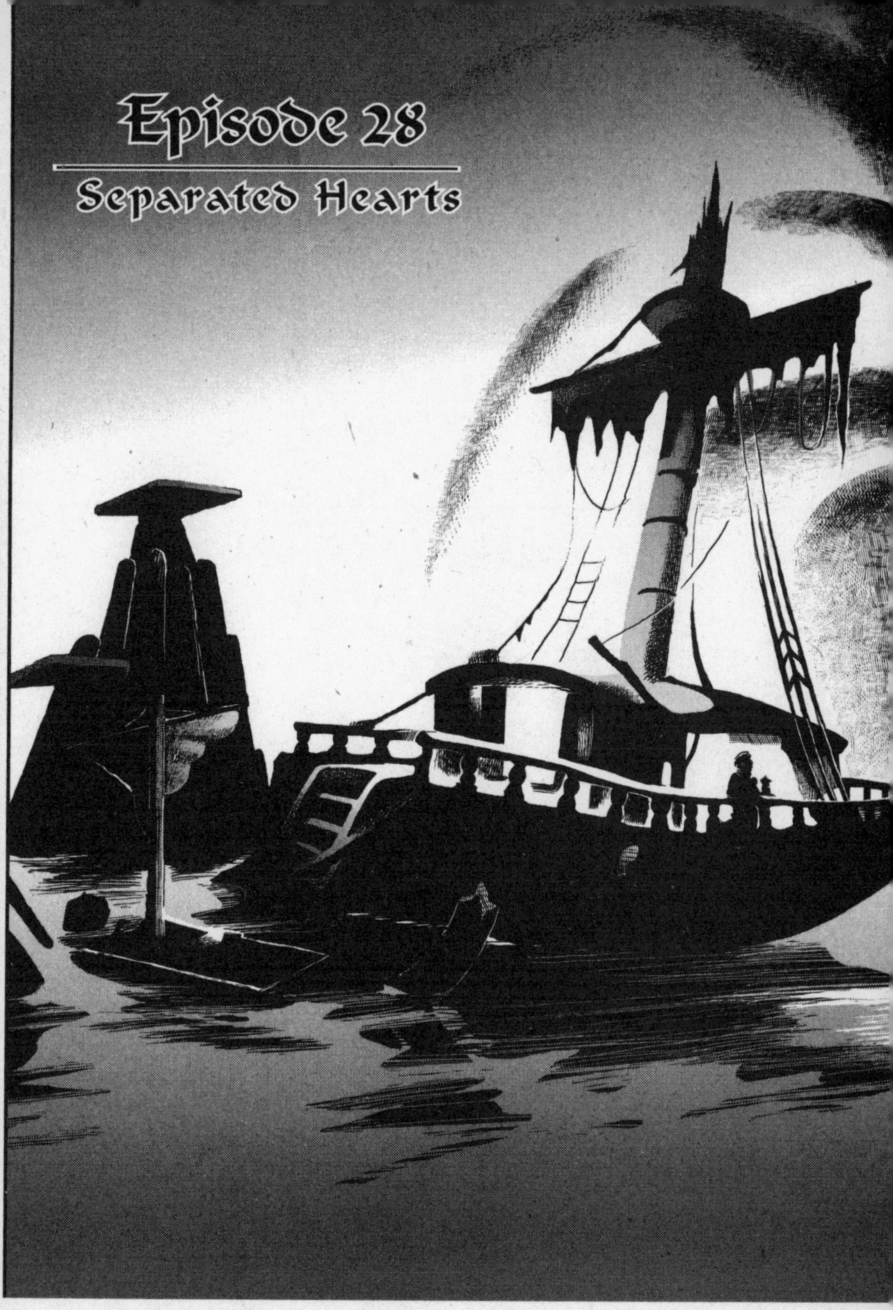
Episode 28
Separated Hearts

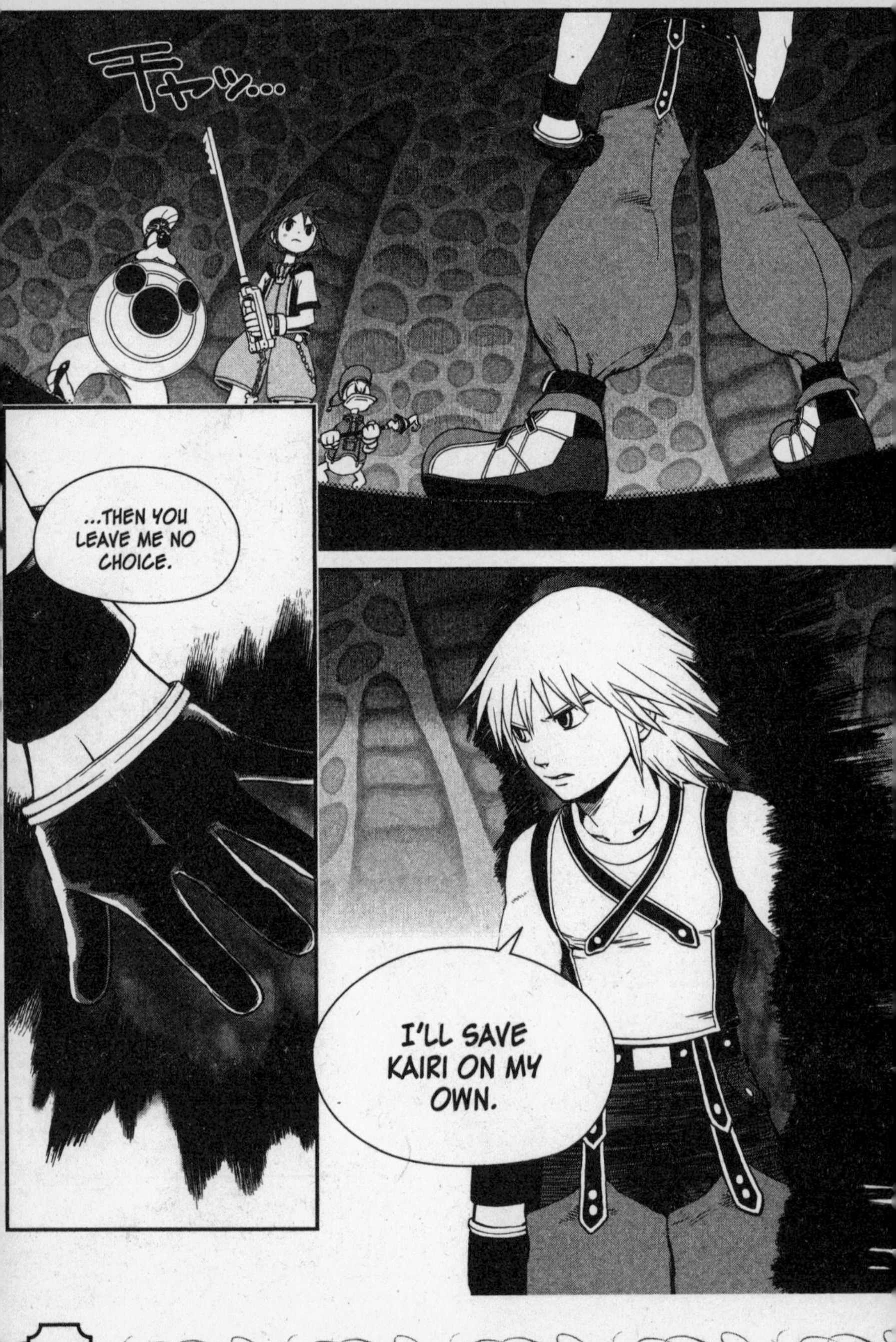
チャッ...
...THEN YOU LEAVE ME NO CHOICE.
I'LL SAVE KAIRI ON MY OWN.

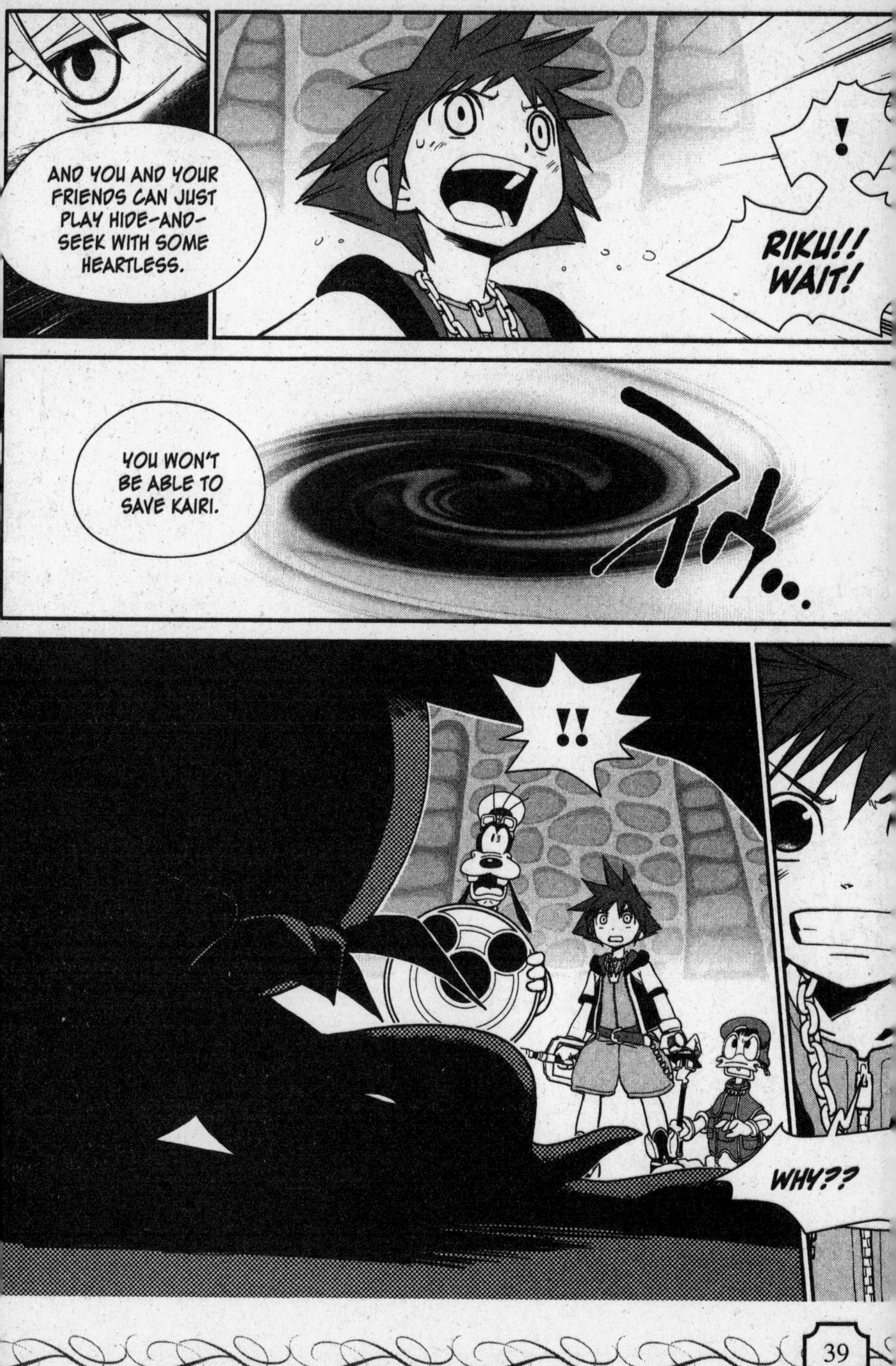
AND YOU AND YOUR FRIENDS CAN JUST PLAY HIDE-AND-SEEK WITH SOME HEARTLESS.
!
RIKU!! WAIT!
YOU WON'T BE ABLE TO SAVE KAIRI.
!!
WHY??

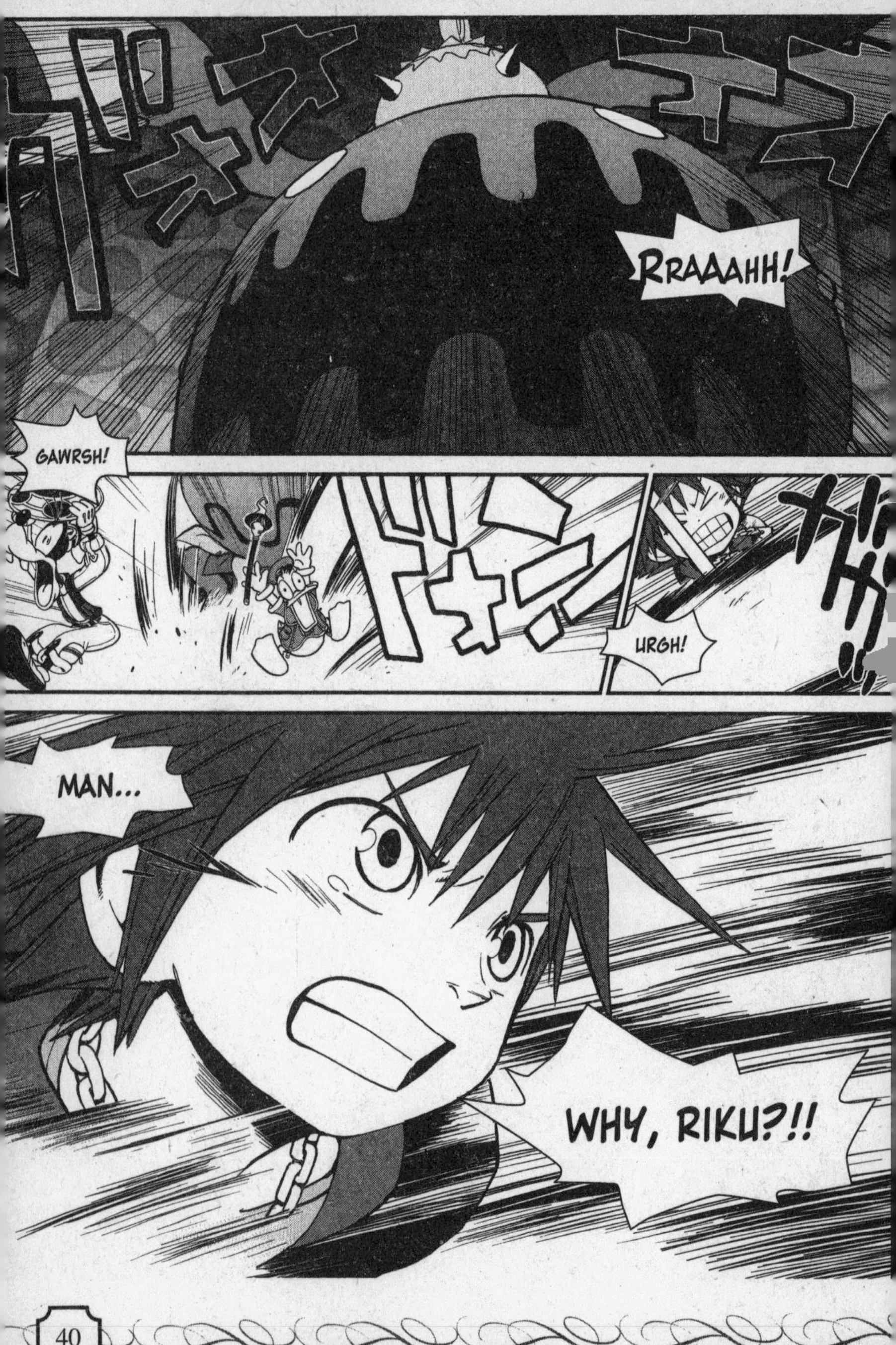
RRAAAHH!
GAWRSH!
URGH!
MAN...
WHY, RIKU?!!

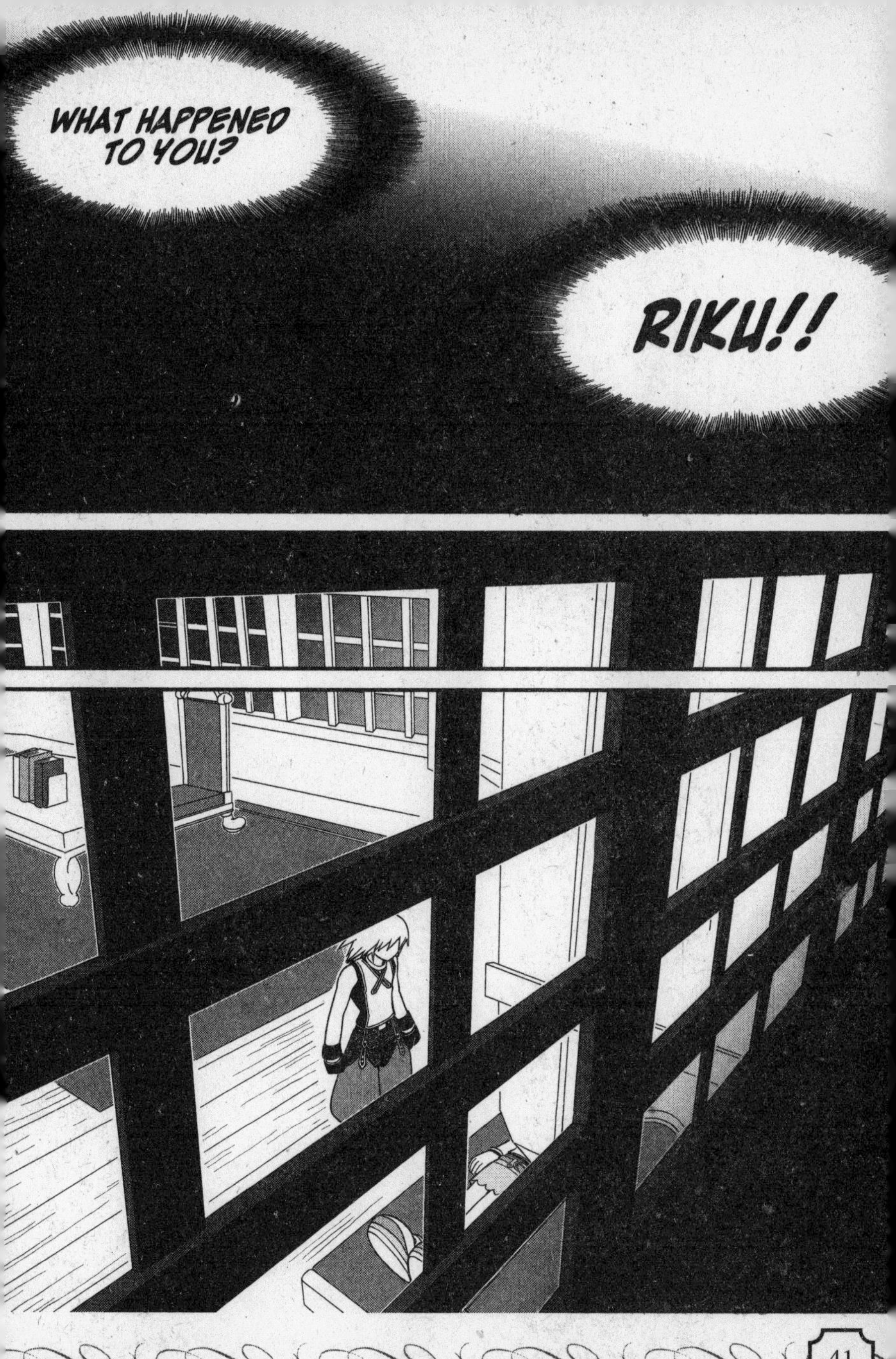
WHAT HAPPENED TO YOU?
RIKU!!

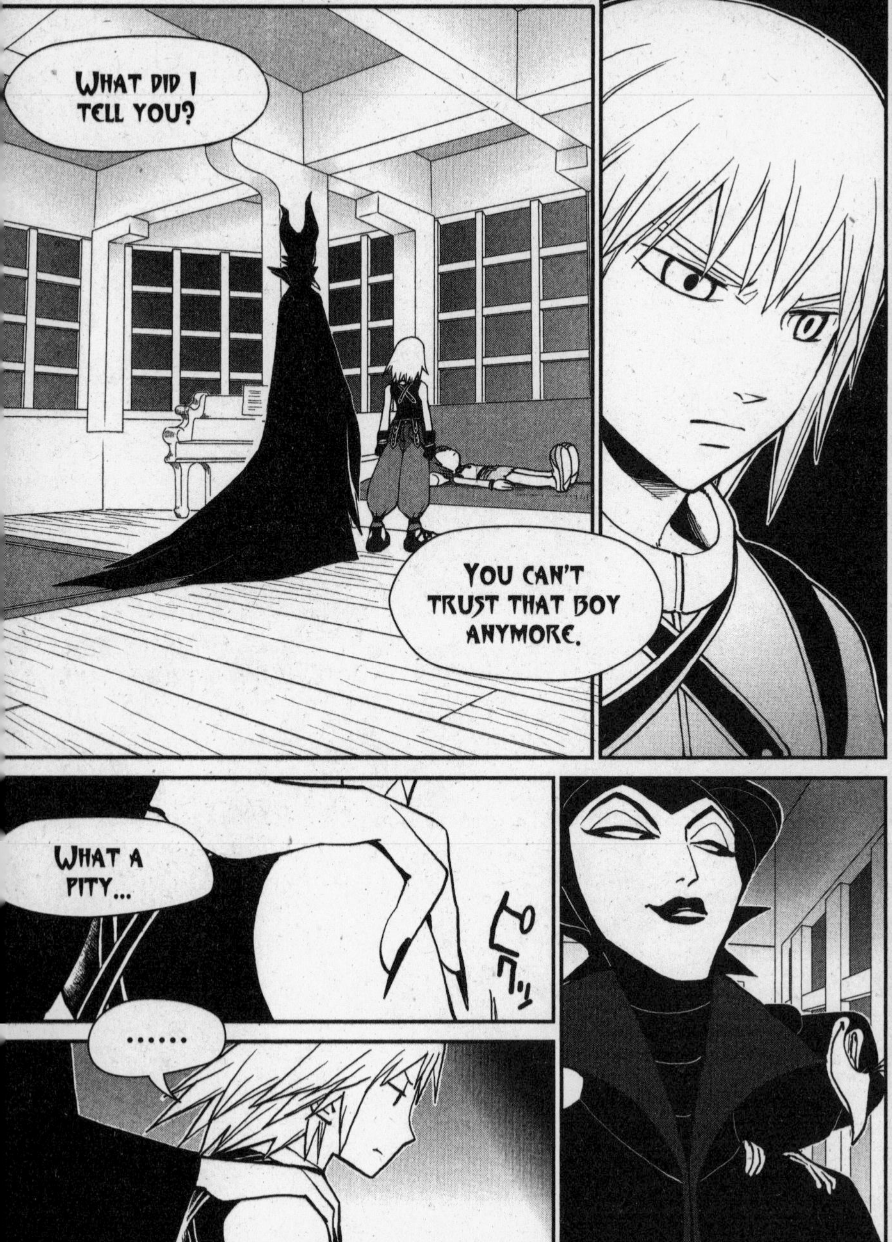
WHAT DID I TELL YOU?
YOU CAN'T TRUST THAT BOY ANYMORE.
WHAT A PITY...
ピクッ
......

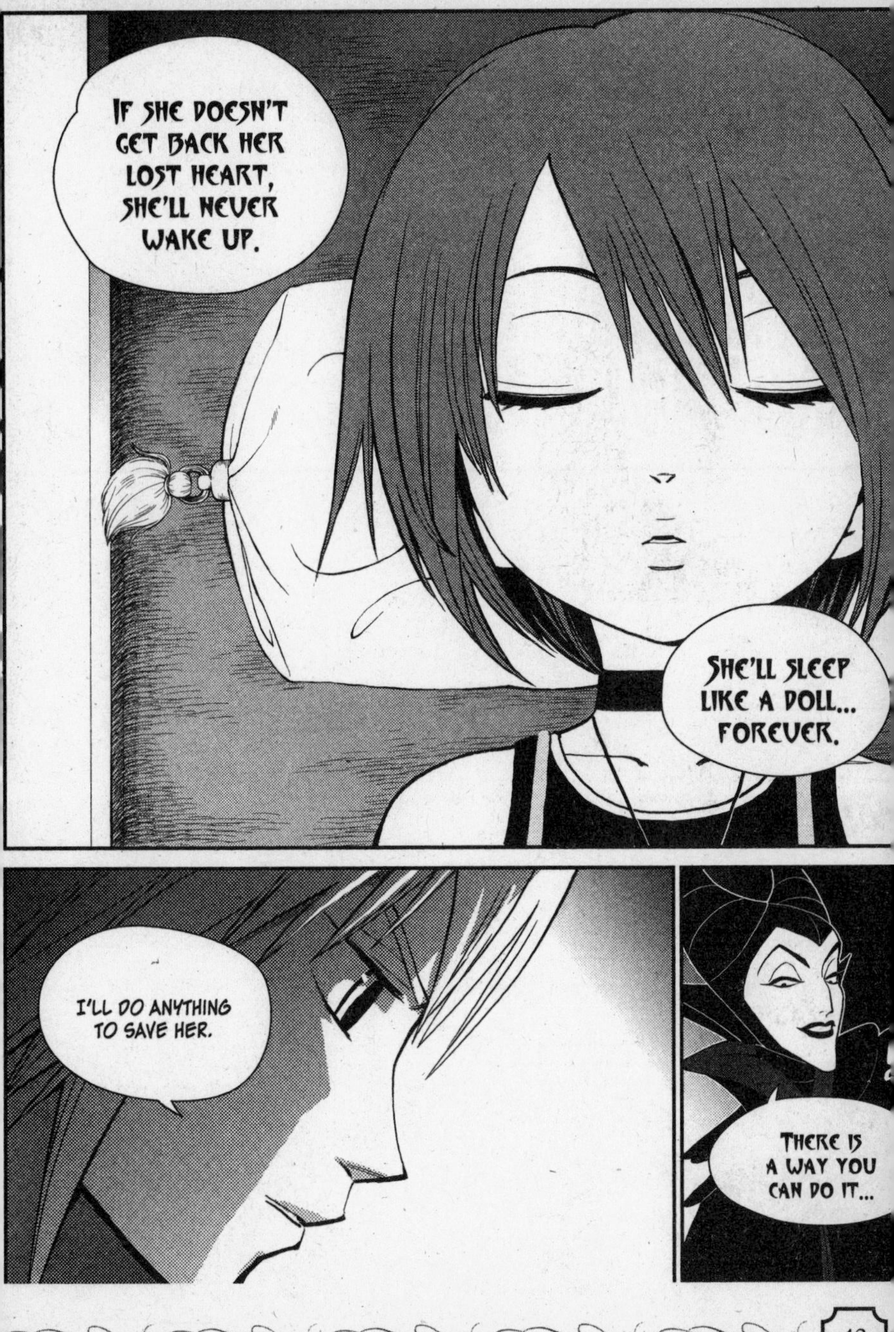
IF SHE DOESN'T GET BACK HER LOST HEART, SHE'LL NEVER WAKE UP.
SHE'LL SLEEP LIKE A DOLL... FOREVER.
I'LL DO ANYTHING TO SAVE HER.
THERE IS A WAY YOU CAN DO IT...

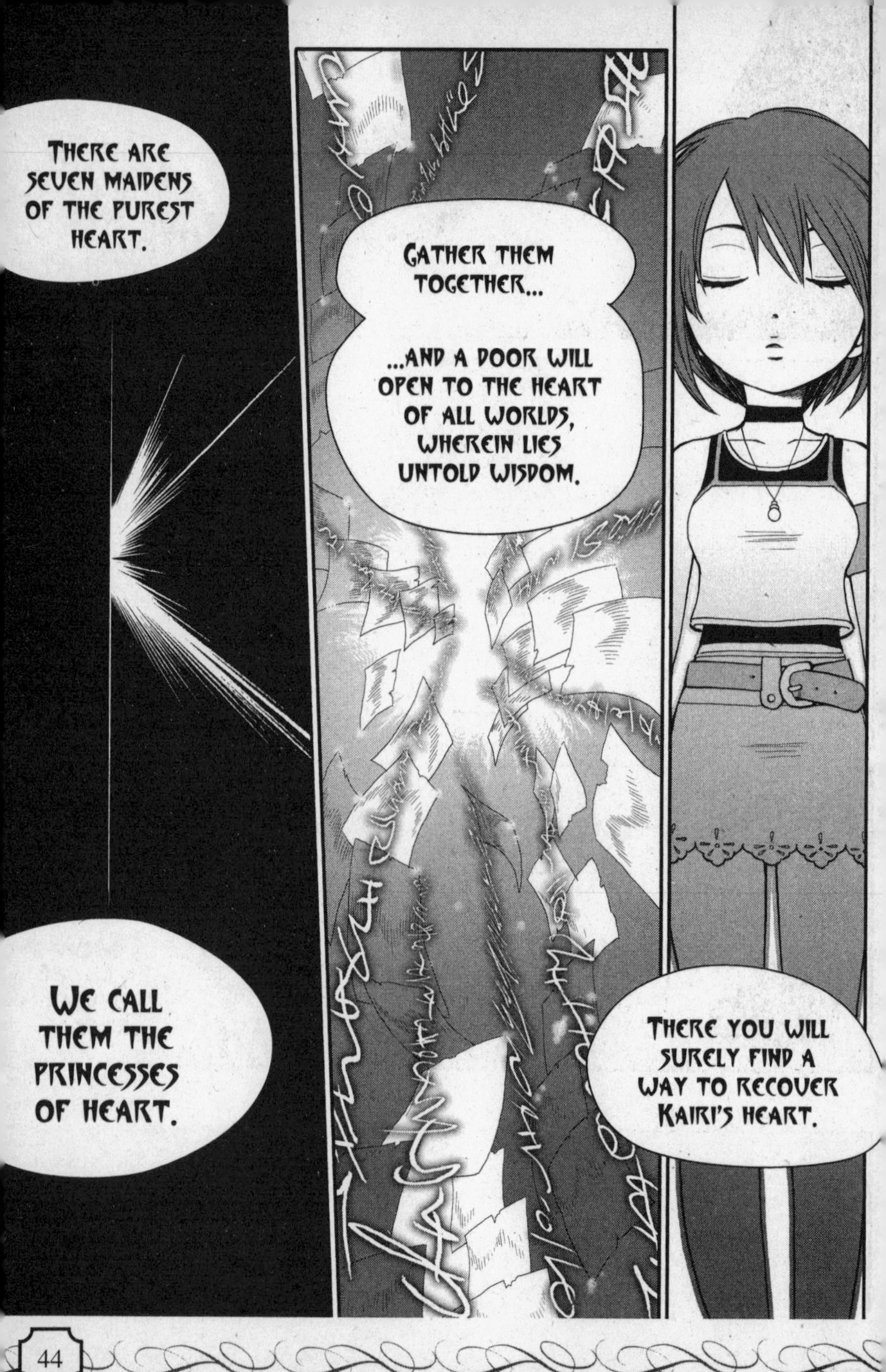
There are seven maidens of the purest heart.
We call them the princesses of heart.
Gather them together...
...and a door will open to the heart of all worlds, wherein lies untold wisdom.
There you will surely find a way to recover Kairi's heart.

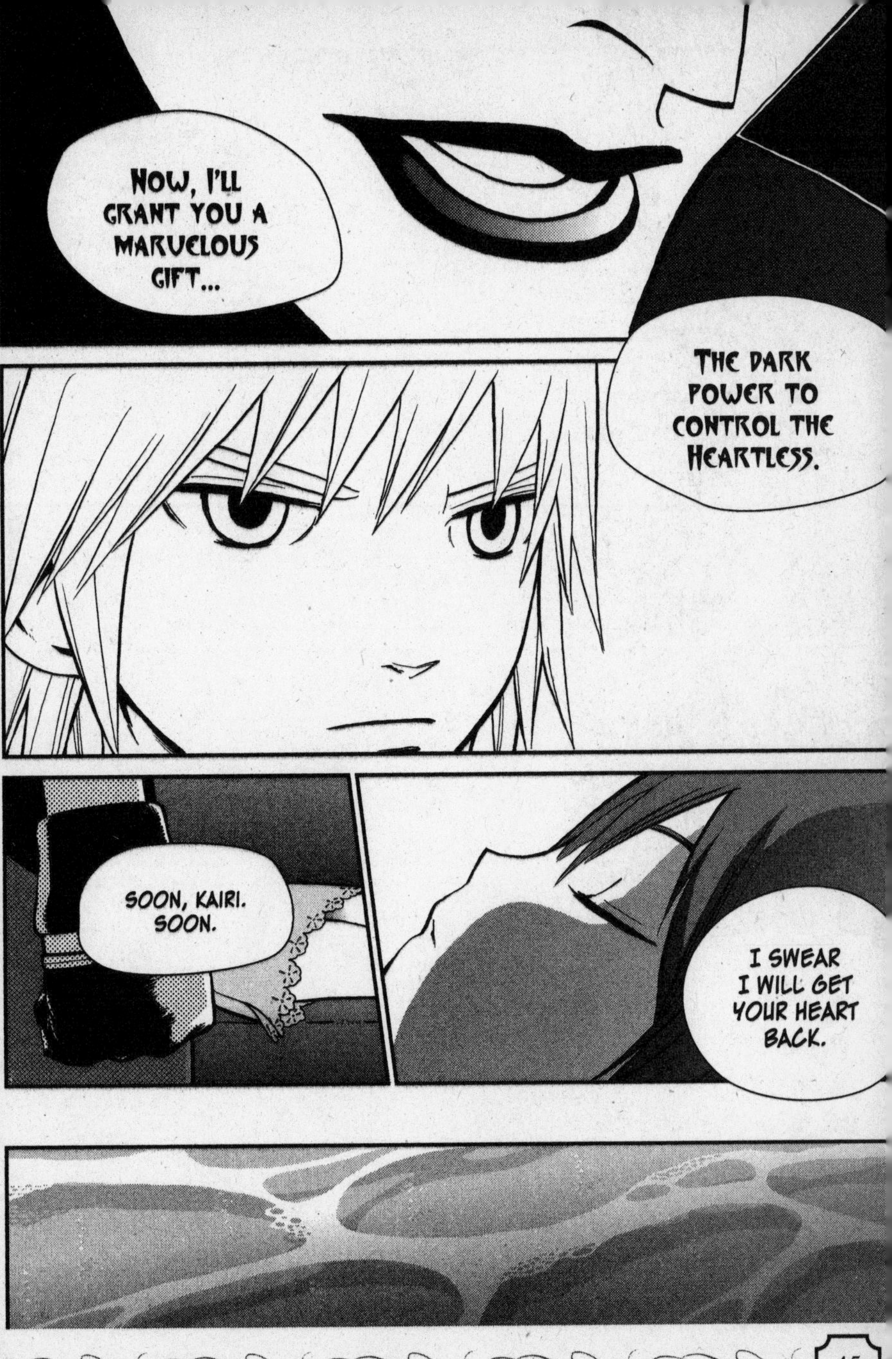
NOW, I'LL GRANT YOU A MARVELOUS GIFT...
THE DARK POWER TO CONTROL THE HEARTLESS.
SOON, KAIRI. SOON.
I SWEAR I WILL GET YOUR HEART BACK.

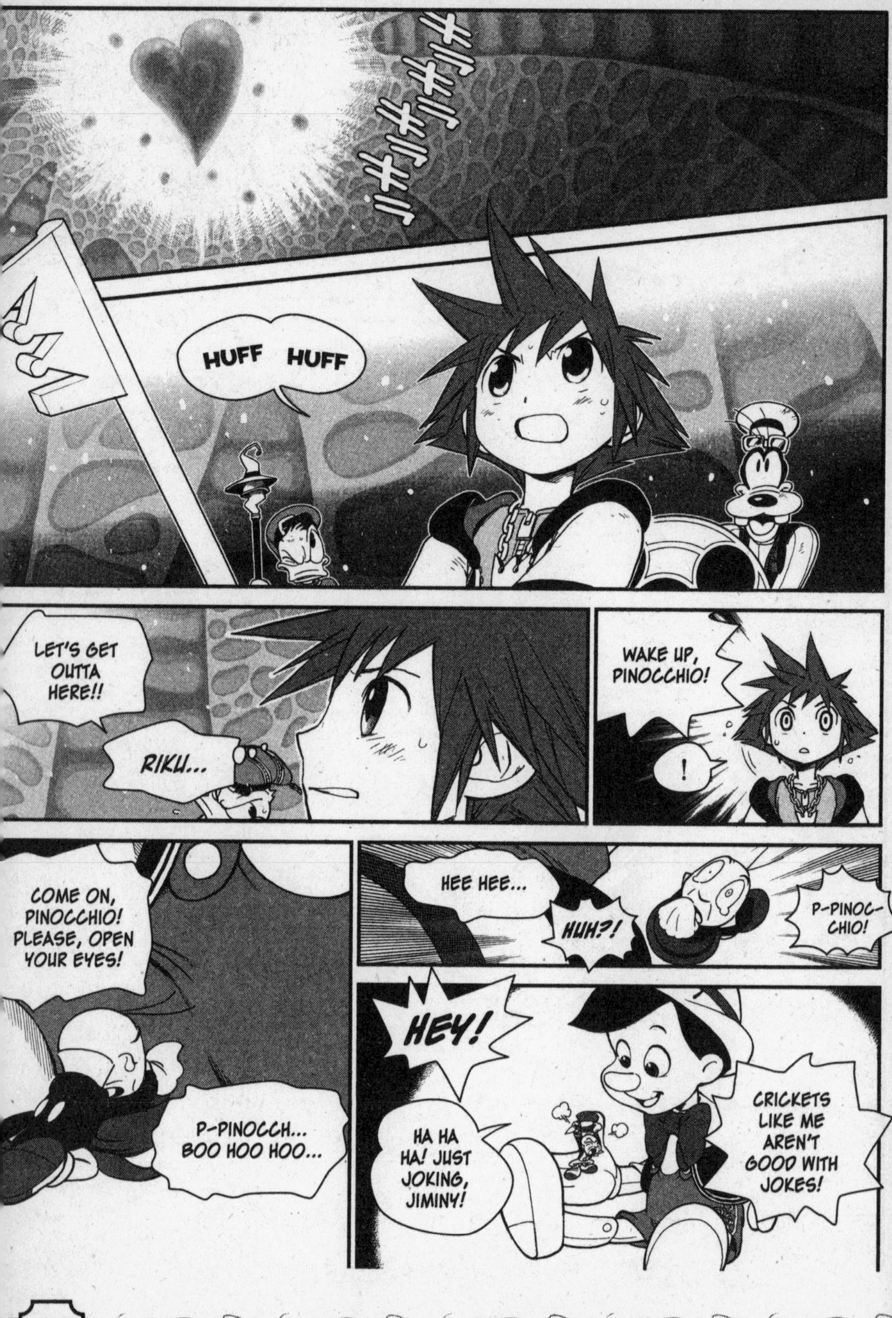
キラキラキラキラ
HUFF HUFF
LET'S GET OUTTA HERE!!
RIKU...
WAKE UP, PINOCCHIO!
!
COME ON, PINOCCHIO! PLEASE, OPEN YOUR EYES!
P-PINOCCH... BOO HOO HOO...
HEE HEE...
HUH?!
P-PINOCCHIO!
HEY!
HA HA HA! JUST JOKING, JIMINY!
CRICKETS LIKE ME AREN'T GOOD WITH JOKES!

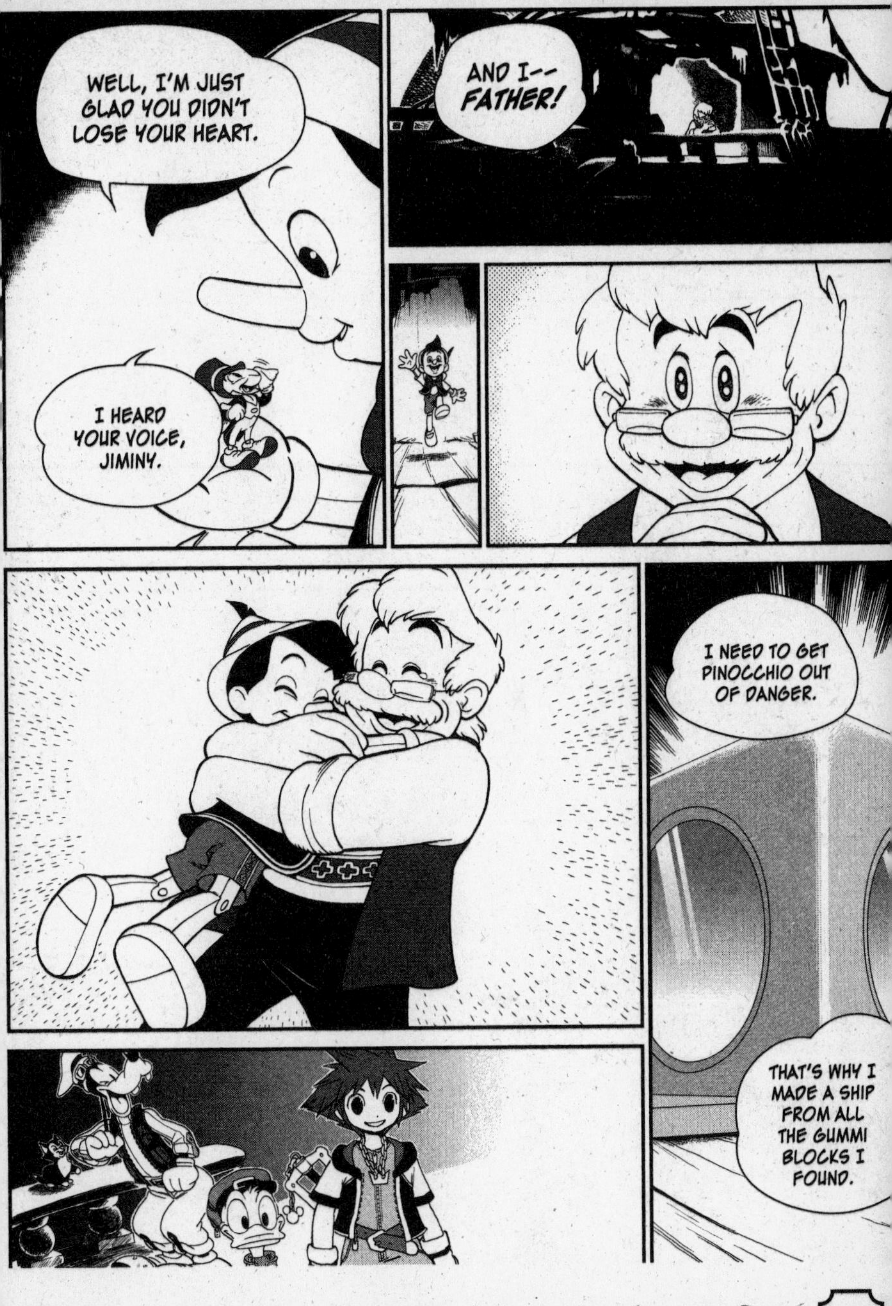
WELL, I'M JUST GLAD YOU DIDN'T LOSE YOUR HEART.
I HEARD YOUR VOICE, JIMINY.
AND I-- FATHER!
I NEED TO GET PINOCCHIO OUT OF DANGER.
THAT'S WHY I MADE A SHIP FROM ALL THE GUMMI BLOCKS I FOUND.

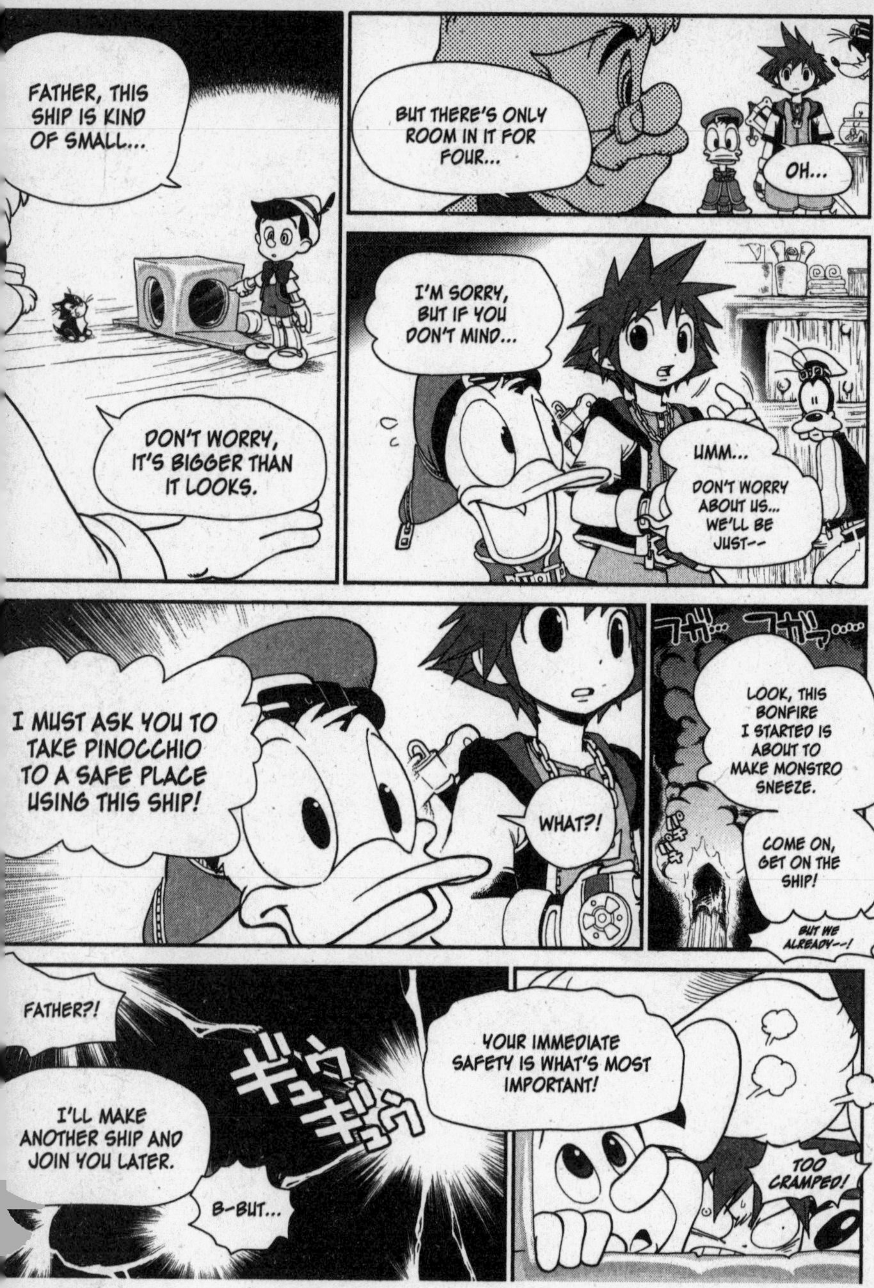
FATHER, THIS SHIP IS KIND OF SMALL...
DON'T WORRY, IT'S BIGGER THAN IT LOOKS.
BUT THERE'S ONLY ROOM IN IT FOR FOUR...
OH...
I'M SORRY, BUT IF YOU DON'T MIND...
UMM...
DON'T WORRY ABOUT US... WE'LL BE JUST--
I MUST ASK YOU TO TAKE PINOCCHIO TO A SAFE PLACE USING THIS SHIP!
WHAT?!
フガ… フガァ…
LOOK, THIS BONFIRE I STARTED IS ABOUT TO MAKE MONSTRO SNEEZE.
COME ON, GET ON THE SHIP!
BUT WE ALREADY--!
FATHER?!
I'LL MAKE ANOTHER SHIP AND JOIN YOU LATER.
ギュウギュウ
B-BUT...
YOUR IMMEDIATE SAFETY IS WHAT'S MOST IMPORTANT!
TOO CRAMPED!

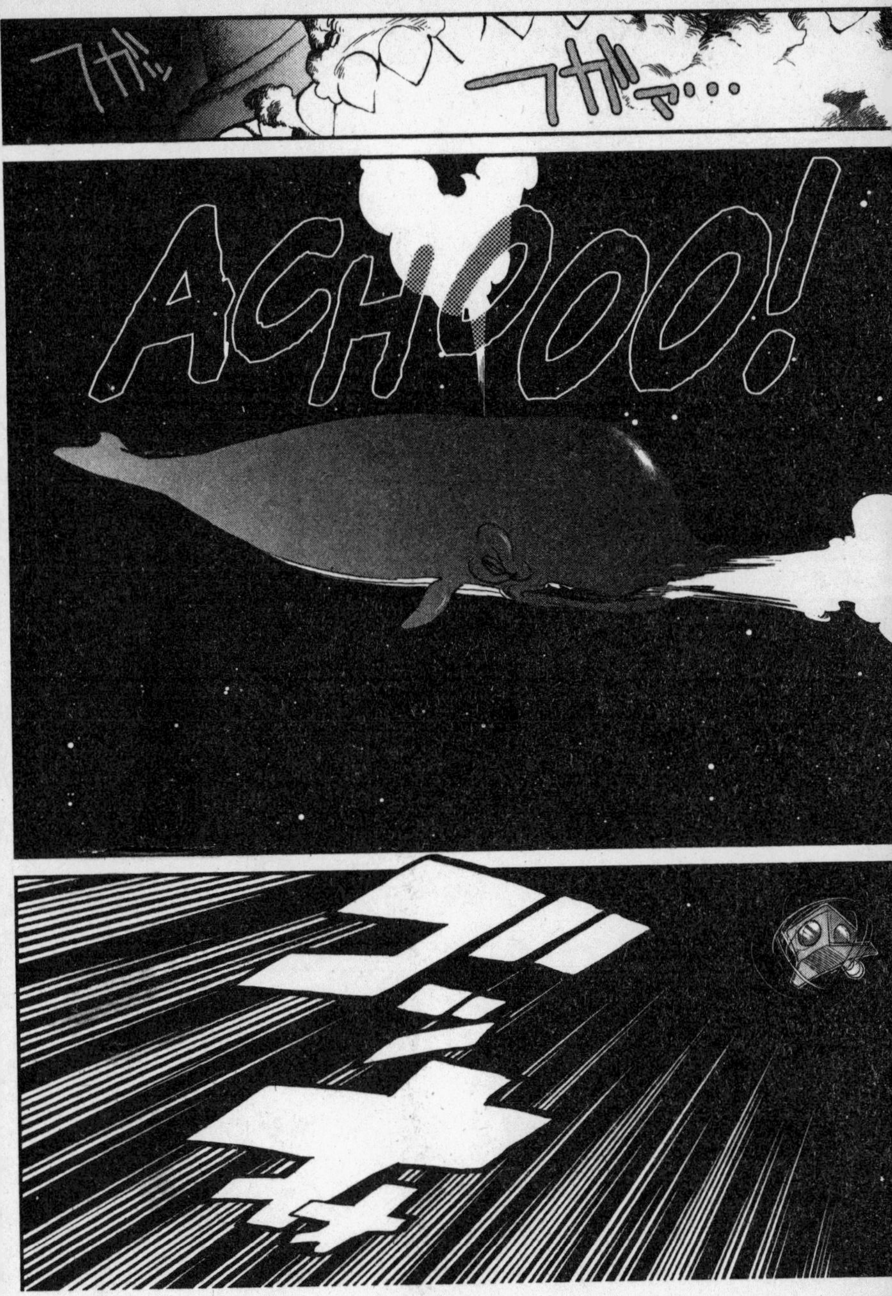
フガッ
フガァ…
ACHOOO!

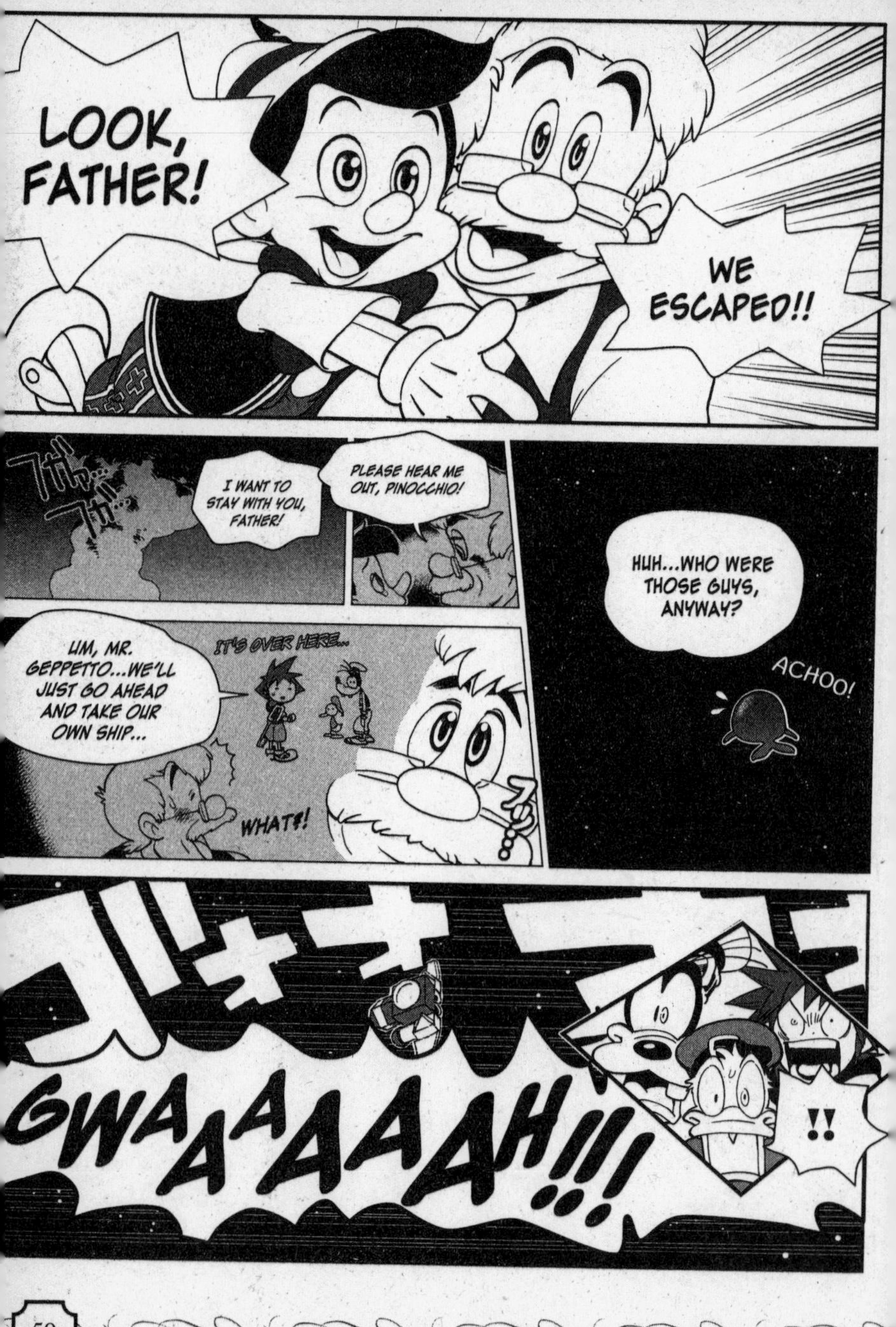
LOOK, FATHER!
WE ESCAPED!!
I WANT TO STAY WITH YOU, FATHER!
PLEASE HEAR ME OUT, PINOCCHIO!
UM, MR. GEPPETTO...WE'LL JUST GO AHEAD AND TAKE OUR OWN SHIP...
IT'S OVER HERE...
WHAT?!
HUH...WHO WERE THOSE GUYS, ANYWAY?
ACHOO!
GWAAAAAH!!!
!!

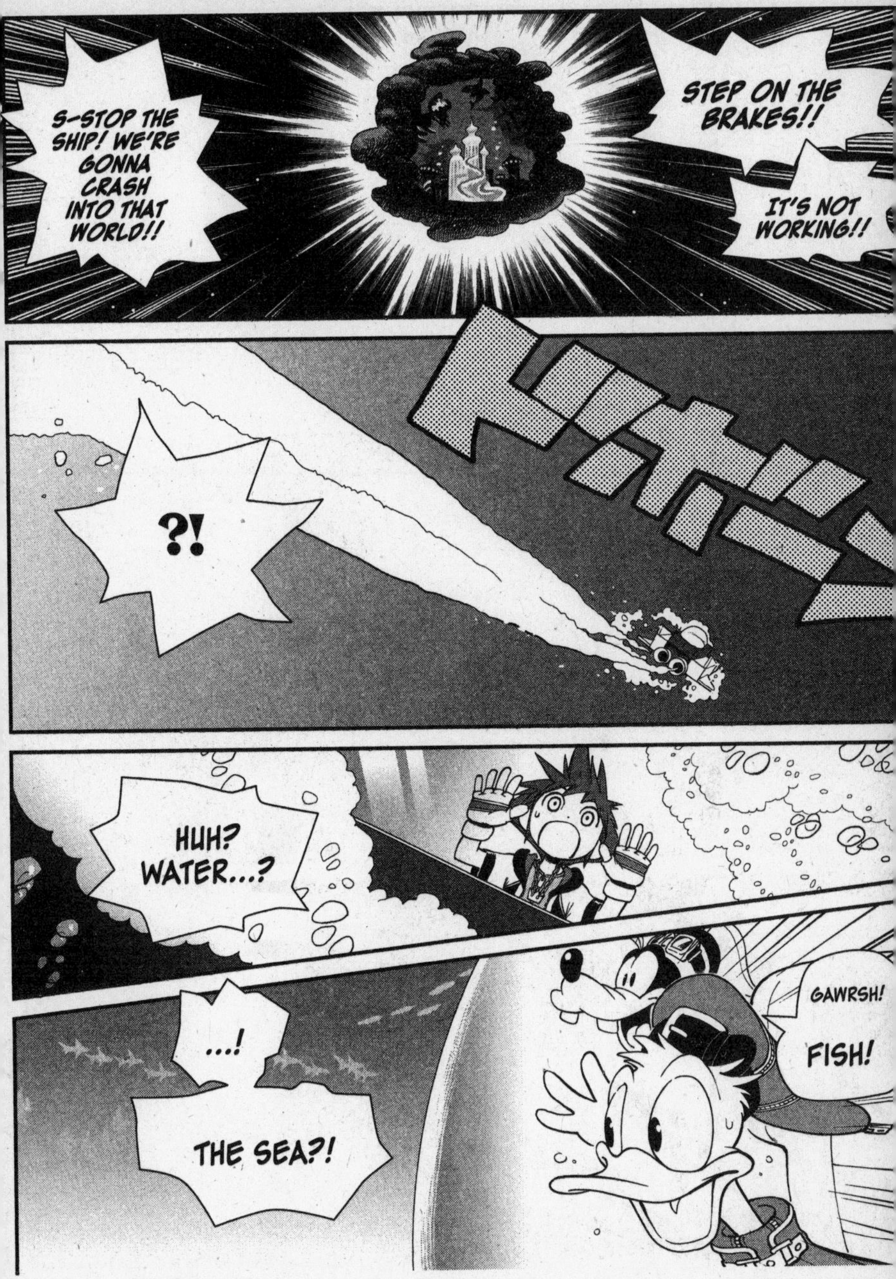

S-STOP THE SHIP! WE'RE GONNA CRASH INTO THAT WORLD!!
STEP ON THE BRAKES!!
IT'S NOT WORKING!!
?!
HUH? WATER...?
...!
THE SEA?!
GAWRSH!
FISH!

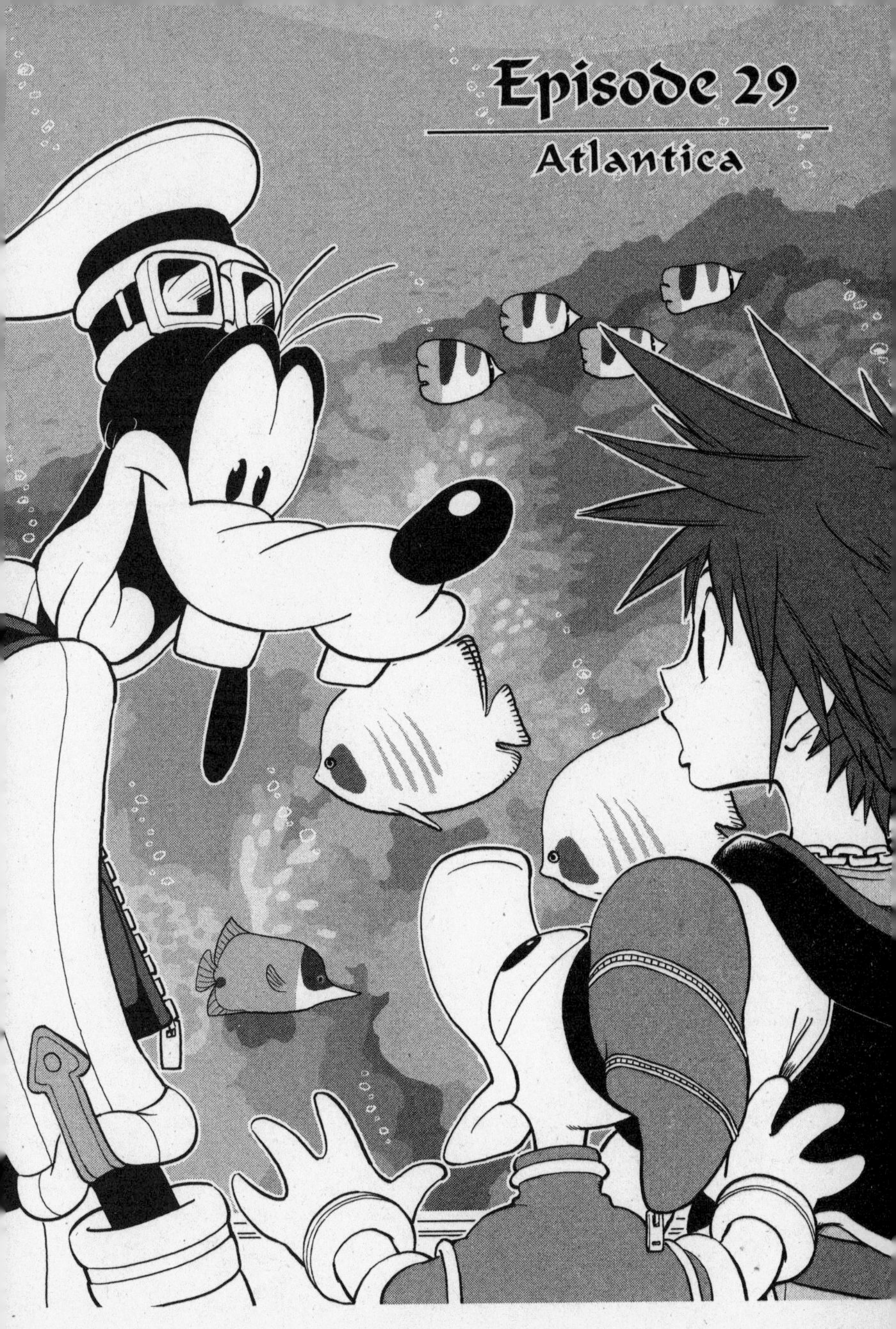
Episode 29
Atlantica

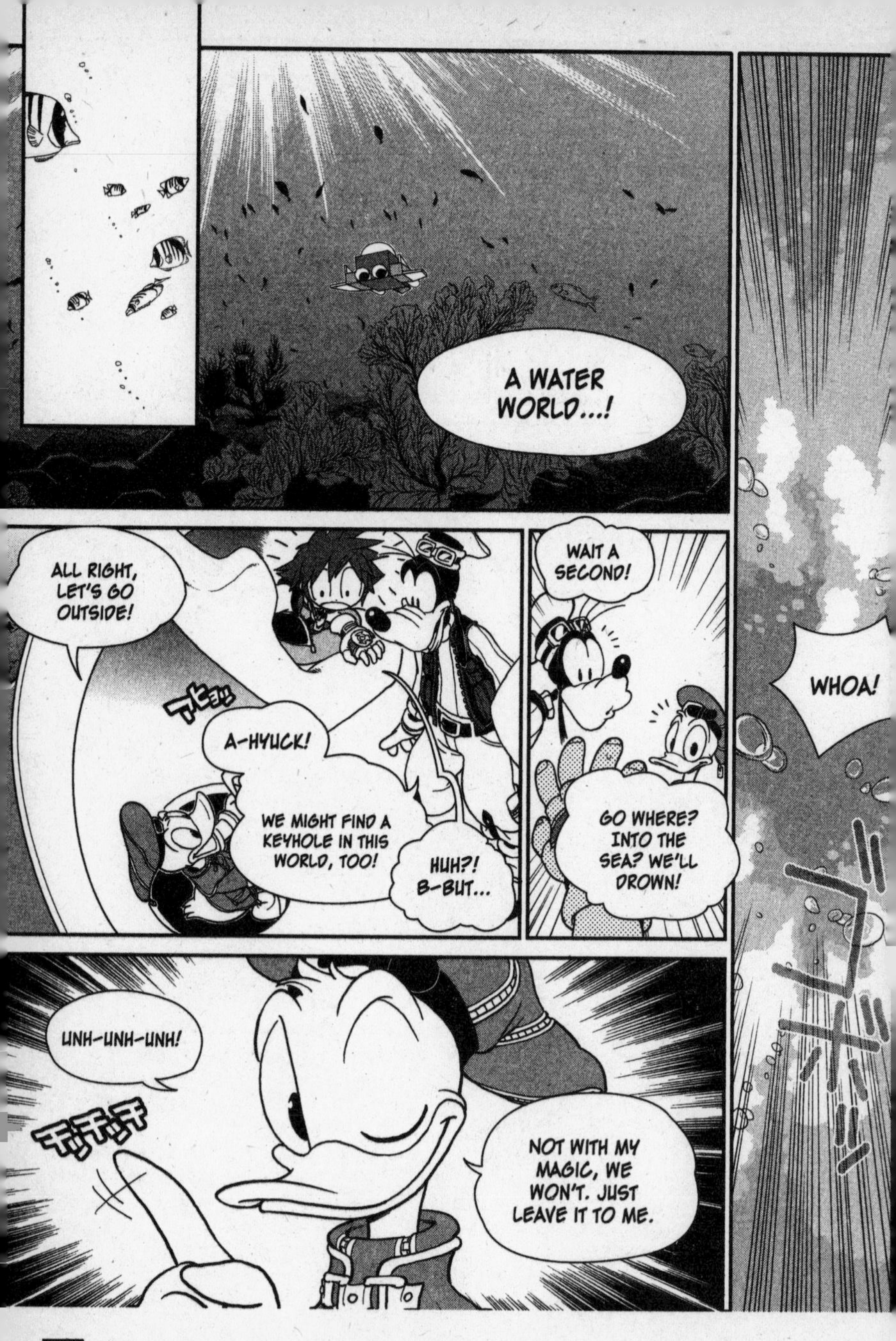
A WATER WORLD...!
ALL RIGHT, LET'S GO OUTSIDE!
A-HYUCK!
WE MIGHT FIND A KEYHOLE IN THIS WORLD, TOO!
HUH?! B-BUT...
WAIT A SECOND!
GO WHERE? INTO THE SEA? WE'LL DROWN!
UNH-UNH-UNH!
NOT WITH MY MAGIC, WE WON'T. JUST LEAVE IT TO ME.
WHOA!

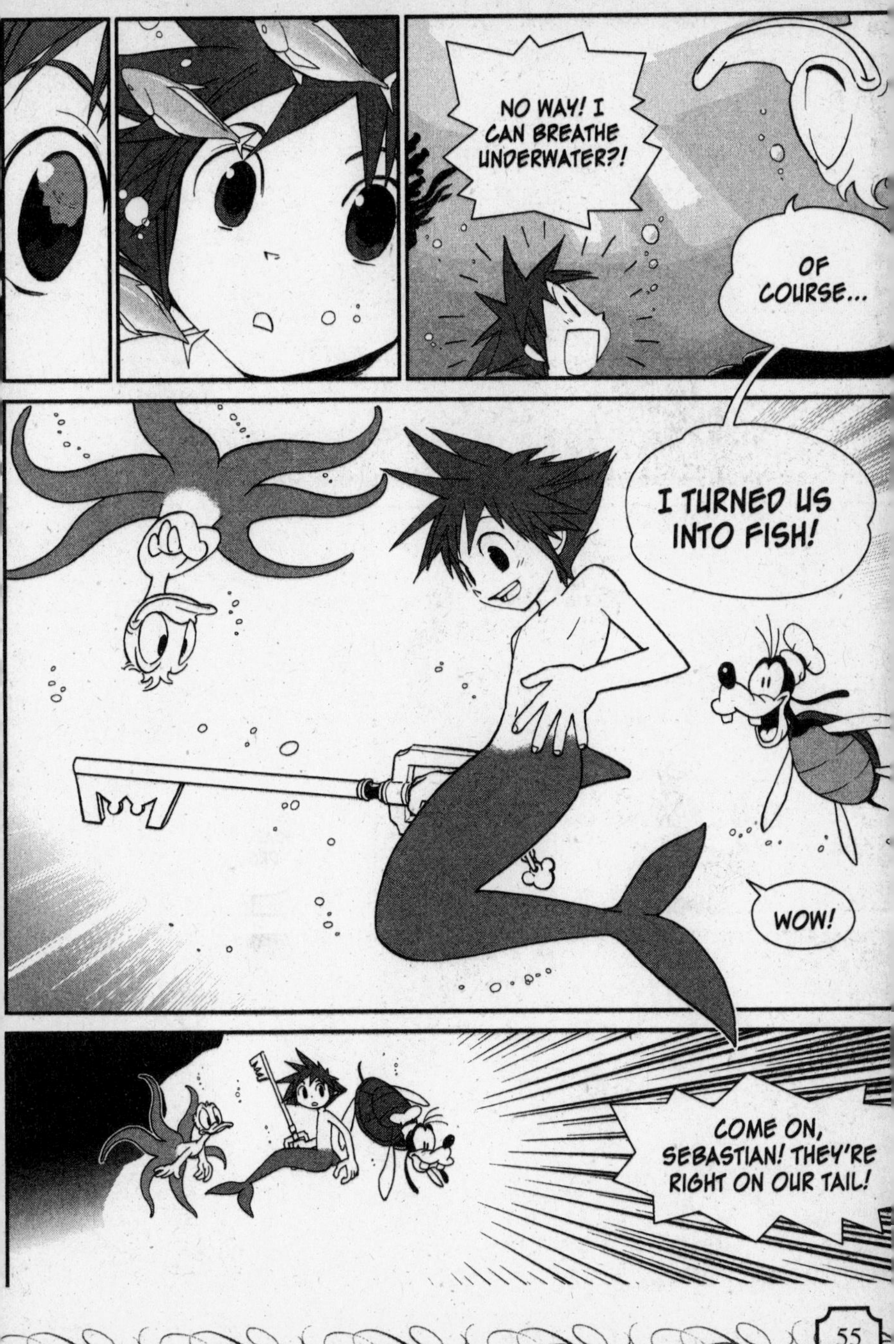
NO WAY! I CAN BREATHE UNDERWATER?!
OF COURSE...
I TURNED US INTO FISH!
WOW!
COME ON, SEBASTIAN! THEY'RE RIGHT ON OUR TAIL!

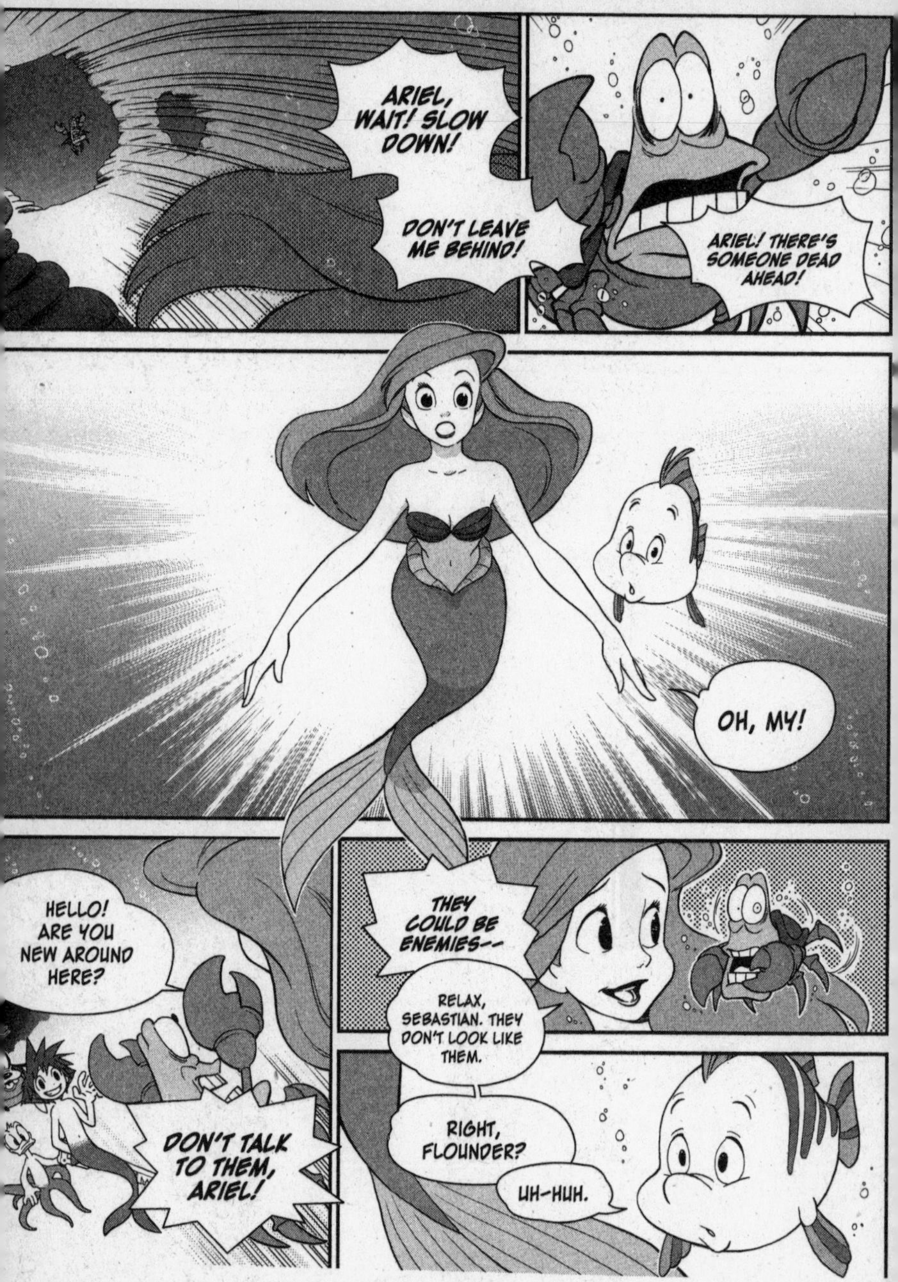
ARIEL, WAIT! SLOW DOWN!
DON'T LEAVE ME BEHIND!
ARIEL! THERE'S SOMEONE DEAD AHEAD!
OH, MY!
HELLO! ARE YOU NEW AROUND HERE?
DON'T TALK TO THEM, ARIEL!
THEY COULD BE ENEMIES--
RELAX, SEBASTIAN. THEY DON'T LOOK LIKE THEM.
RIGHT, FLOUNDER?
UH-HUH.

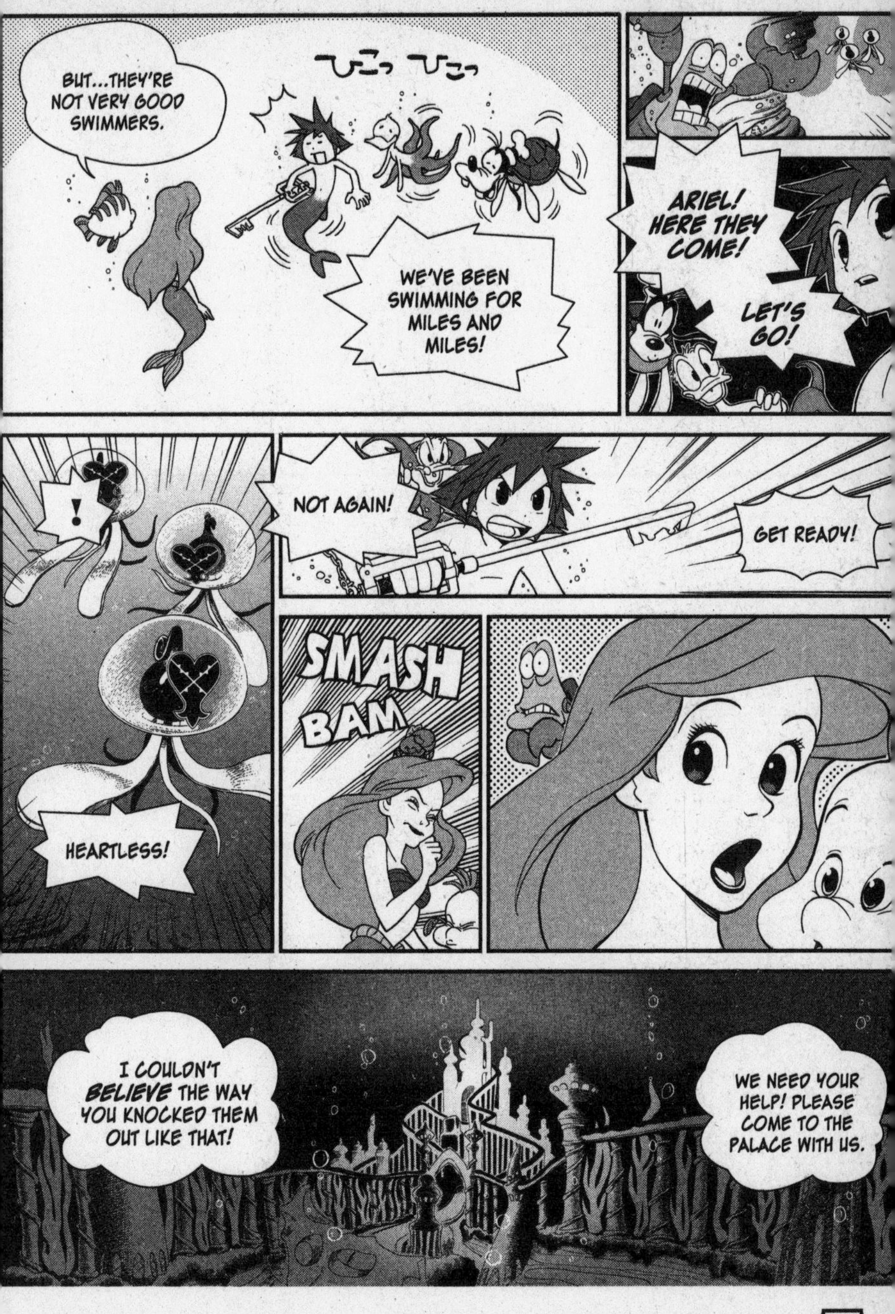
BUT...THEY'RE NOT VERY GOOD SWIMMERS.
ひこっ ひこっ
WE'VE BEEN SWIMMING FOR MILES AND MILES!
ARIEL! HERE THEY COME!
LET'S GO!
!
HEARTLESS!
NOT AGAIN!
GET READY!
SMASH
BAM
I COULDN'T *BELIEVE* THE WAY YOU KNOCKED THEM OUT LIKE THAT!
WE NEED YOUR HELP! PLEASE COME TO THE PALACE WITH US.

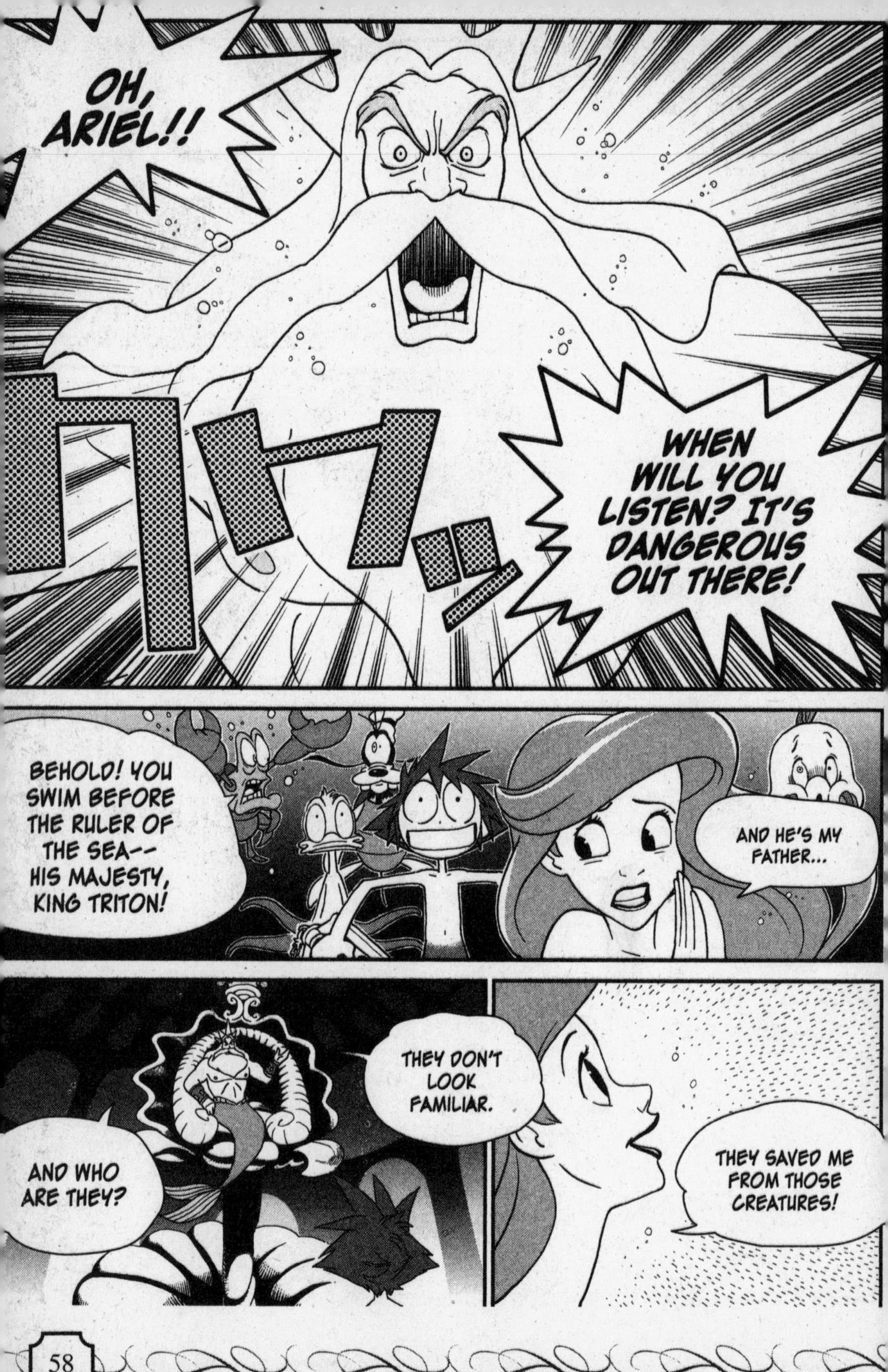
OH, ARIEL!!
WHEN WILL YOU LISTEN? IT'S DANGEROUS OUT THERE!
BEHOLD! YOU SWIM BEFORE THE RULER OF THE SEA-- HIS MAJESTY, KING TRITON!
AND HE'S MY FATHER...
AND WHO ARE THEY?
THEY DON'T LOOK FAMILIAR.
THEY SAVED ME FROM THOSE CREATURES!

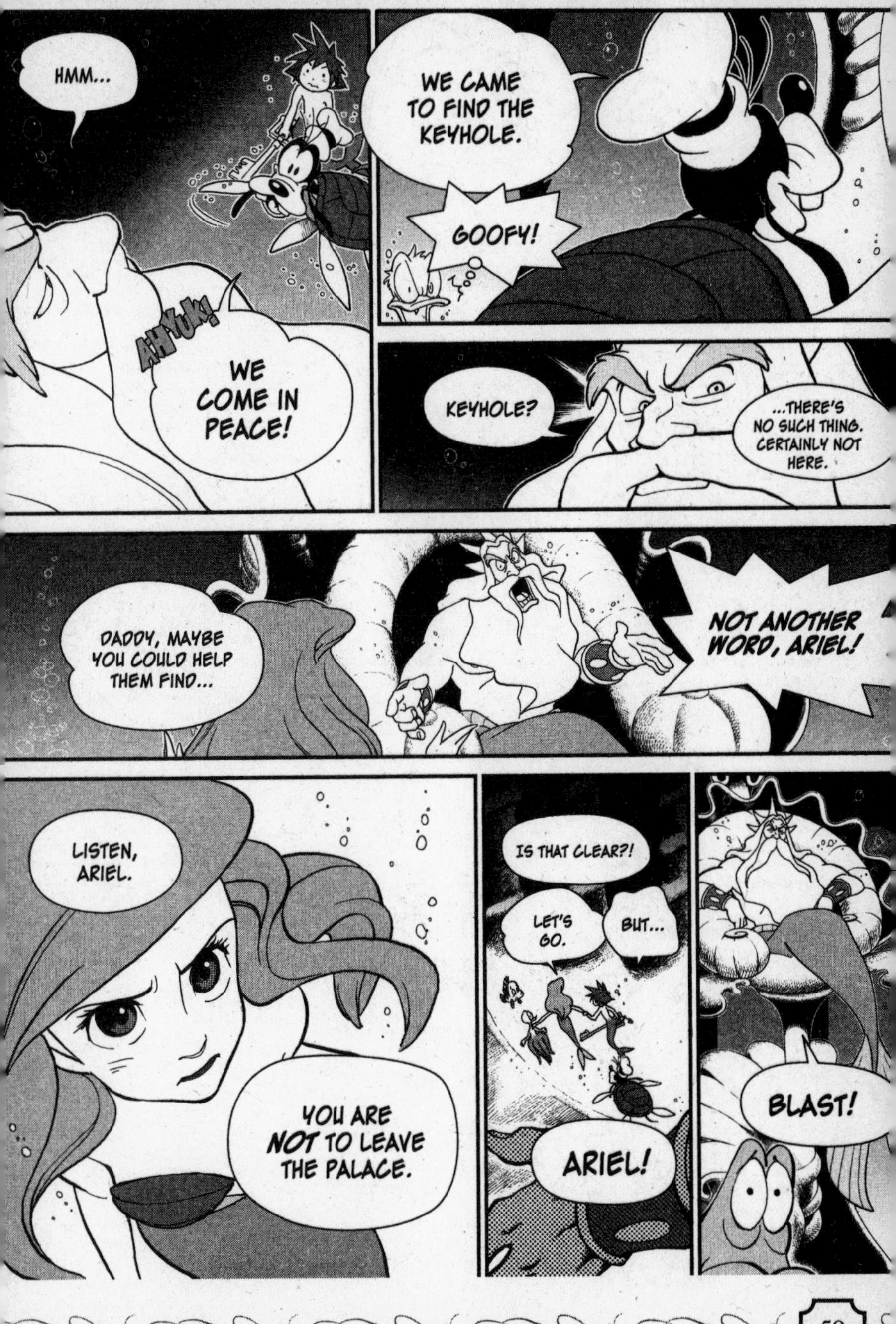
HMM...
AHYUK!
WE COME IN PEACE!
WE CAME TO FIND THE KEYHOLE.
GOOFY!
KEYHOLE?
...THERE'S NO SUCH THING. CERTAINLY NOT HERE.
DADDY, MAYBE YOU COULD HELP THEM FIND...
NOT ANOTHER WORD, ARIEL!
LISTEN, ARIEL.
YOU ARE NOT TO LEAVE THE PALACE.
IS THAT CLEAR?!
LET'S GO.
BUT...
ARIEL!
BLAST!

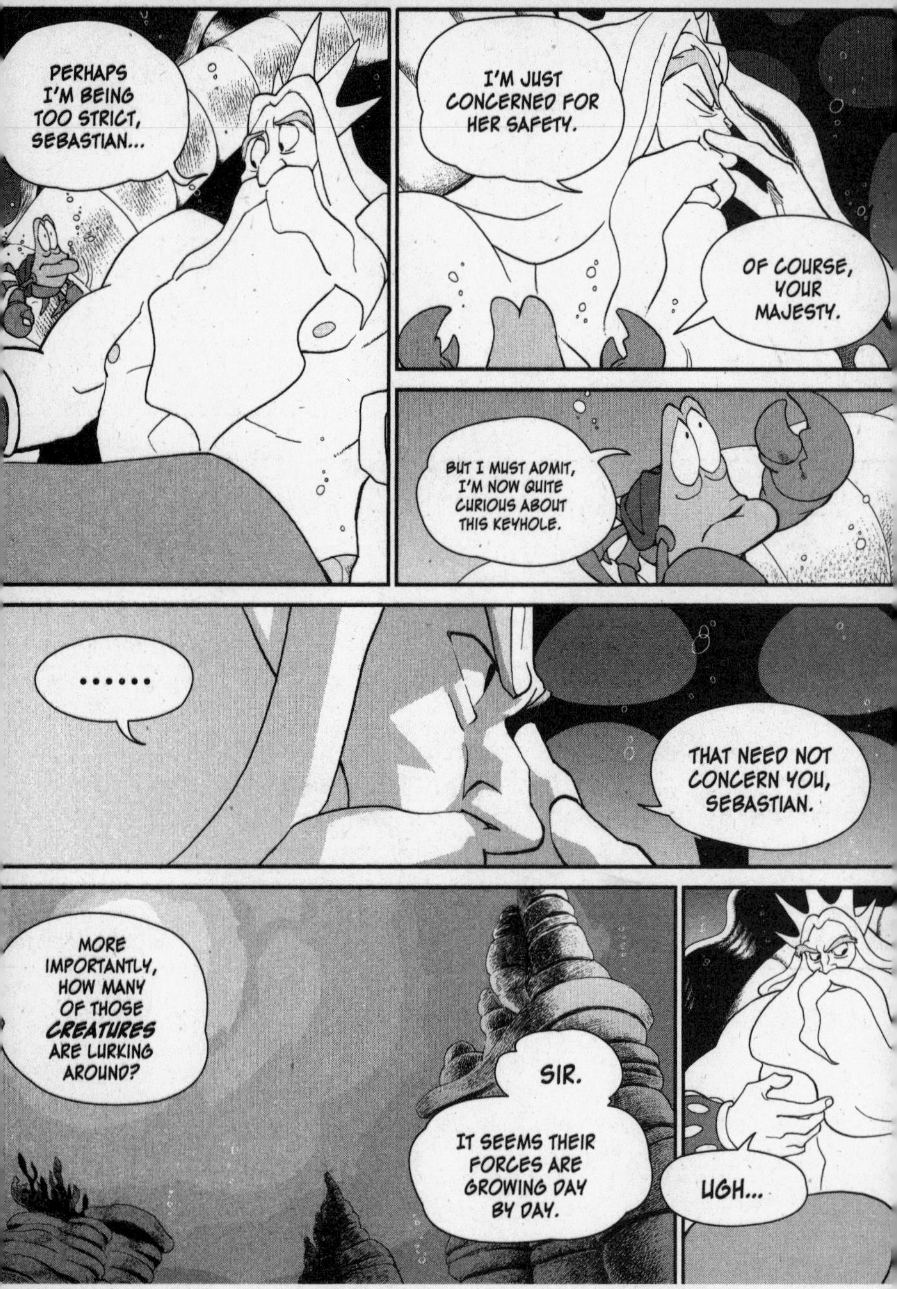
PERHAPS I'M BEING TOO STRICT, SEBASTIAN...
I'M JUST CONCERNED FOR HER SAFETY.
OF COURSE, YOUR MAJESTY.
BUT I MUST ADMIT, I'M NOW QUITE CURIOUS ABOUT THIS KEYHOLE.
......
THAT NEED NOT CONCERN YOU, SEBASTIAN.
MORE IMPORTANTLY, HOW MANY OF THOSE ***CREATURES*** ARE LURKING AROUND?
SIR.
IT SEEMS THEIR FORCES ARE GROWING DAY BY DAY.
UGH...

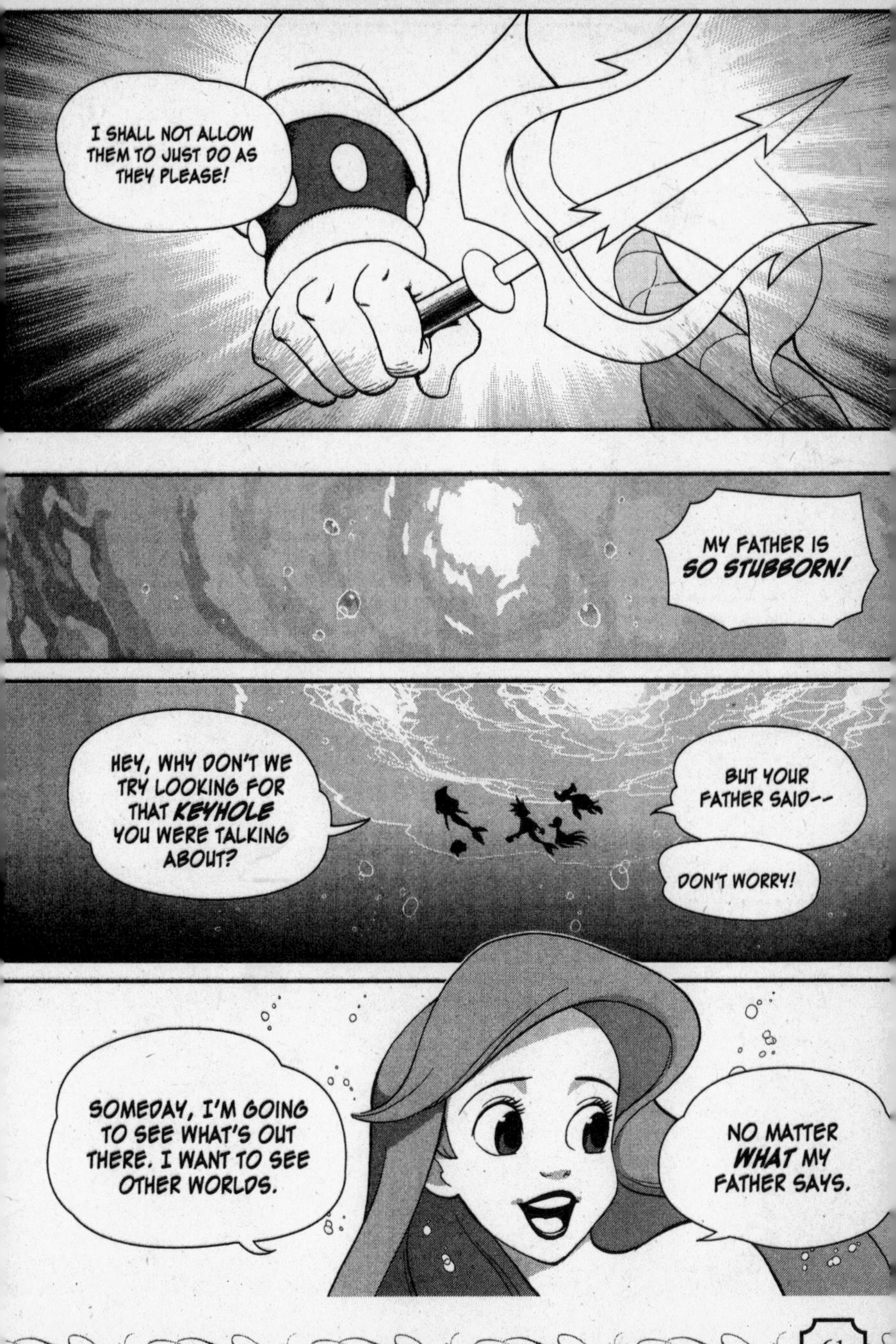
I SHALL NOT ALLOW THEM TO JUST DO AS THEY PLEASE!
MY FATHER IS SO STUBBORN!
HEY, WHY DON'T WE TRY LOOKING FOR THAT KEYHOLE YOU WERE TALKING ABOUT?
BUT YOUR FATHER SAID--
DON'T WORRY!
SOMEDAY, I'M GOING TO SEE WHAT'S OUT THERE. I WANT TO SEE OTHER WORLDS.
NO MATTER WHAT MY FATHER SAYS.

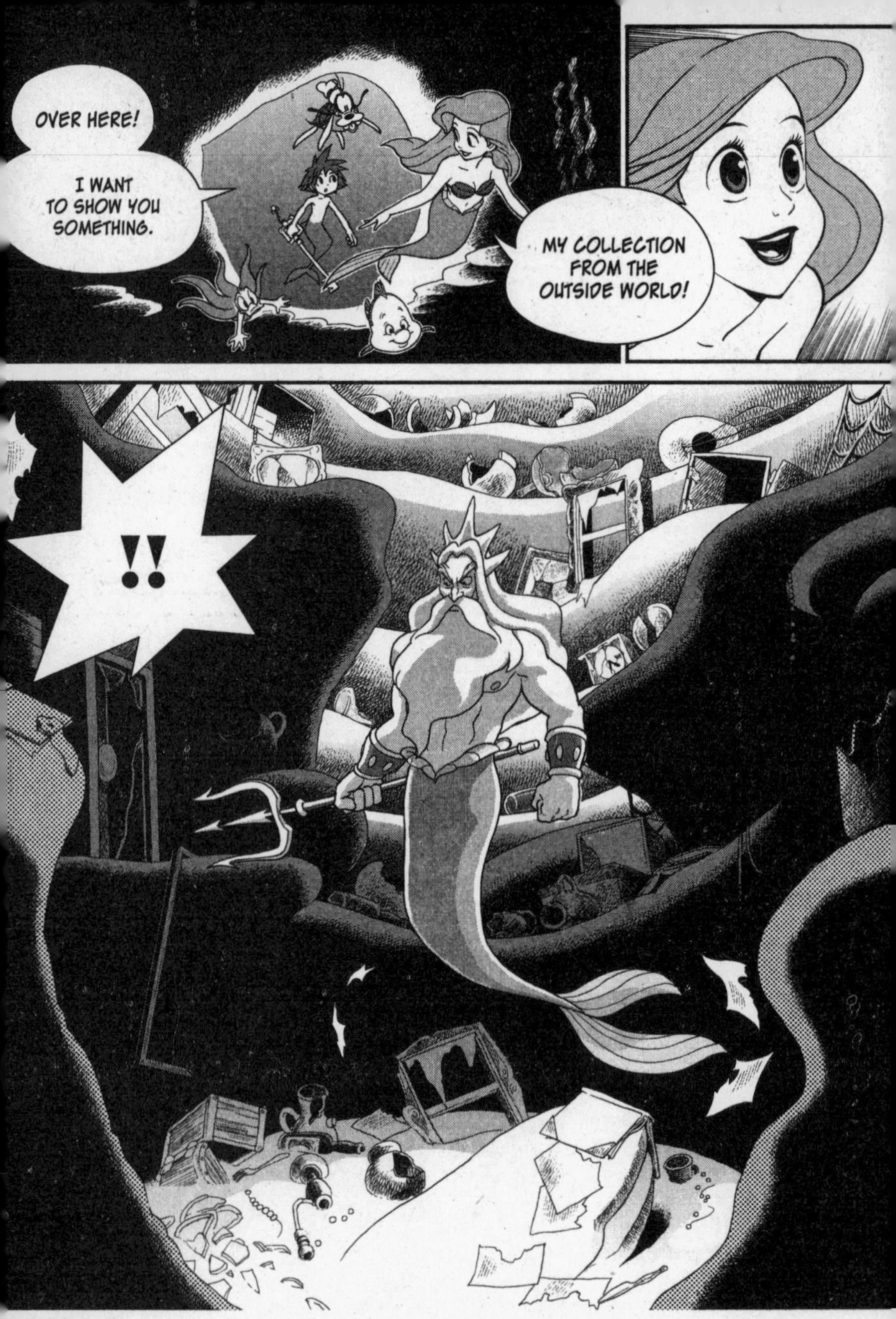
OVER HERE!
I WANT TO SHOW YOU SOMETHING.
MY COLLECTION FROM THE OUTSIDE WORLD!
!!

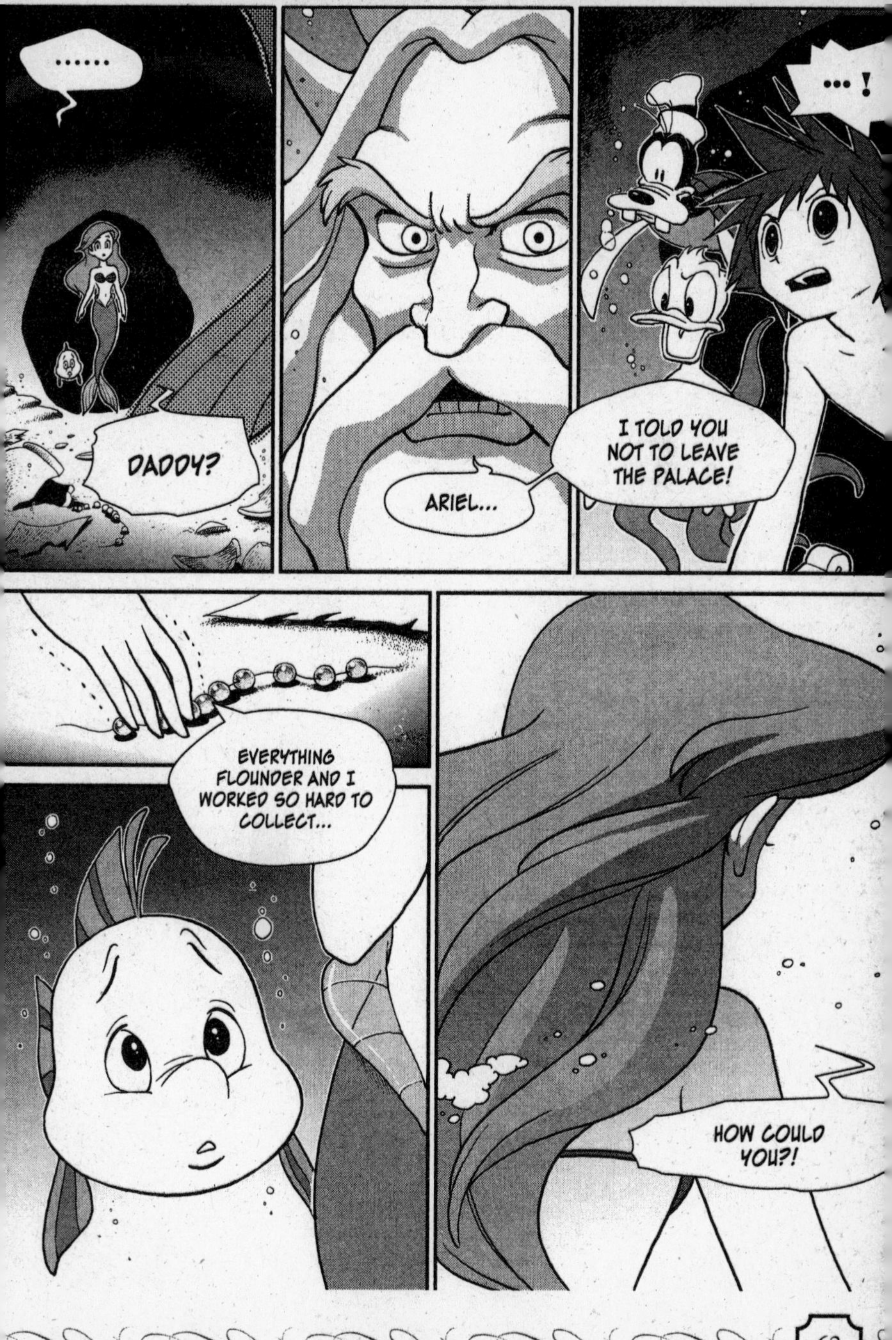
......
DADDY?
ARIEL...
I TOLD YOU NOT TO LEAVE THE PALACE!
... !
EVERYTHING FLOUNDER AND I WORKED SO HARD TO COLLECT...
HOW COULD YOU?!

ARIEL!!

FATHER OR NOT, THAT WASN'T VERY NICE!

IT WASN'T ME.

YOU ARE ALL FROM ANOTHER WORLD, AREN'T YOU?

THEN *YOU* MUST BE THE KEY BEARER.

!!

THOSE DARK CREATURES WERE IN THIS ROOM.

AS THE KEY BEARER, YOU MUST ALREADY KNOW...

ONE MUST NOT MEDDLE IN THE AFFAIRS OF OTHER WORLDS.

BUT...

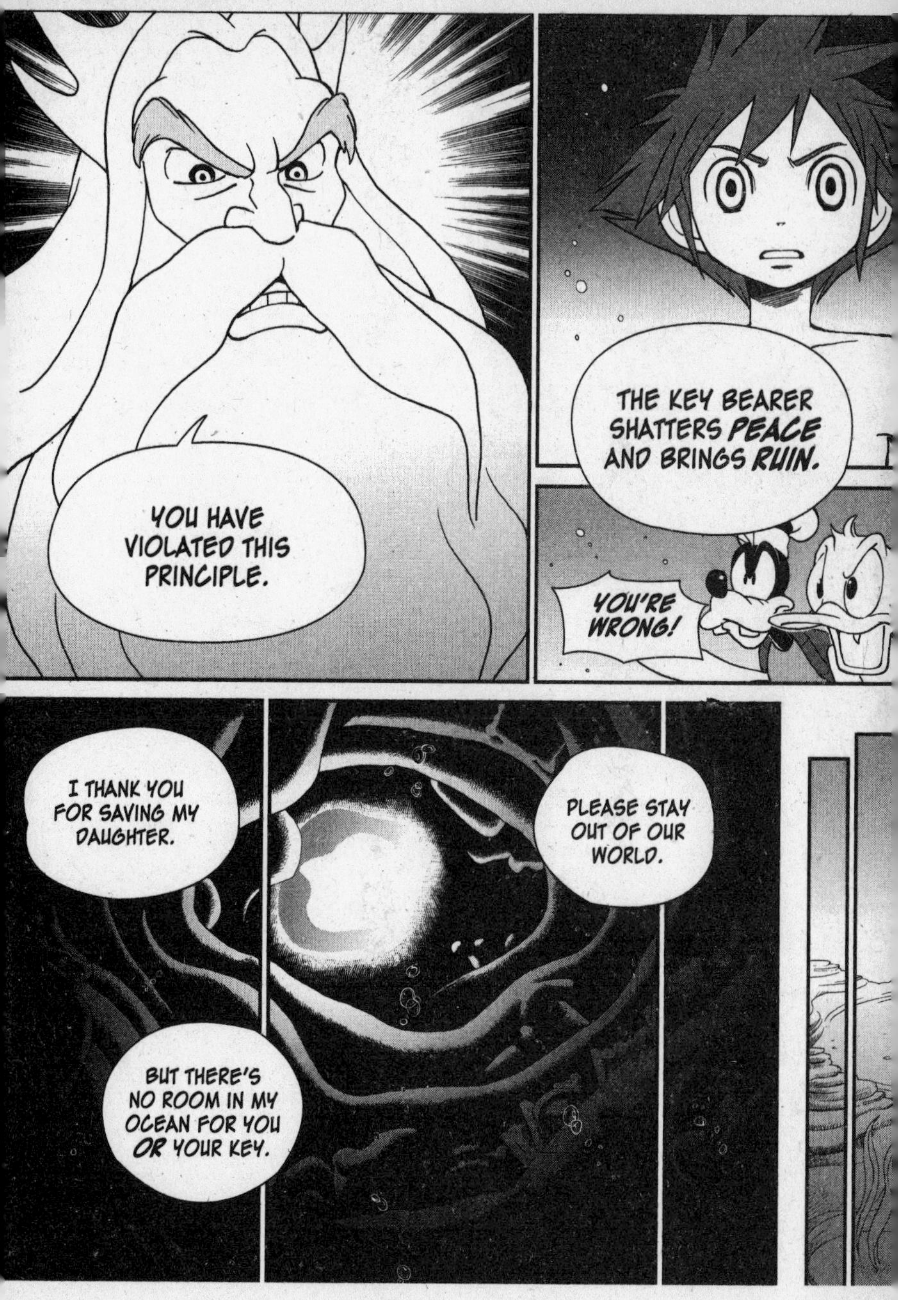

YOU HAVE VIOLATED THIS PRINCIPLE.
THE KEY BEARER SHATTERS PEACE AND BRINGS RUIN.
YOU'RE WRONG!
I THANK YOU FOR SAVING MY DAUGHTER.
BUT THERE'S NO ROOM IN MY OCEAN FOR YOU OR YOUR KEY.
PLEASE STAY OUT OF OUR WORLD.

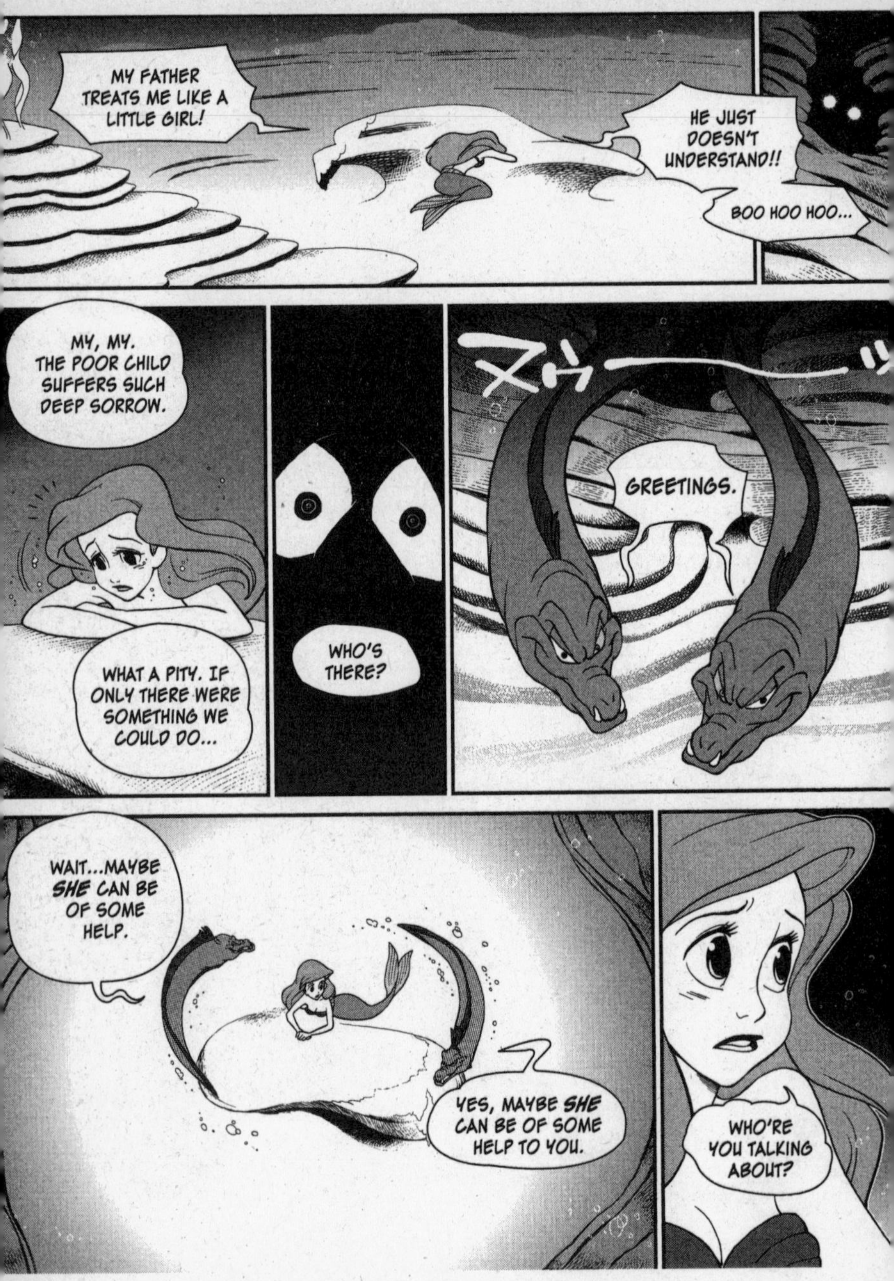
MY FATHER TREATS ME LIKE A LITTLE GIRL!
HE JUST DOESN'T UNDERSTAND!!
BOO HOO HOO...
MY, MY. THE POOR CHILD SUFFERS SUCH DEEP SORROW.
WHAT A PITY. IF ONLY THERE WERE SOMETHING WE COULD DO...
WHO'S THERE?
GREETINGS.
WAIT...MAYBE *SHE* CAN BE OF SOME HELP.
YES, MAYBE *SHE* CAN BE OF SOME HELP TO YOU.
WHO'RE YOU TALKING ABOUT?

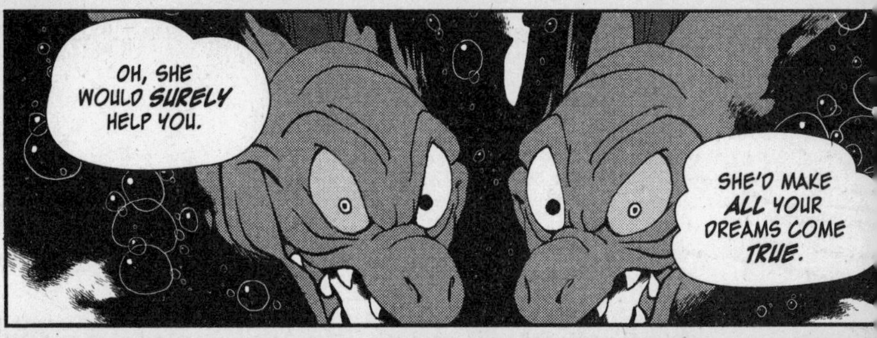
OH, SHE WOULD SURELY HELP YOU.
SHE'D MAKE ALL YOUR DREAMS COME TRUE.

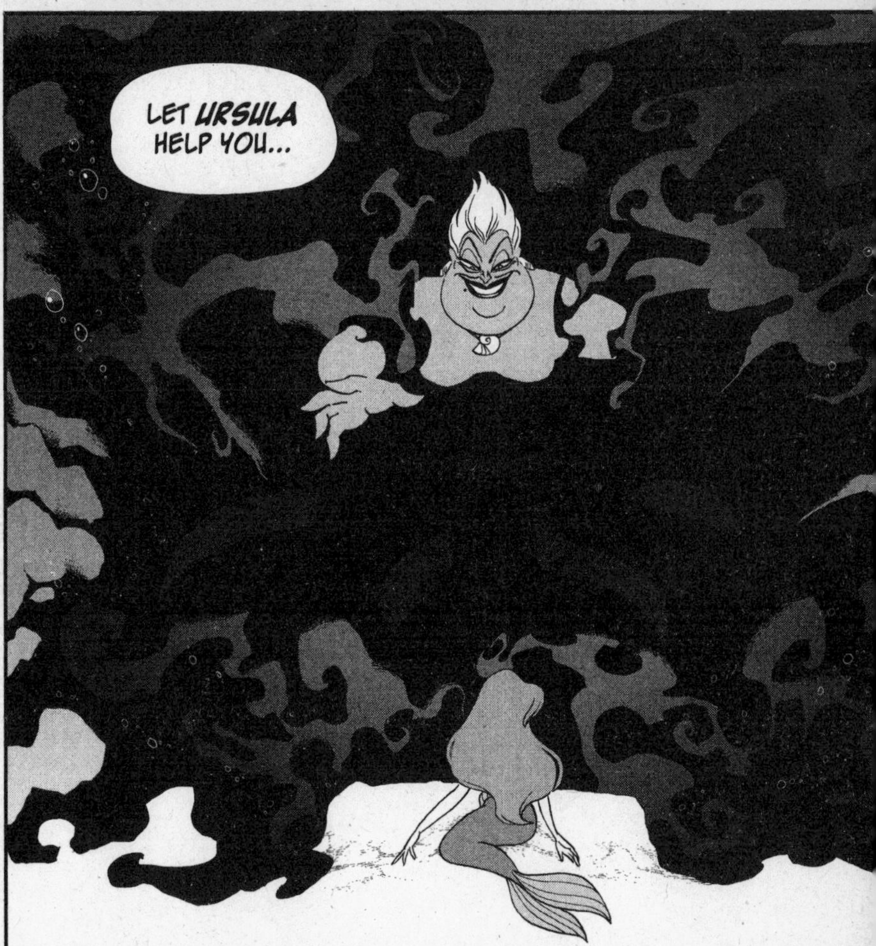
LET URSULA HELP YOU...

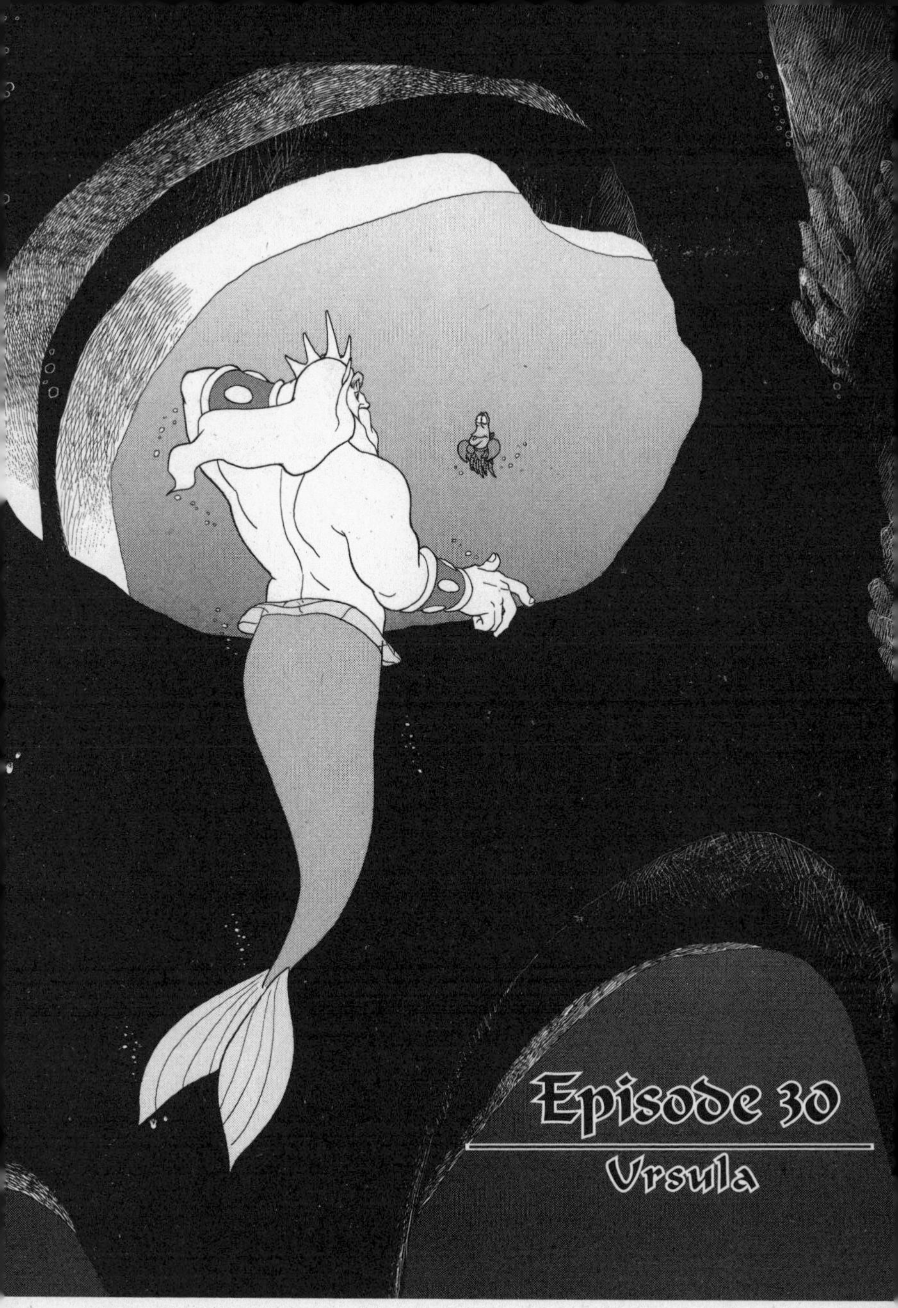
Episode 30
Ursula

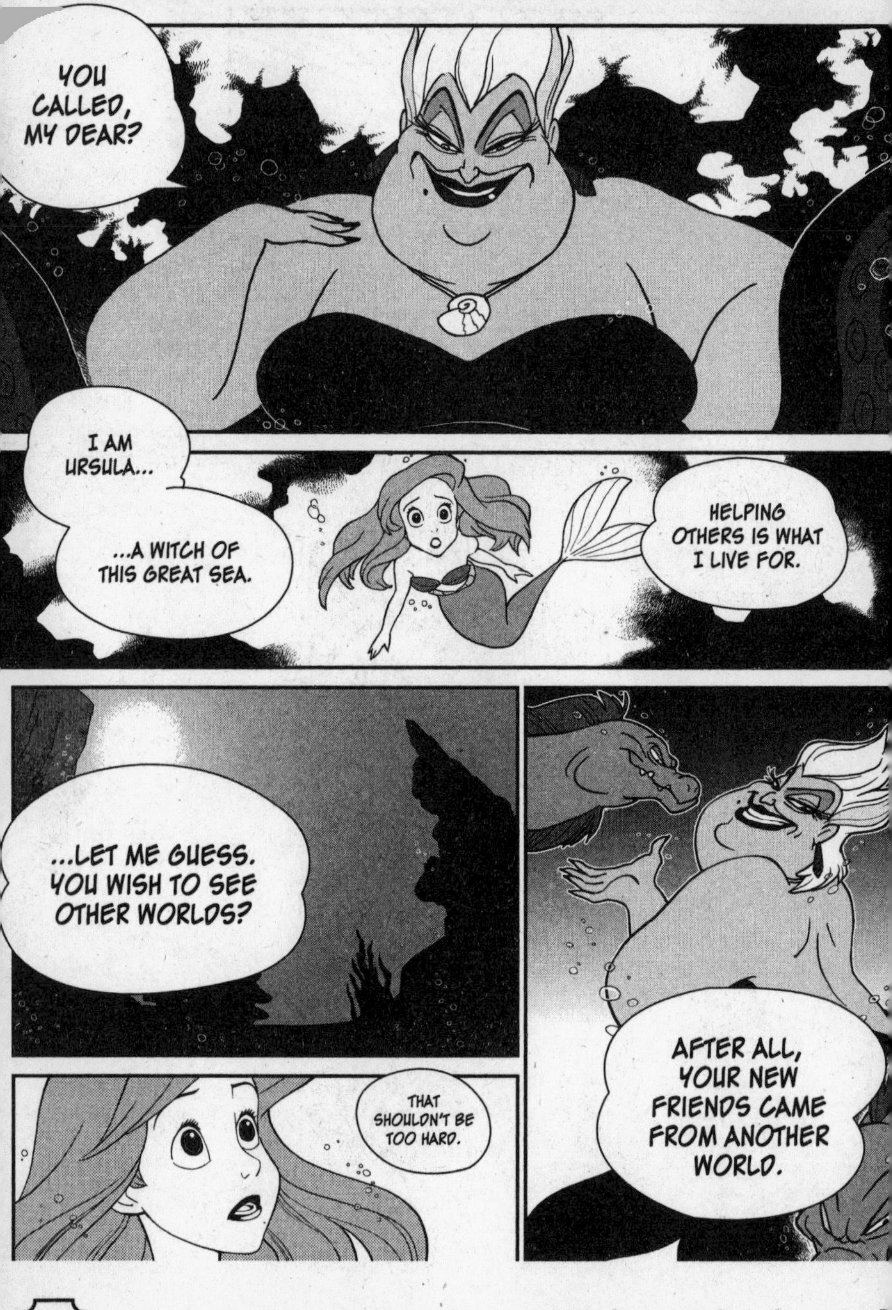
YOU CALLED, MY DEAR?
I AM URSULA...
...A WITCH OF THIS GREAT SEA.
HELPING OTHERS IS WHAT I LIVE FOR.
...LET ME GUESS. YOU WISH TO SEE OTHER WORLDS?
THAT SHOULDN'T BE TOO HARD.
AFTER ALL, YOUR NEW FRIENDS CAME FROM ANOTHER WORLD.

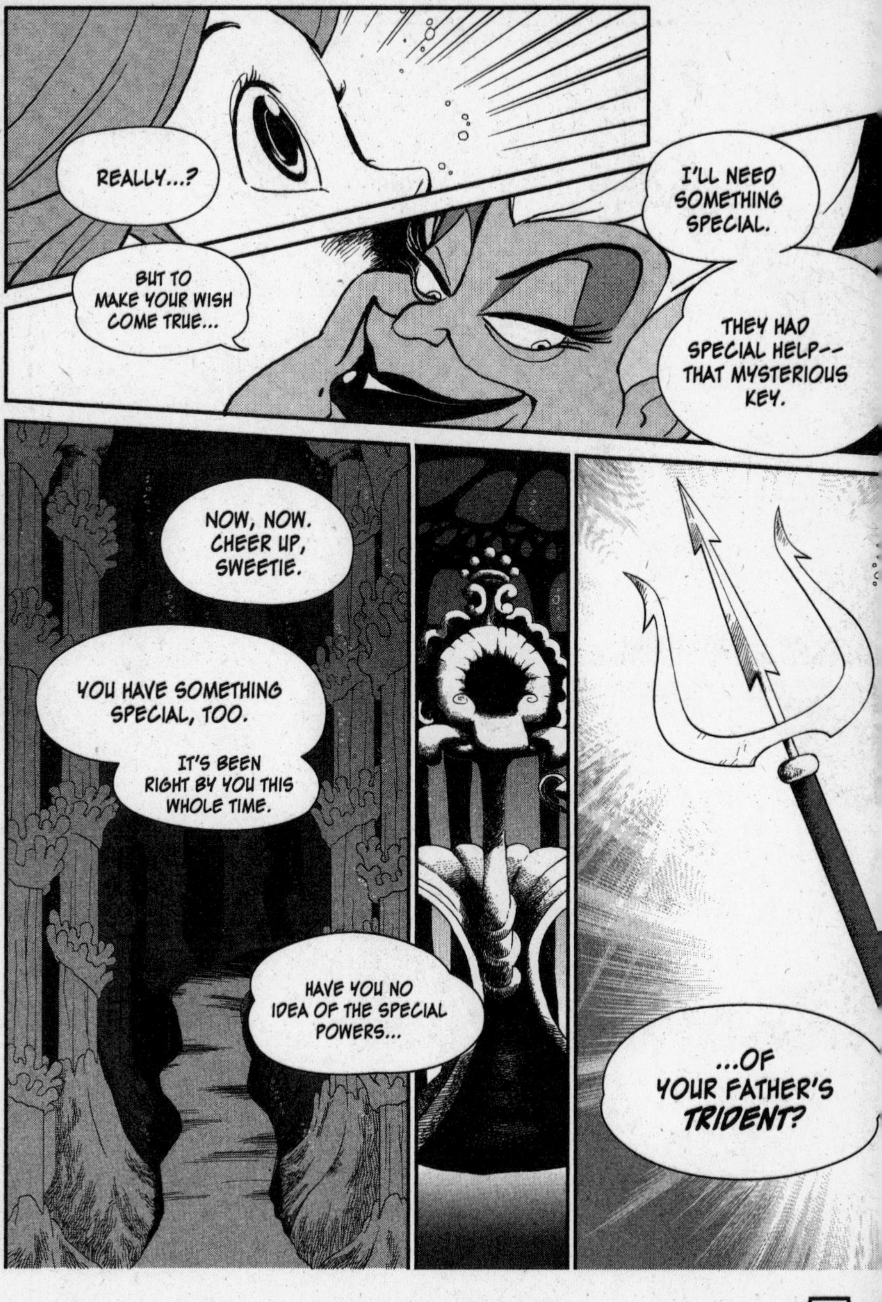
REALLY...?
BUT TO MAKE YOUR WISH COME TRUE...
I'LL NEED SOMETHING SPECIAL.
THEY HAD SPECIAL HELP-- THAT MYSTERIOUS KEY.
NOW, NOW. CHEER UP, SWEETIE.
YOU HAVE SOMETHING SPECIAL, TOO.
IT'S BEEN RIGHT BY YOU THIS WHOLE TIME.
HAVE YOU NO IDEA OF THE SPECIAL POWERS...
...OF YOUR FATHER'S TRIDENT?

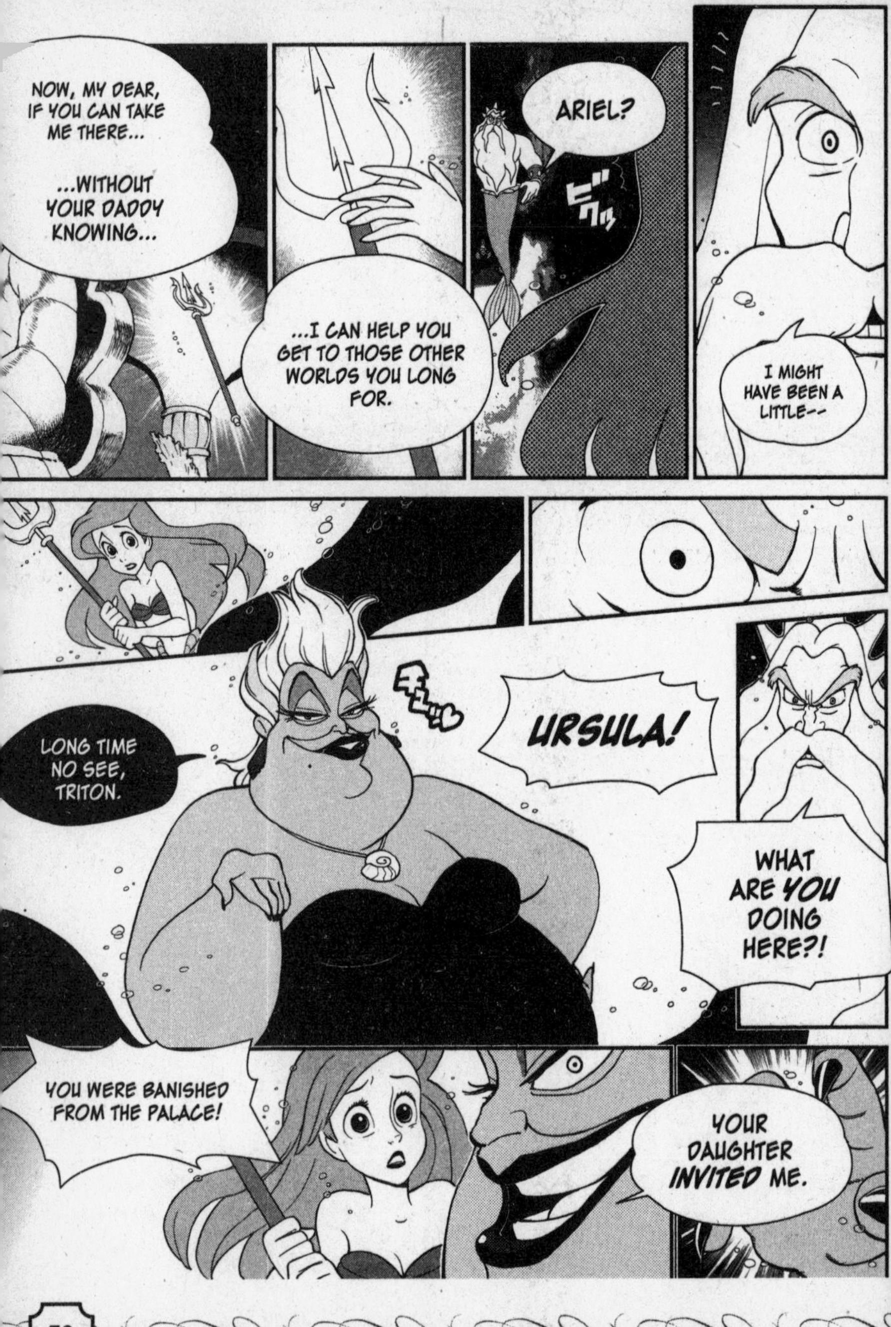
NOW, MY DEAR, IF YOU CAN TAKE ME THERE...
...WITHOUT YOUR DADDY KNOWING...
...I CAN HELP YOU GET TO THOSE OTHER WORLDS YOU LONG FOR.
ARIEL?
I MIGHT HAVE BEEN A LITTLE--
LONG TIME NO SEE, TRITON.
URSULA!
WHAT ARE YOU DOING HERE?!
YOU WERE BANISHED FROM THE PALACE!
YOUR DAUGHTER INVITED ME.

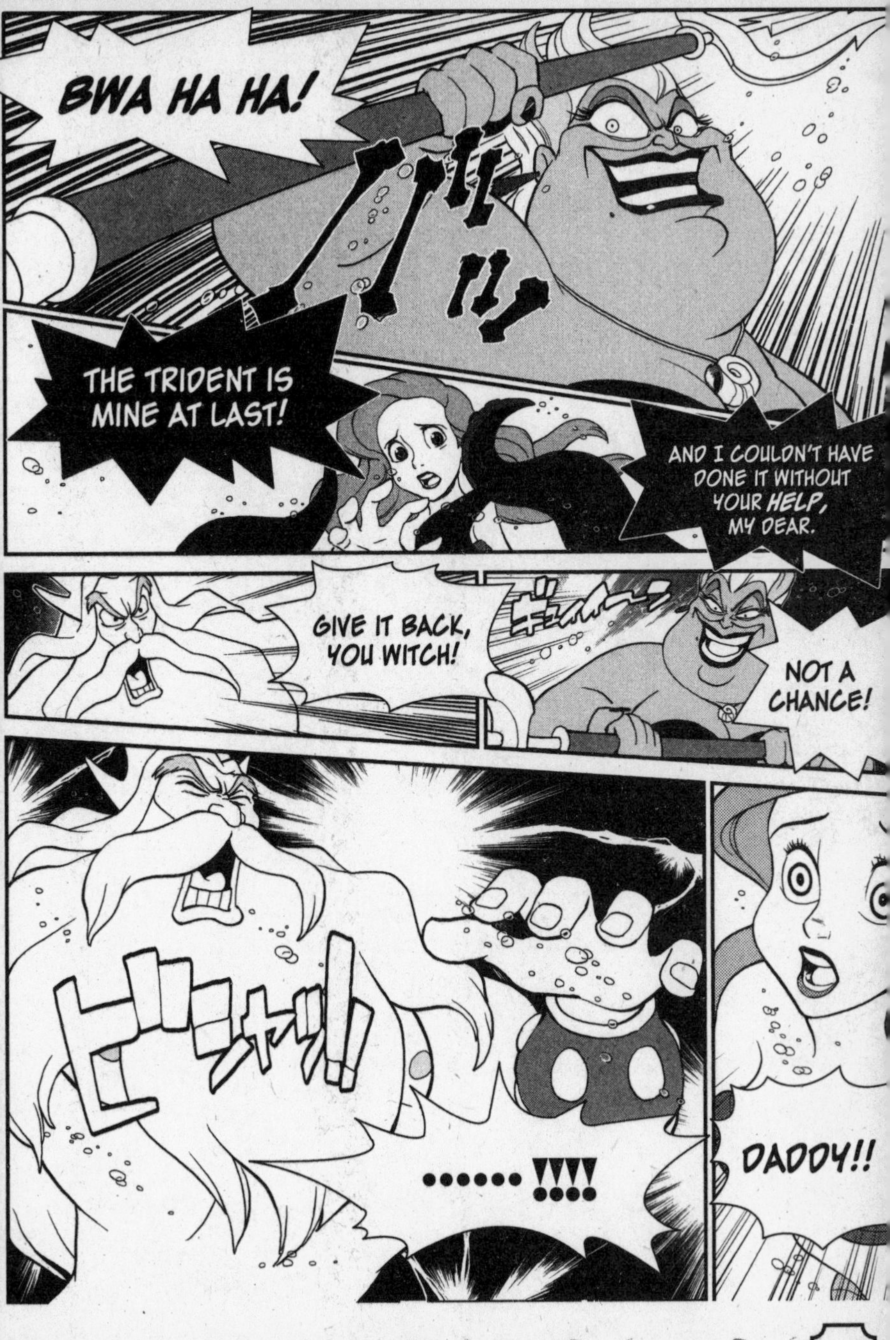
BWA HA HA!
THE TRIDENT IS MINE AT LAST!
AND I COULDN'T HAVE DONE IT WITHOUT YOUR HELP, MY DEAR.
GIVE IT BACK, YOU WITCH!
NOT A CHANCE!
......!!!!
DADDY!!

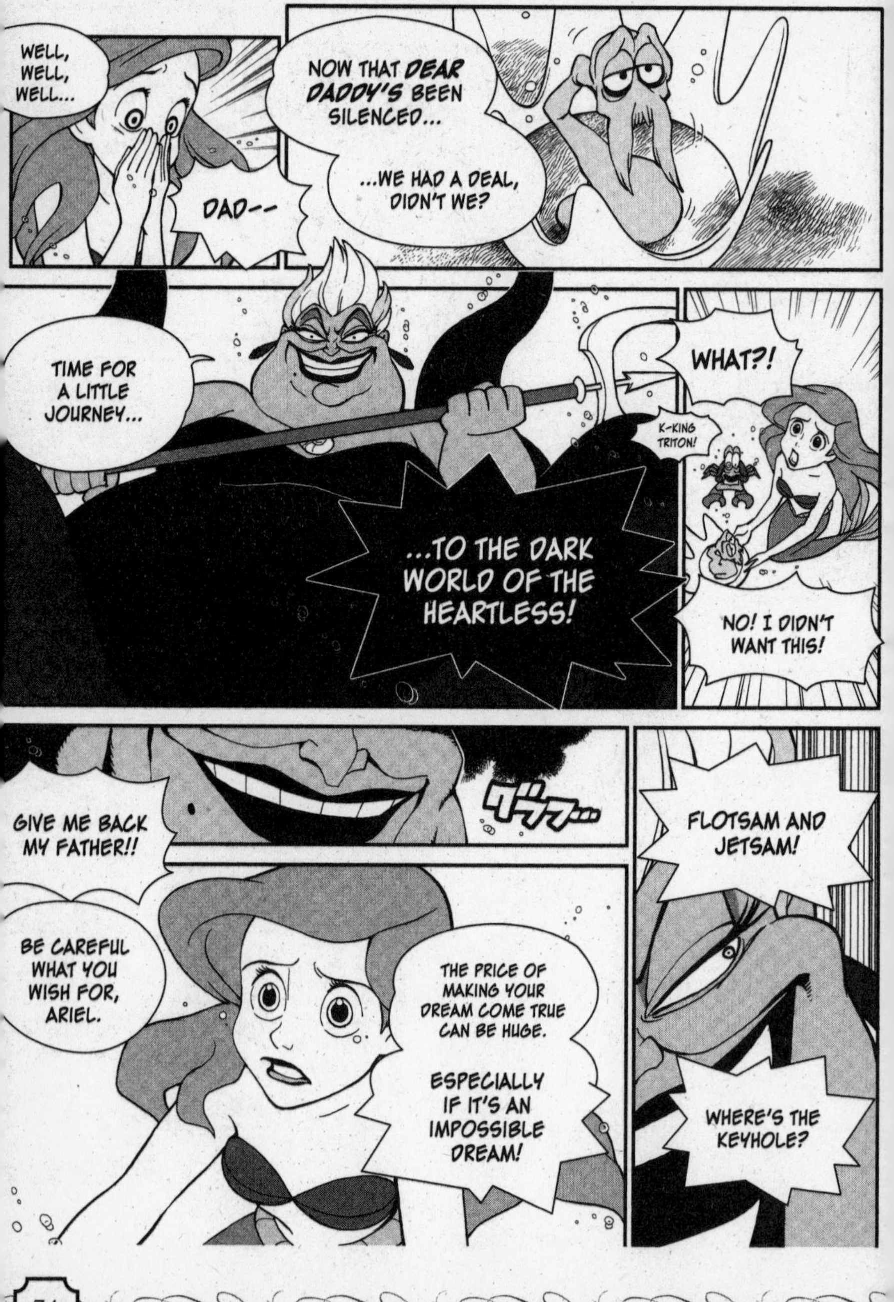
WELL, WELL, WELL...
DAD--
NOW THAT *DEAR DADDY'S* BEEN SILENCED...
...WE HAD A DEAL, DIDN'T WE?
TIME FOR A LITTLE JOURNEY...
...TO THE DARK WORLD OF THE HEARTLESS!
WHAT?!
K-KING TRITON!
NO! I DIDN'T WANT THIS!
GIVE ME BACK MY FATHER!!
BE CAREFUL WHAT YOU WISH FOR, ARIEL.
THE PRICE OF MAKING YOUR DREAM COME TRUE CAN BE HUGE.
ESPECIALLY IF IT'S AN IMPOSSIBLE DREAM!
FLOTSAM AND JETSAM!
WHERE'S THE KEYHOLE?

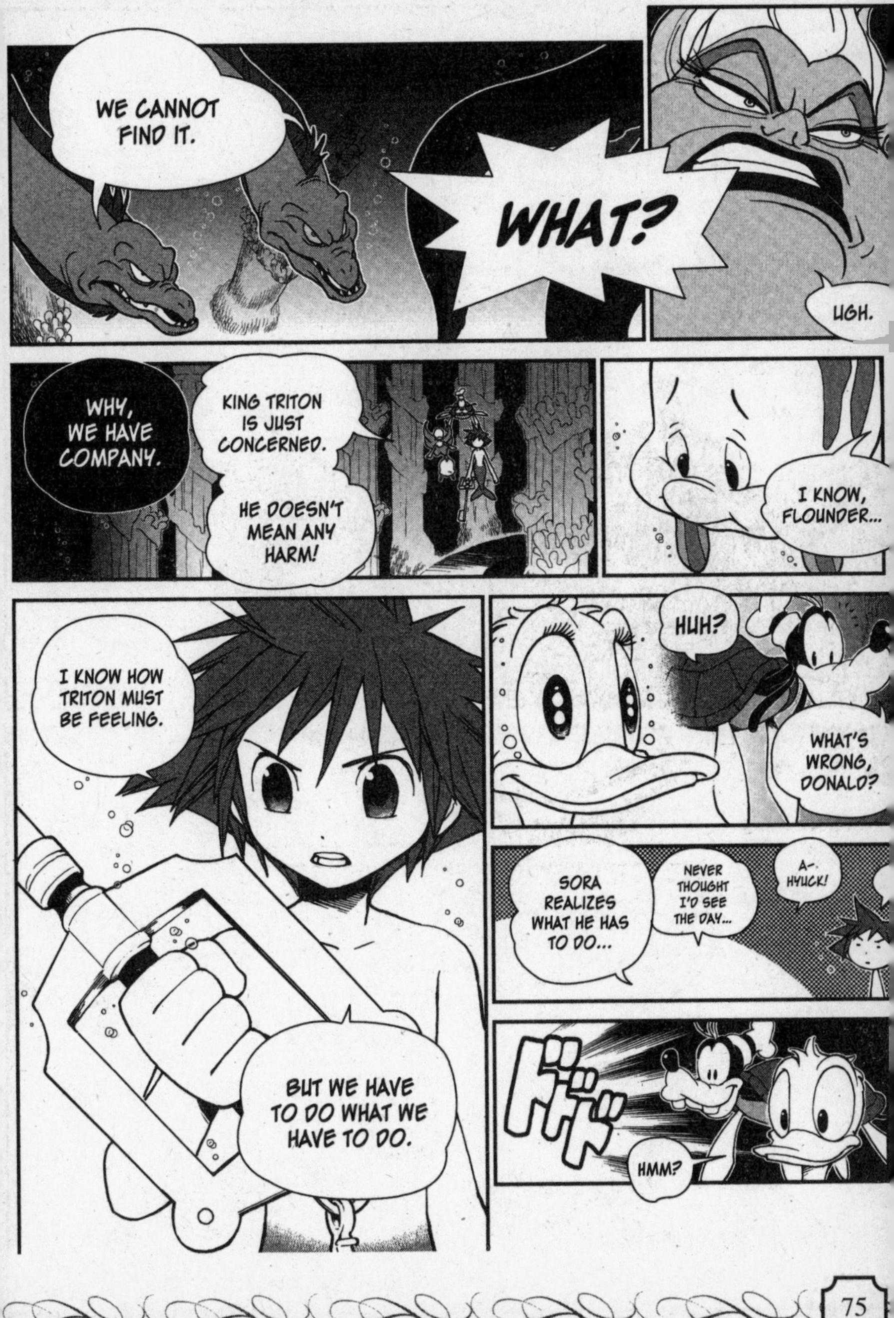
WE CANNOT FIND IT.
WHAT?
UGH.
WHY, WE HAVE COMPANY.
KING TRITON IS JUST CONCERNED.
HE DOESN'T MEAN ANY HARM!
I KNOW, FLOUNDER...
I KNOW HOW TRITON MUST BE FEELING.
BUT WE HAVE TO DO WHAT WE HAVE TO DO.
HUH?
WHAT'S WRONG, DONALD?
SORA REALIZES WHAT HE HAS TO DO...
NEVER THOUGHT I'D SEE THE DAY...
A-HYUCK!
HMM?

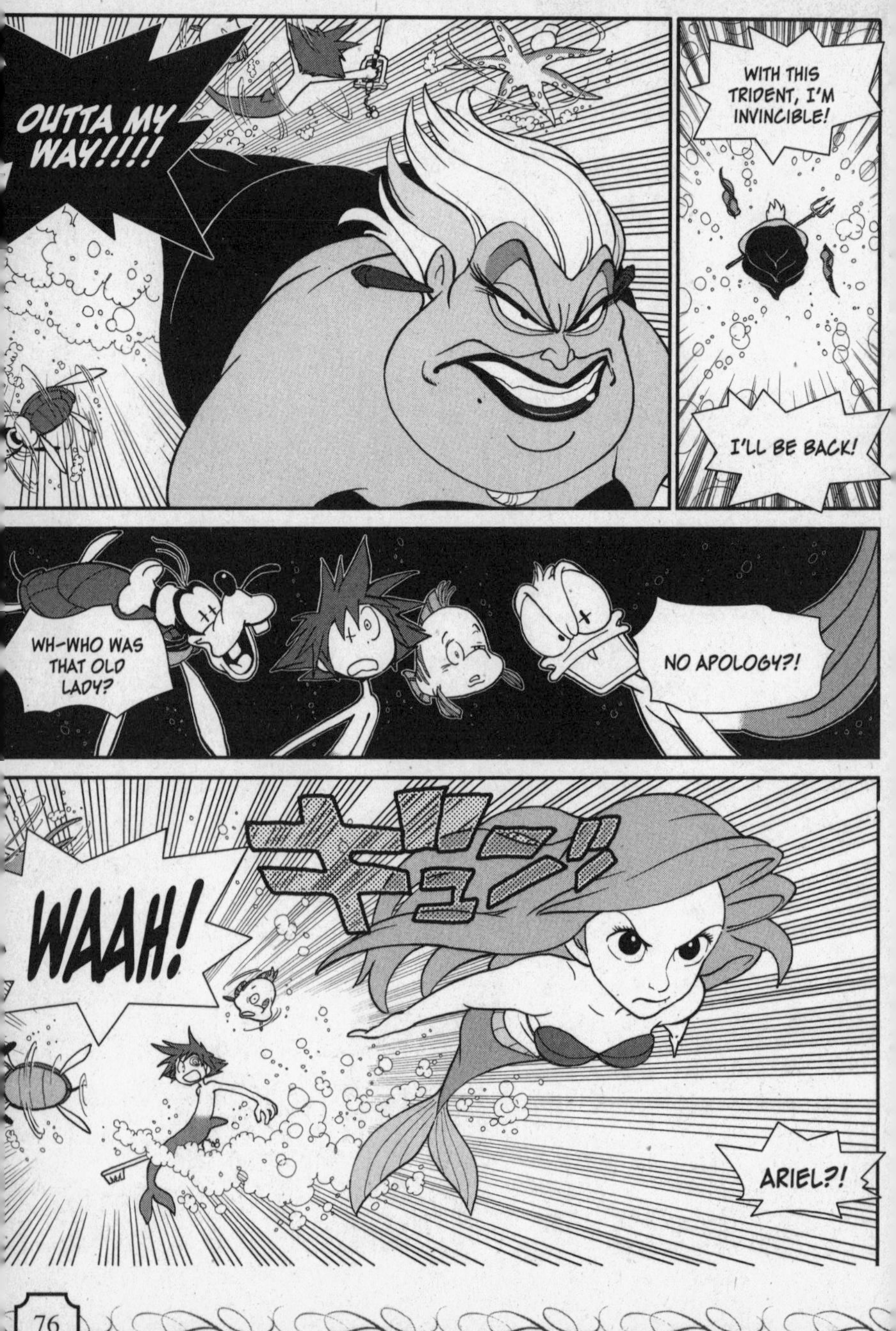
OUTTA MY WAY!!!!
WITH THIS TRIDENT, I'M INVINCIBLE!
I'LL BE BACK!
WH-WHO WAS THAT OLD LADY?
NO APOLOGY?!
キュン
WAAH!
ARIEL?!

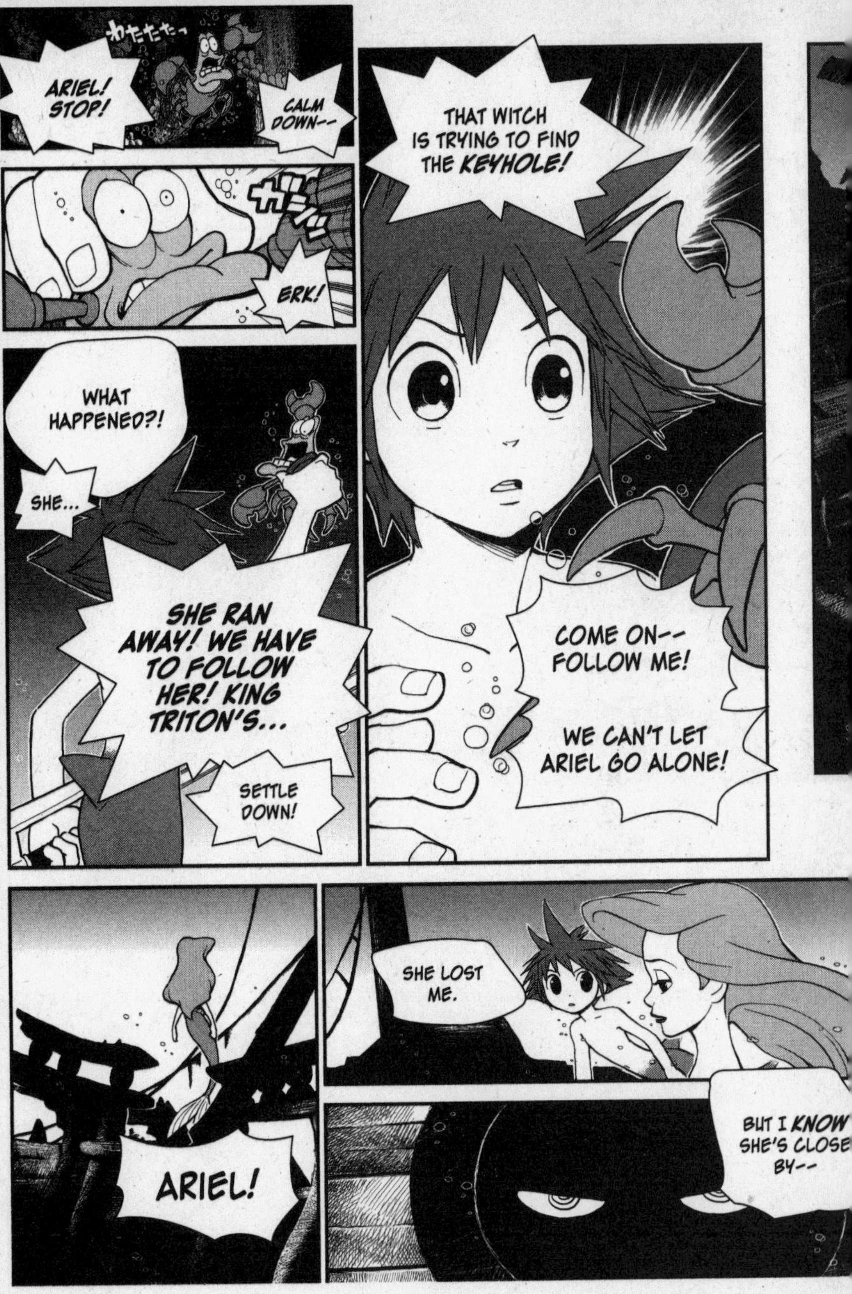
わたたたっ
ARIEL! STOP!
CALM DOWN--
ERK!
WHAT HAPPENED?!
SHE...
SHE RAN AWAY! WE HAVE TO FOLLOW HER! KING TRITON'S...
SETTLE DOWN!
THAT WITCH IS TRYING TO FIND THE *KEYHOLE!*
COME ON-- FOLLOW ME!
WE CAN'T LET ARIEL GO ALONE!
ARIEL!
SHE LOST ME.
BUT I *KNOW* SHE'S CLOSE BY--

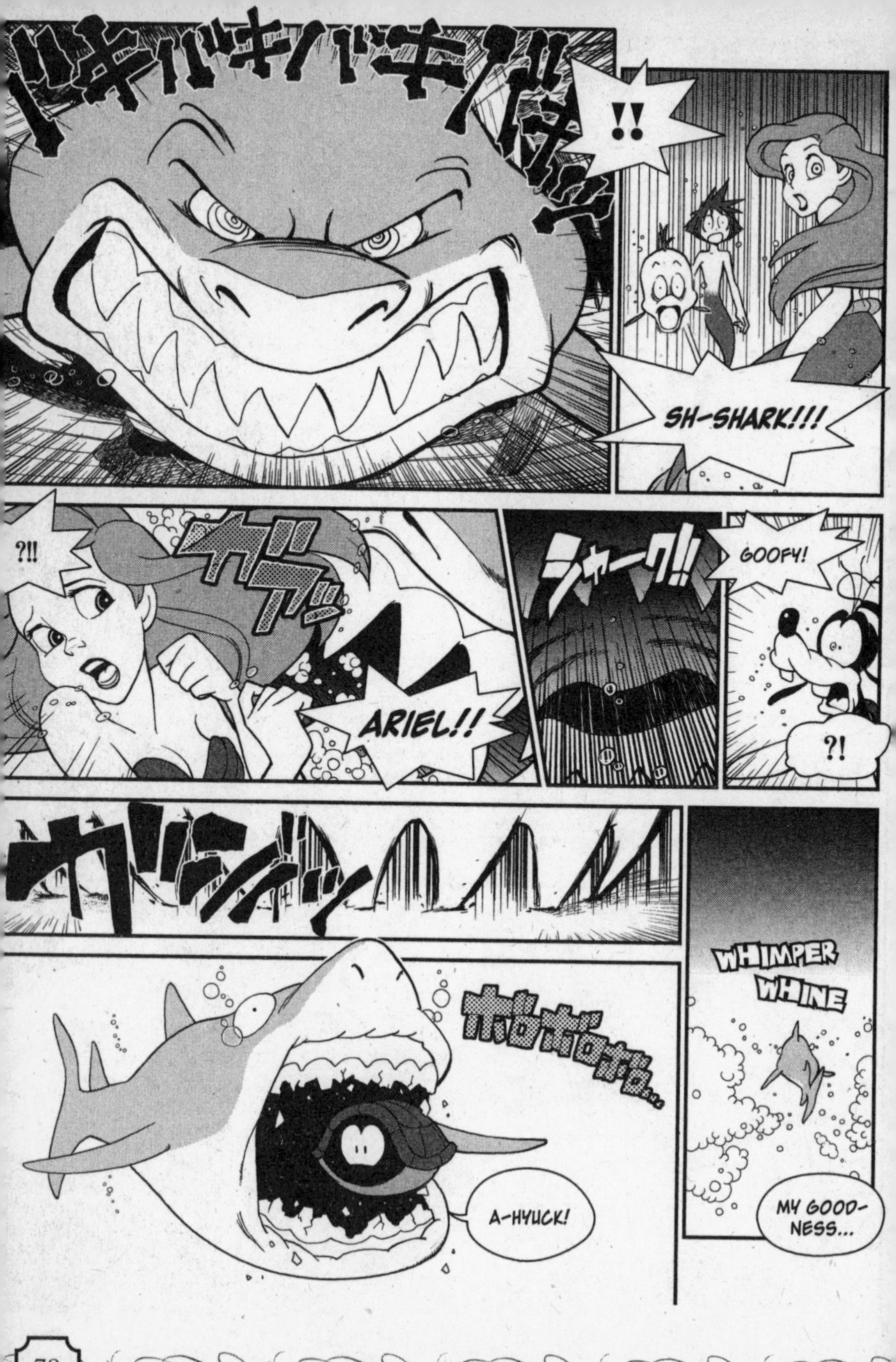
!!
SH-SHARK!!!
?!!
ARIEL!!
GOOFY!
?!
WHIMPER
WHINE
A-HYUCK!
MY GOOD-
NESS...

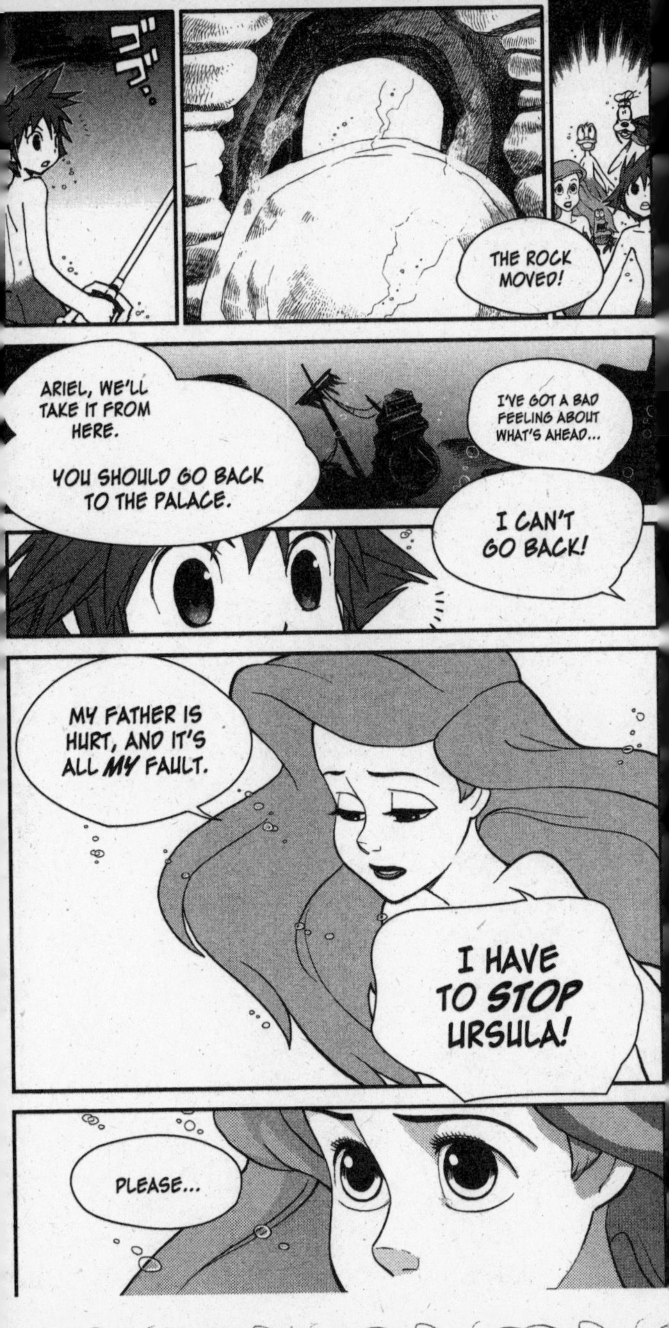

ゴゴ
THE ROCK MOVED!
ARIEL, WE'LL TAKE IT FROM HERE.
YOU SHOULD GO BACK TO THE PALACE.
I'VE GOT A BAD FEELING ABOUT WHAT'S AHEAD...
I CAN'T GO BACK!
MY FATHER IS HURT, AND IT'S ALL *MY* FAULT.
I HAVE TO *STOP* URSULA!
PLEASE...

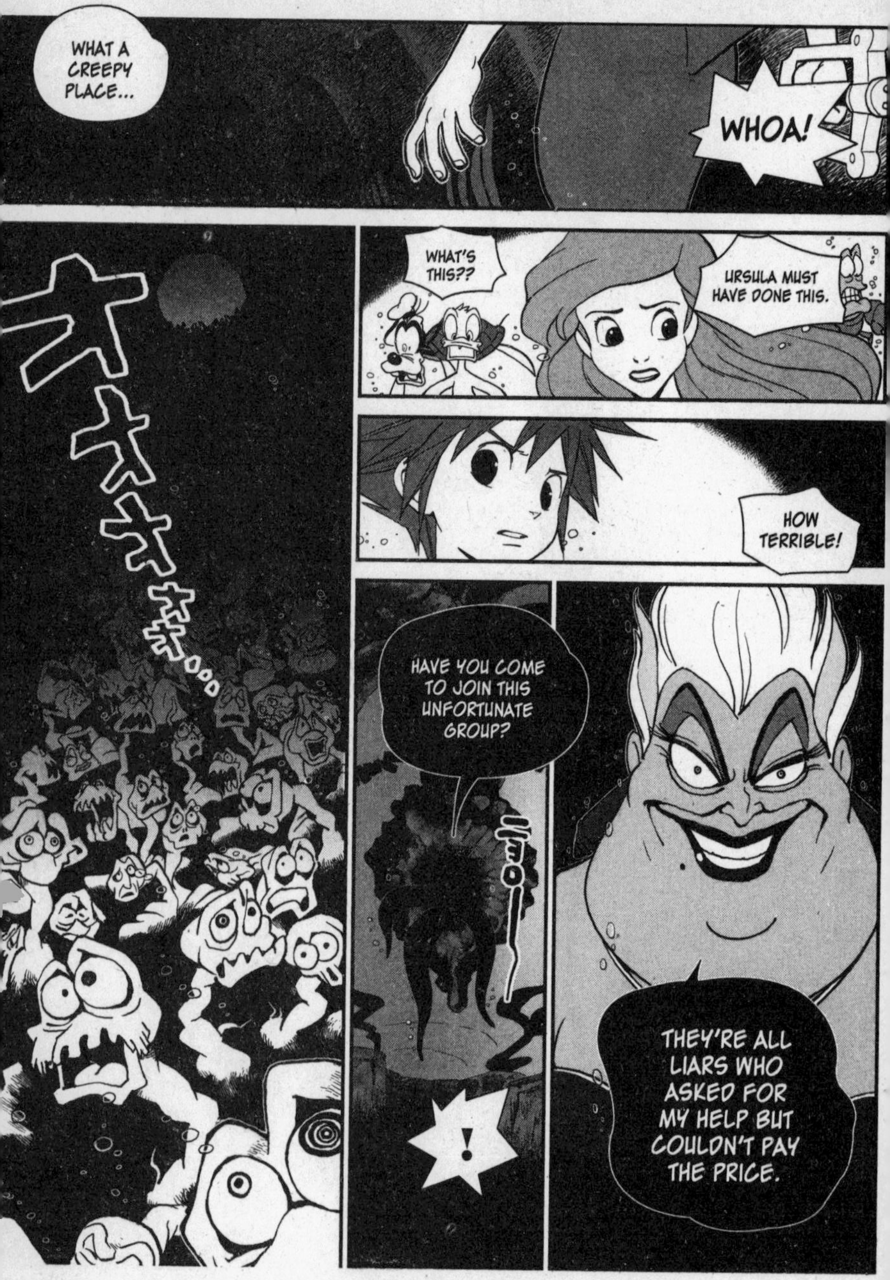

WHAT A CREEPY PLACE...
WHOA!
オォォォォ…
WHAT'S THIS??
URSULA MUST HAVE DONE THIS.
HOW TERRIBLE!
HAVE YOU COME TO JOIN THIS UNFORTUNATE GROUP?
!
THEY'RE ALL LIARS WHO ASKED FOR MY HELP BUT COULDN'T PAY THE PRICE.

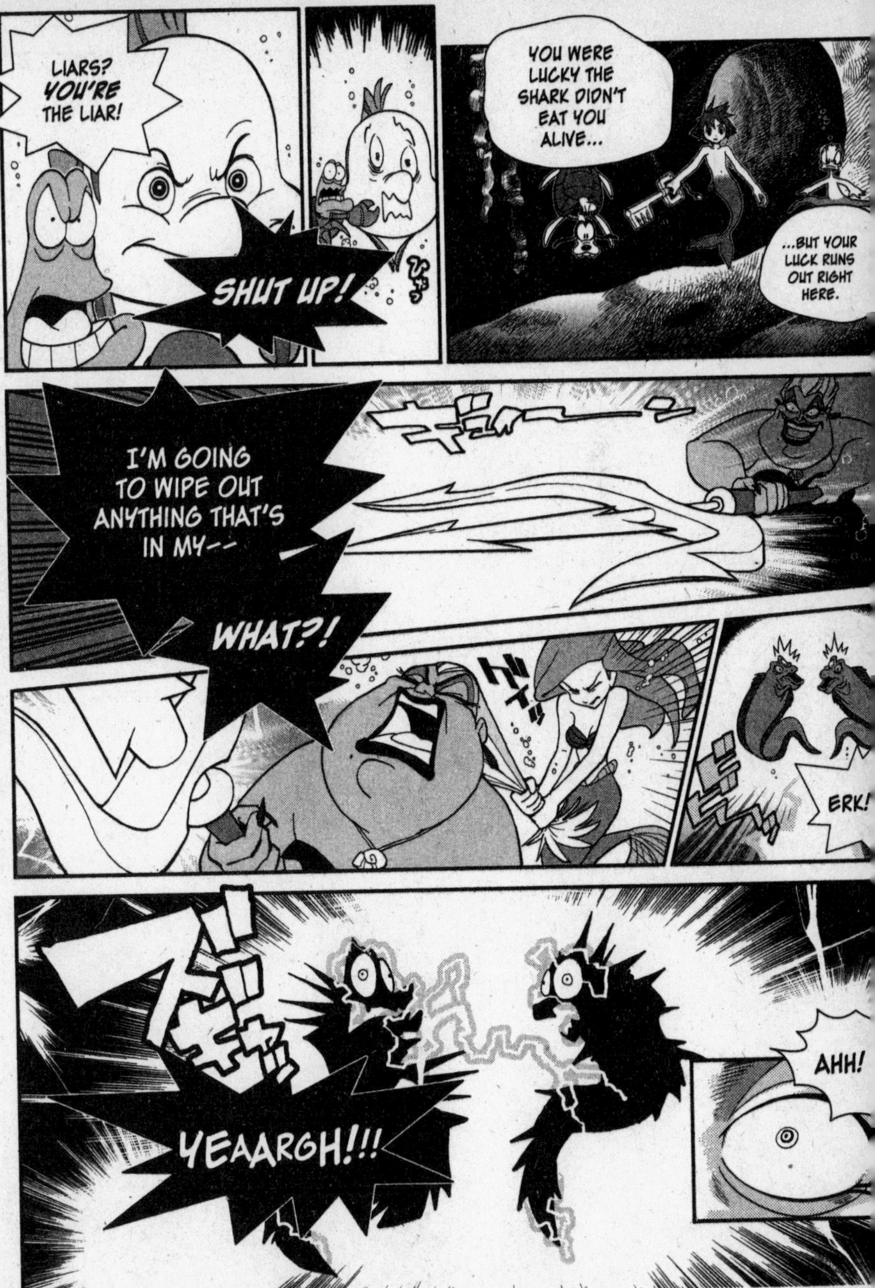
LIARS? YOU'RE THE LIAR!
SHUT UP!
YOU WERE LUCKY THE SHARK DIDN'T EAT YOU ALIVE...
...BUT YOUR LUCK RUNS OUT RIGHT HERE.
I'M GOING TO WIPE OUT ANYTHING THAT'S IN MY--
WHAT?!
ERK!
YEAARGH!!!
AHH!

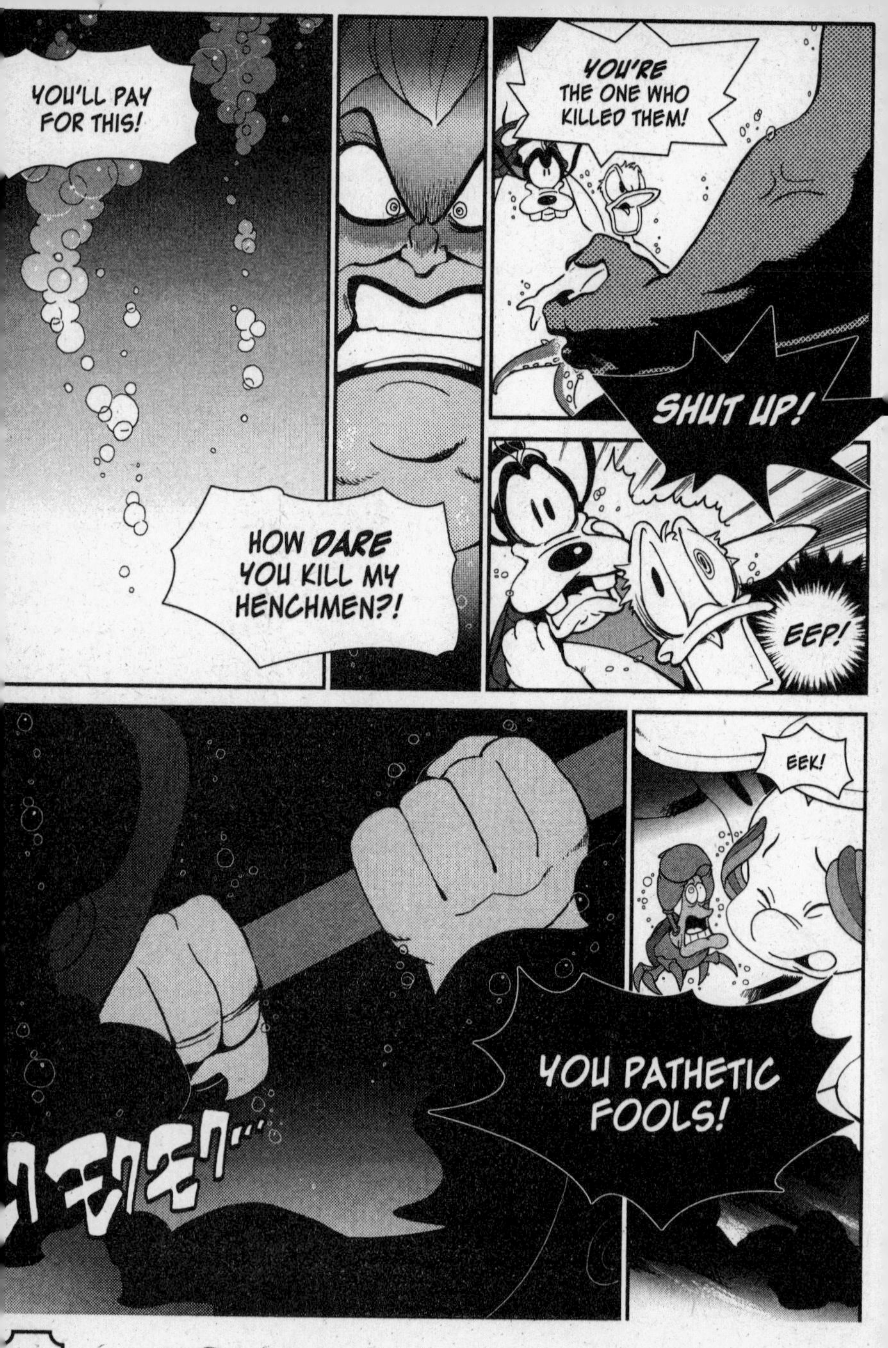
YOU'RE THE ONE WHO KILLED THEM!
SHUT UP!
EEP!
HOW DARE YOU KILL MY HENCHMEN?!
YOU'LL PAY FOR THIS!
EEK!
YOU PATHETIC FOOLS!

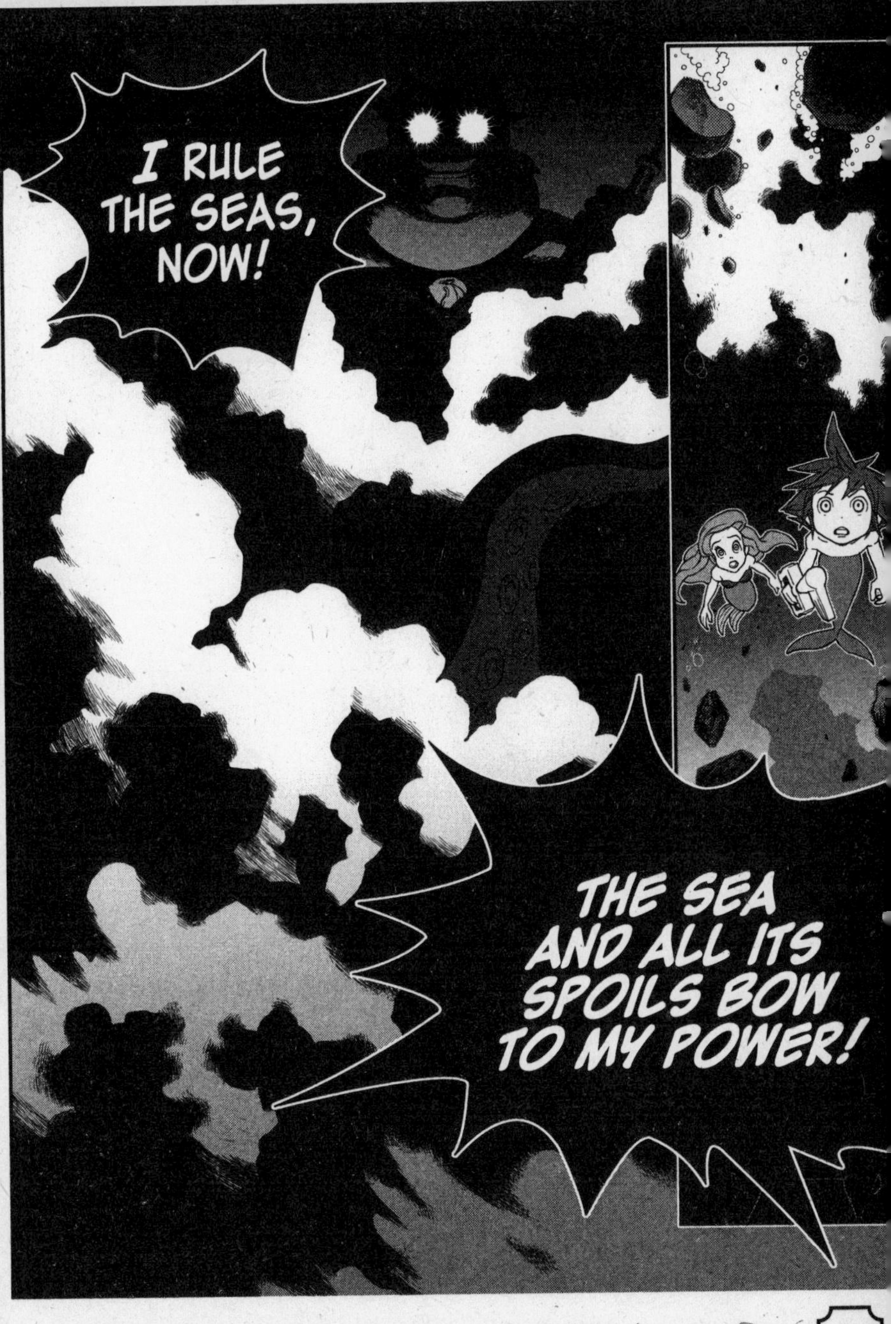
I RULE THE SEAS, NOW!
THE SEA AND ALL ITS SPOILS BOW TO MY POWER!

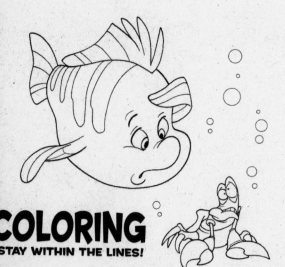

# COLORING
**STAY WITHIN THE LINES!**

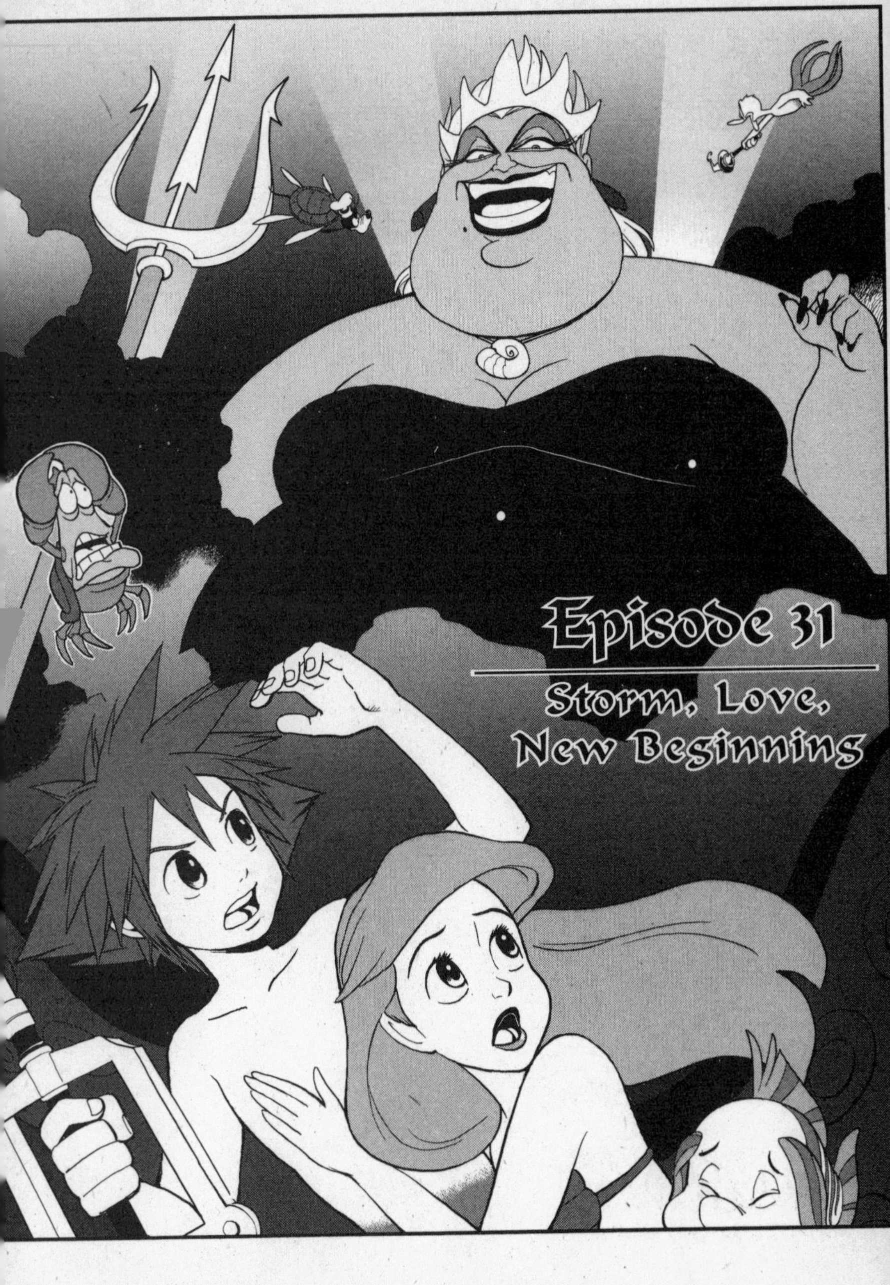

Episode 31
Storm, Love, New Beginning

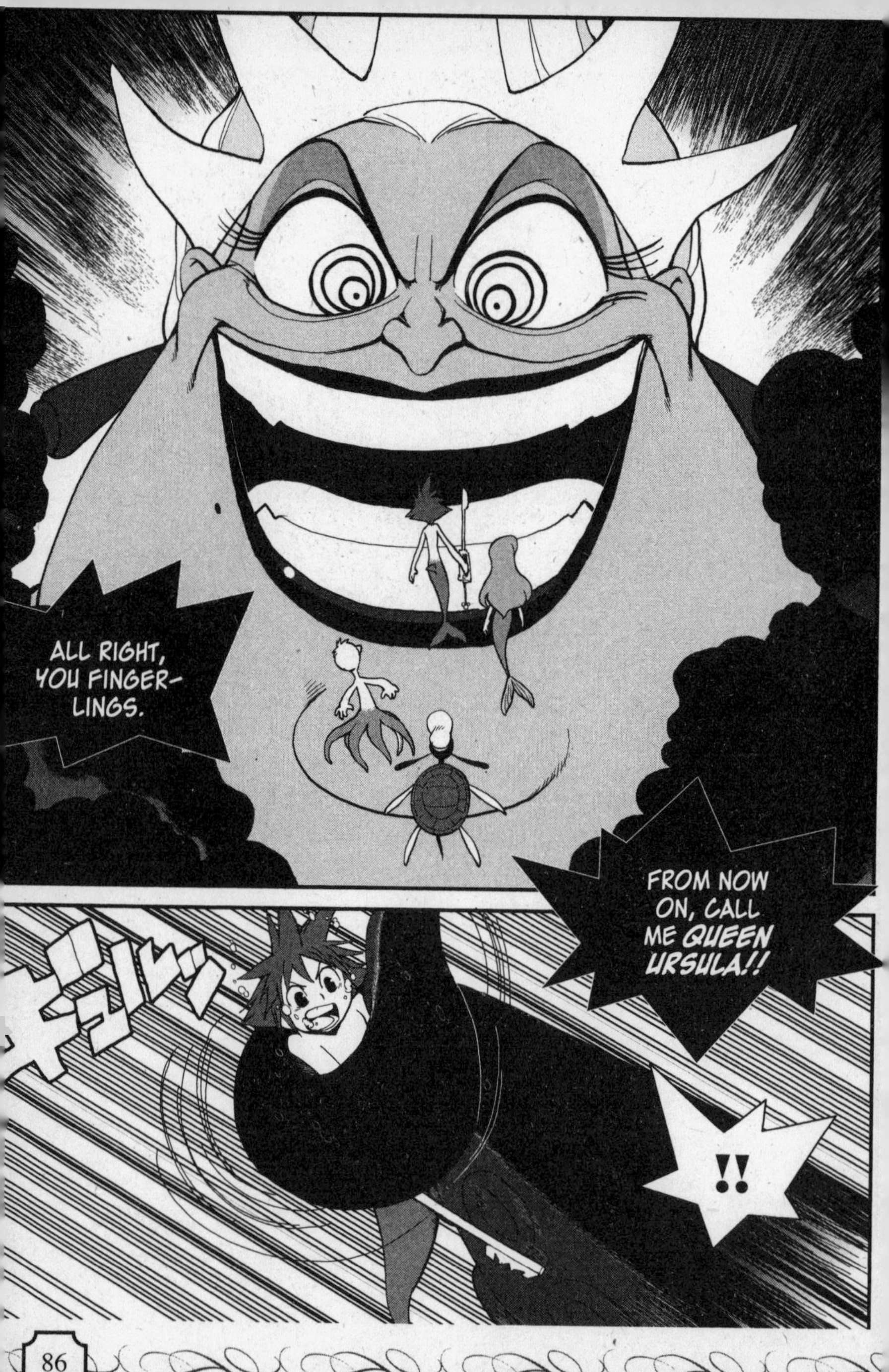
ALL RIGHT, YOU FINGER-LINGS.
FROM NOW ON, CALL ME QUEEN URSULA!!
!!

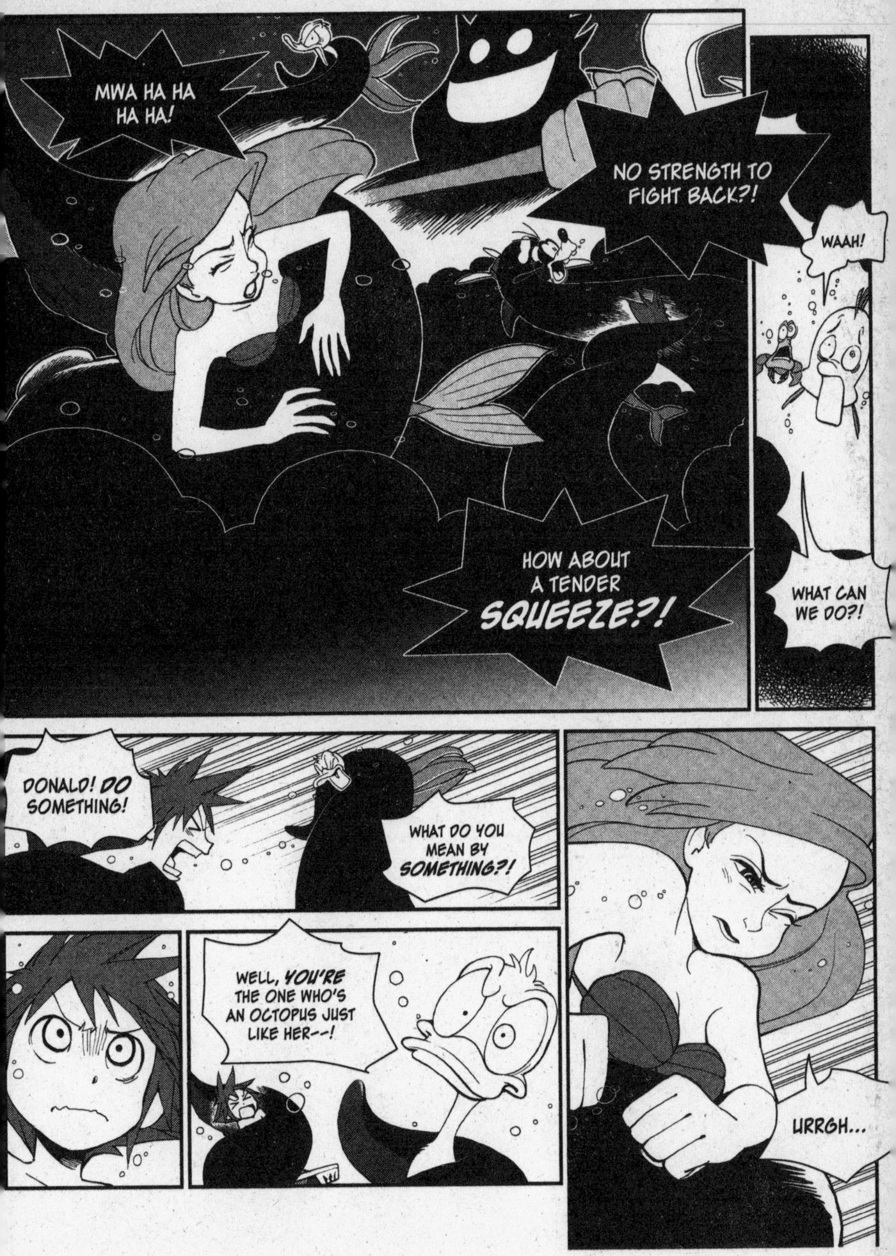
MWA HA HA HA HA!
NO STRENGTH TO FIGHT BACK?!
HOW ABOUT A TENDER SQUEEZE?!
WAAH!
WHAT CAN WE DO?!
DONALD! DO SOMETHING!
WHAT DO YOU MEAN BY SOMETHING?!
URRGH...
WELL, YOU'RE THE ONE WHO'S AN OCTOPUS JUST LIKE HER--!

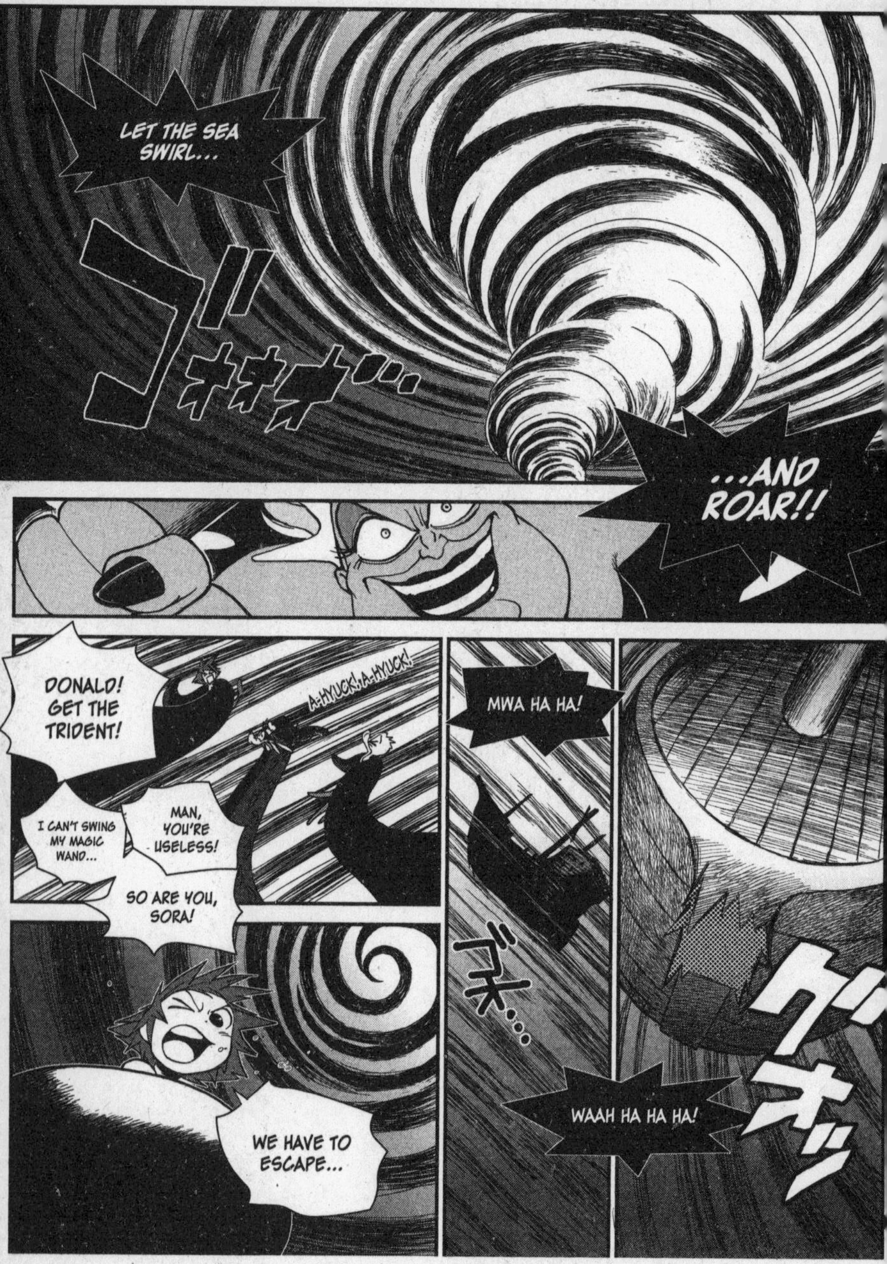
LET THE SEA SWIRL...
...AND ROAR!!
DONALD! GET THE TRIDENT!
A-HYUCK! A-HYUCK!
I CAN'T SWING MY MAGIC WAND...
MAN, YOU'RE USELESS!
SO ARE YOU, SORA!
WE HAVE TO ESCAPE...
MWA HA HA!
WAAH HA HA HA!

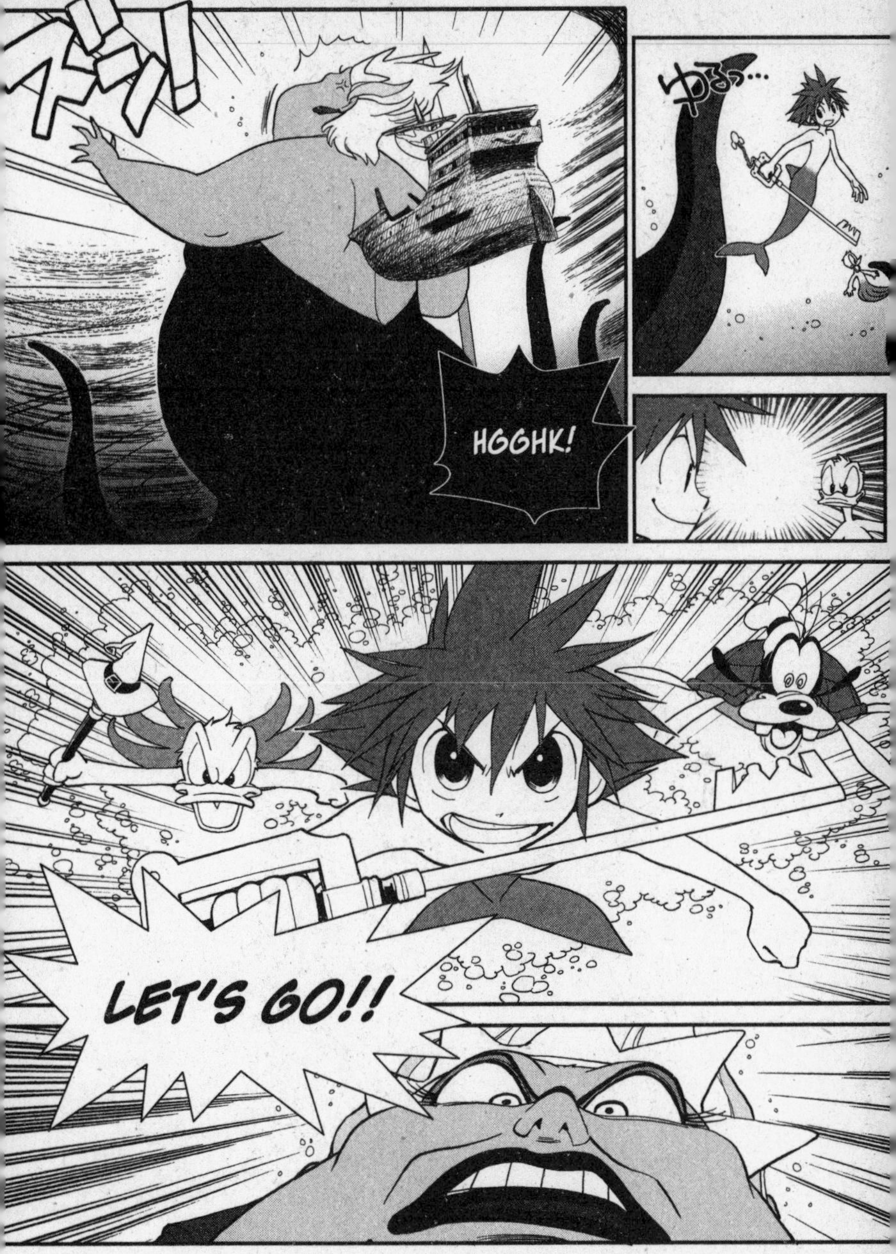
ズン!
ゆるっ…
HGGHK!
LET'S GO!!

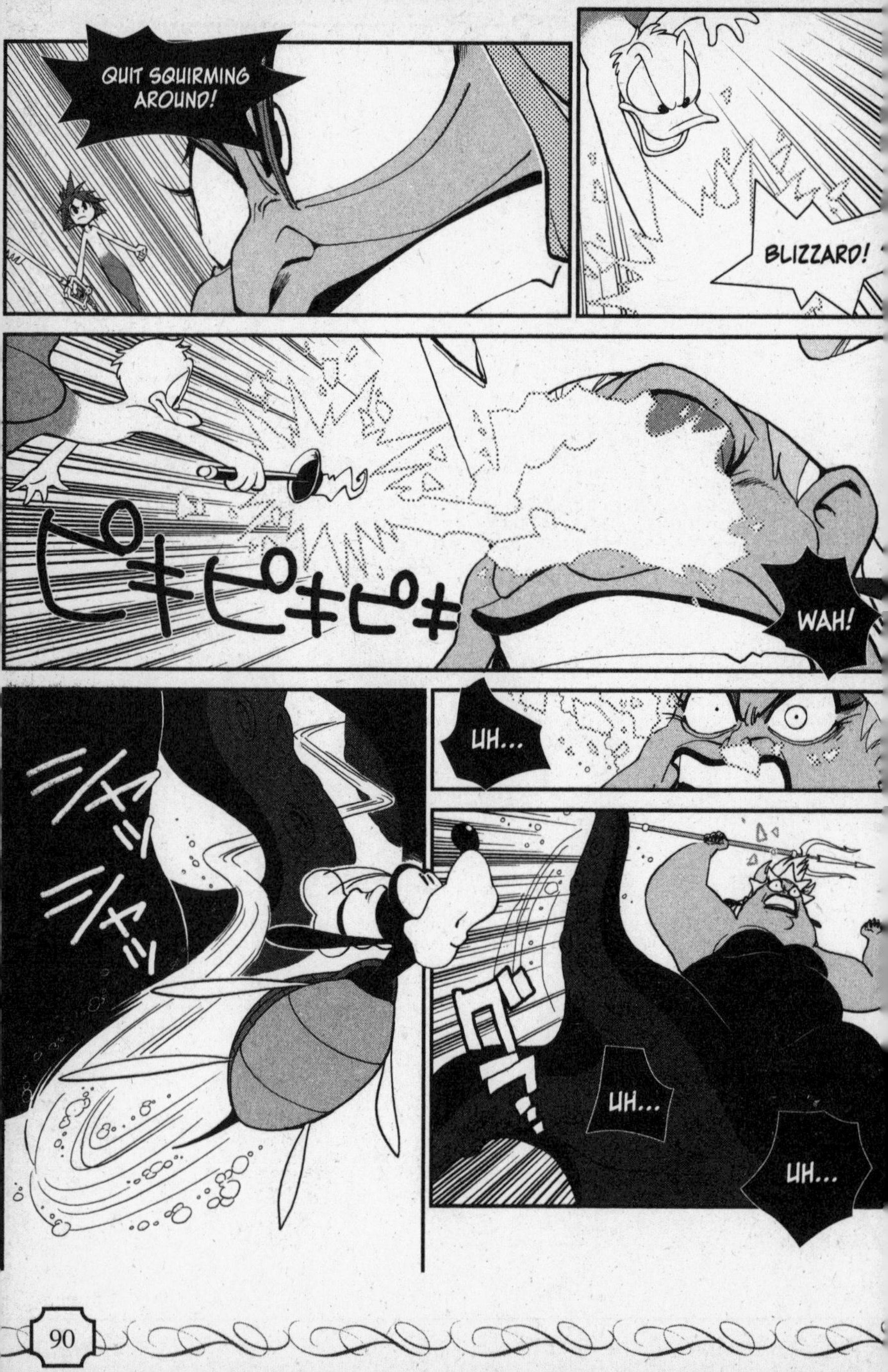
QUIT SQUIRMING AROUND!
BLIZZARD!
ピキピキピキ
WAH!
シャッ
シャッ
UH...
UH...
UH...

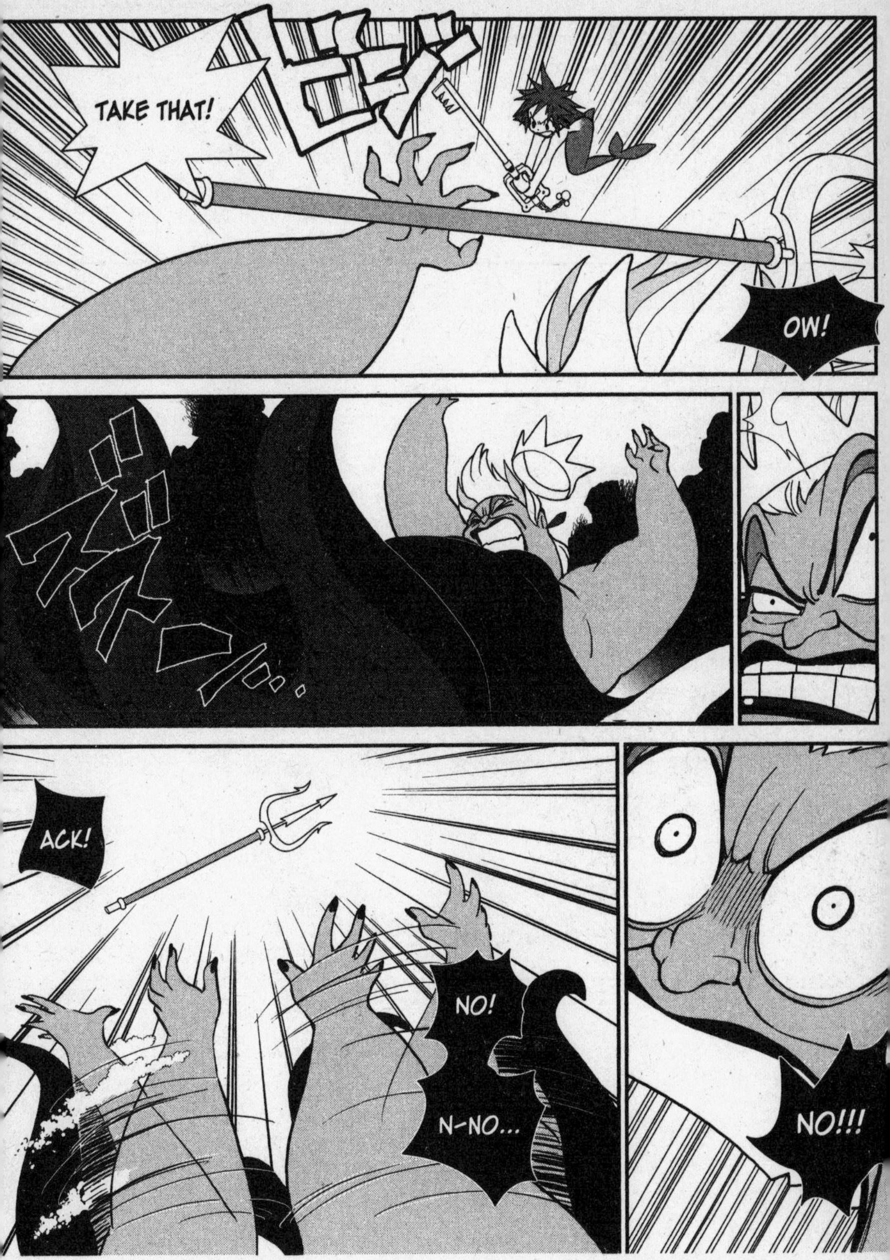
TAKE THAT!
OW!
ACK!
NO!
N-NO...
NO!!!

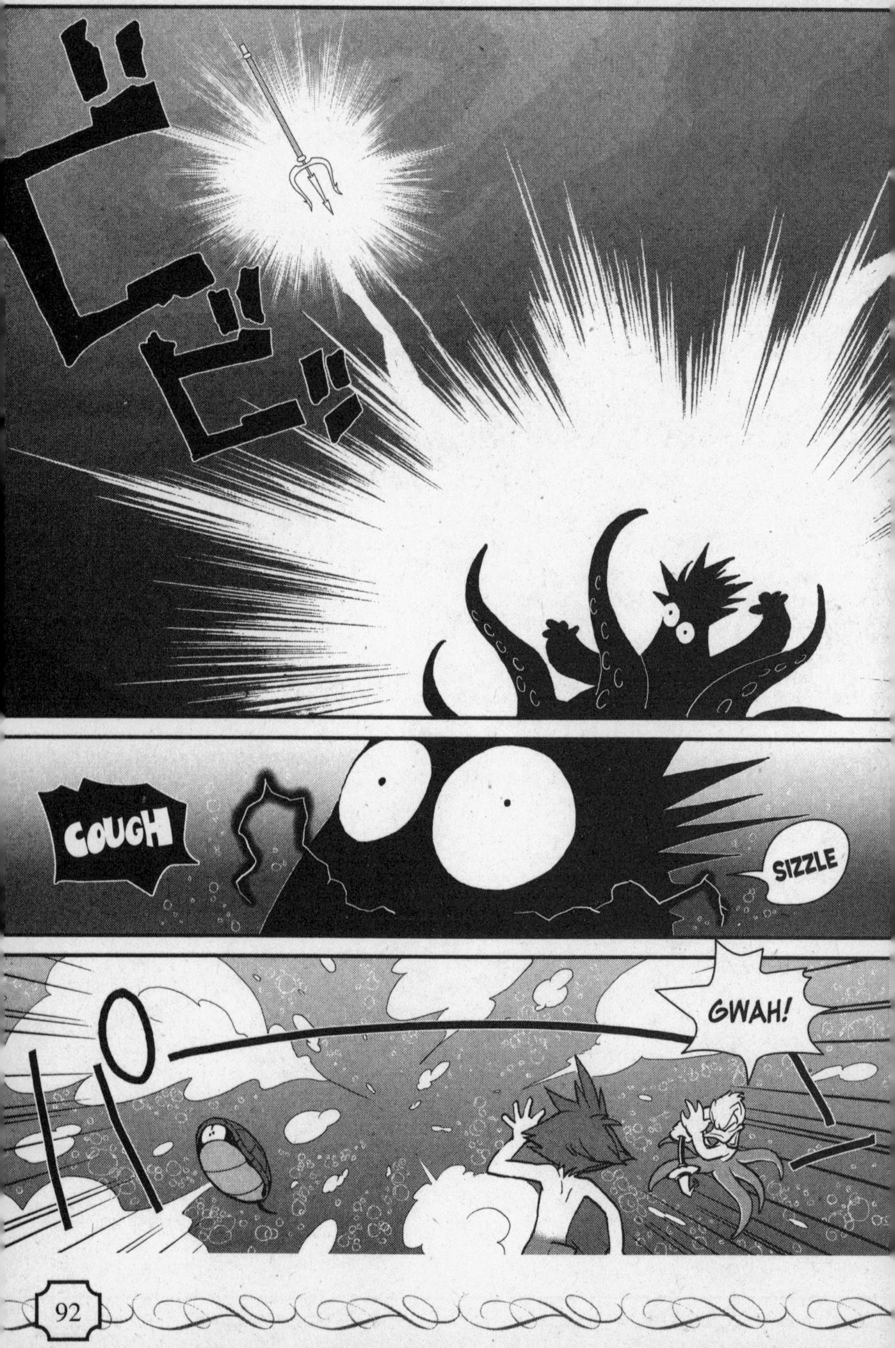
COUGH
SIZZLE
GWAH!

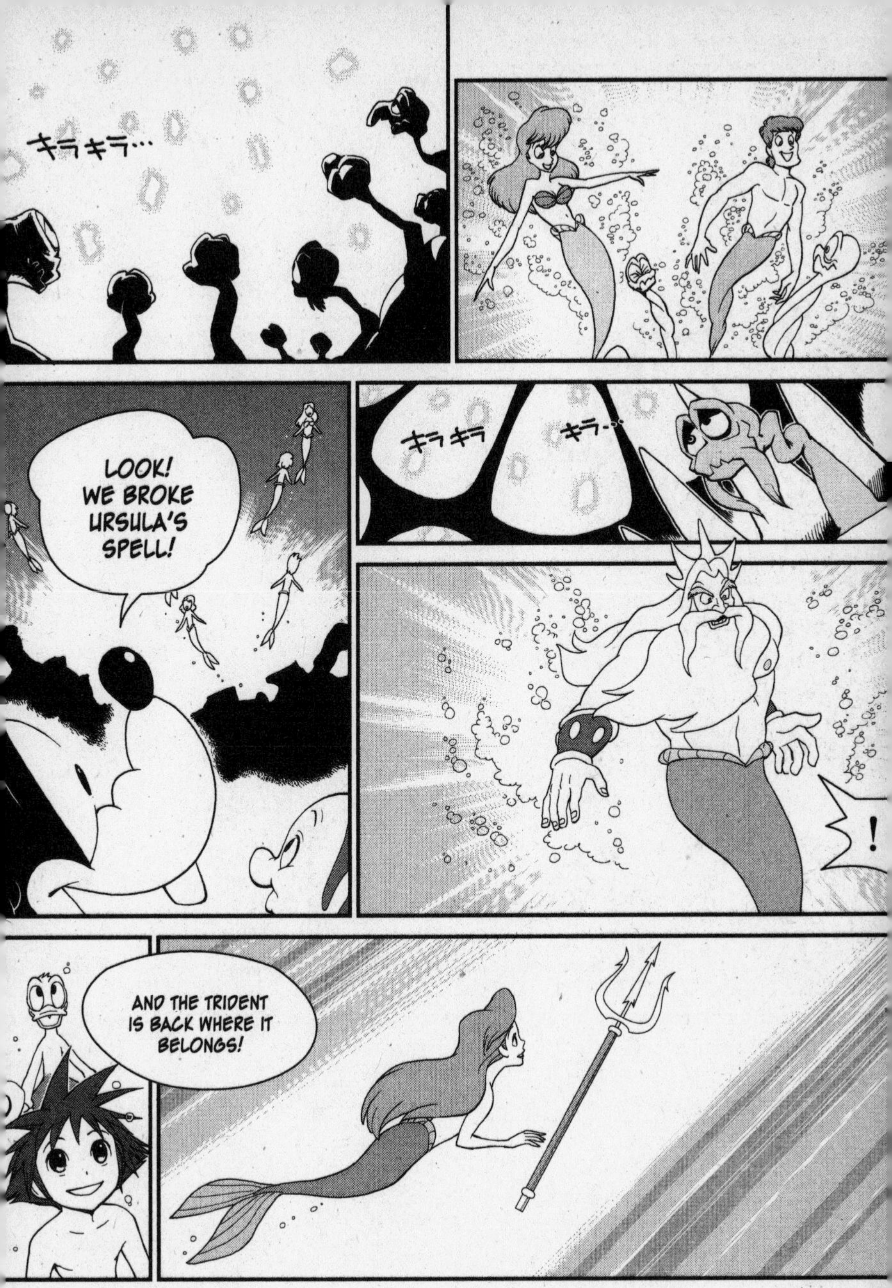

キラキラ…
LOOK! WE BROKE URSULA'S SPELL!
キラキラ
キラ…
!
AND THE TRIDENT IS BACK WHERE IT BELONGS!

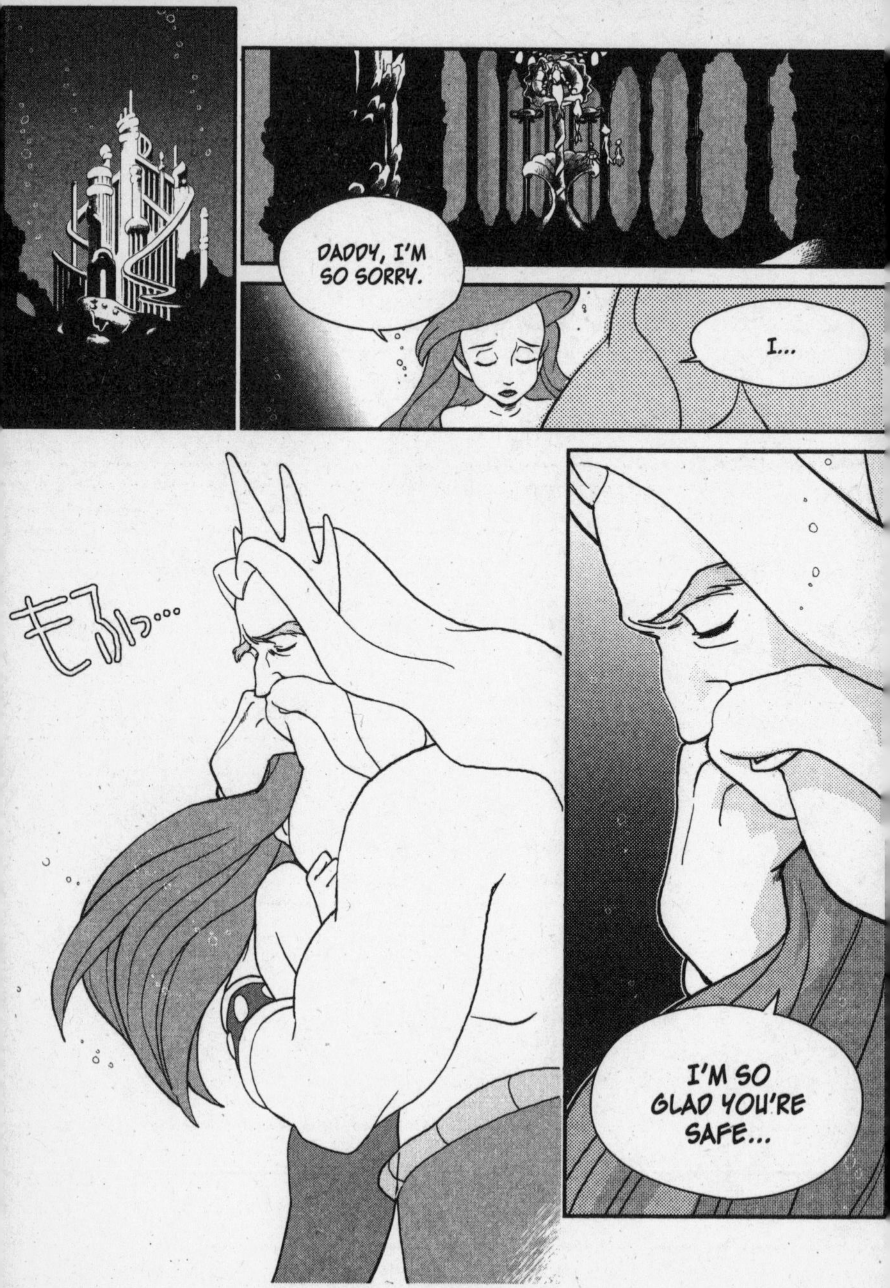
DADDY, I'M SO SORRY.
I...
もふっ…
I'M SO GLAD YOU'RE SAFE...

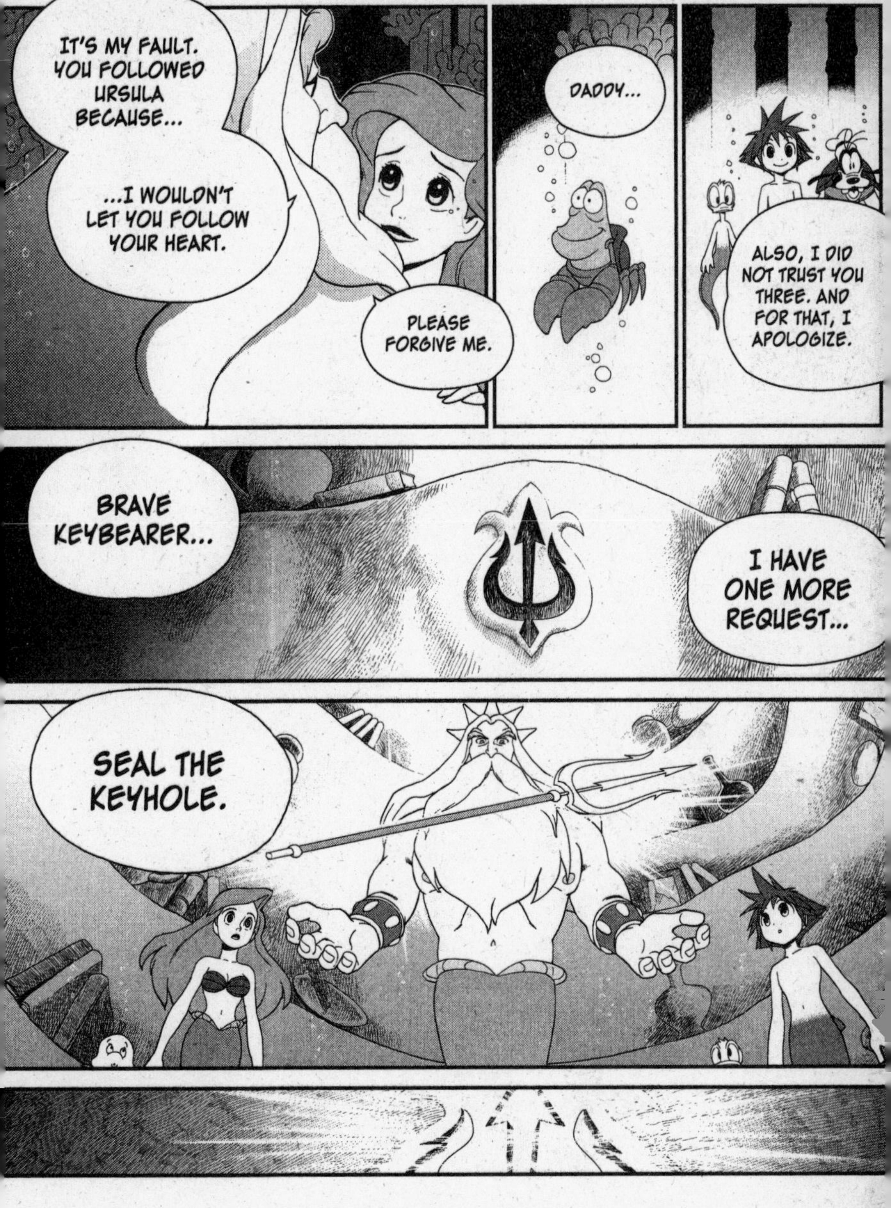
IT'S MY FAULT. YOU FOLLOWED URSULA BECAUSE...
...I WOULDN'T LET YOU FOLLOW YOUR HEART.
PLEASE FORGIVE ME.
DADDY...
ALSO, I DID NOT TRUST YOU THREE. AND FOR THAT, I APOLOGIZE.
BRAVE KEYBEARER...
I HAVE ONE MORE REQUEST...
SEAL THE KEYHOLE.

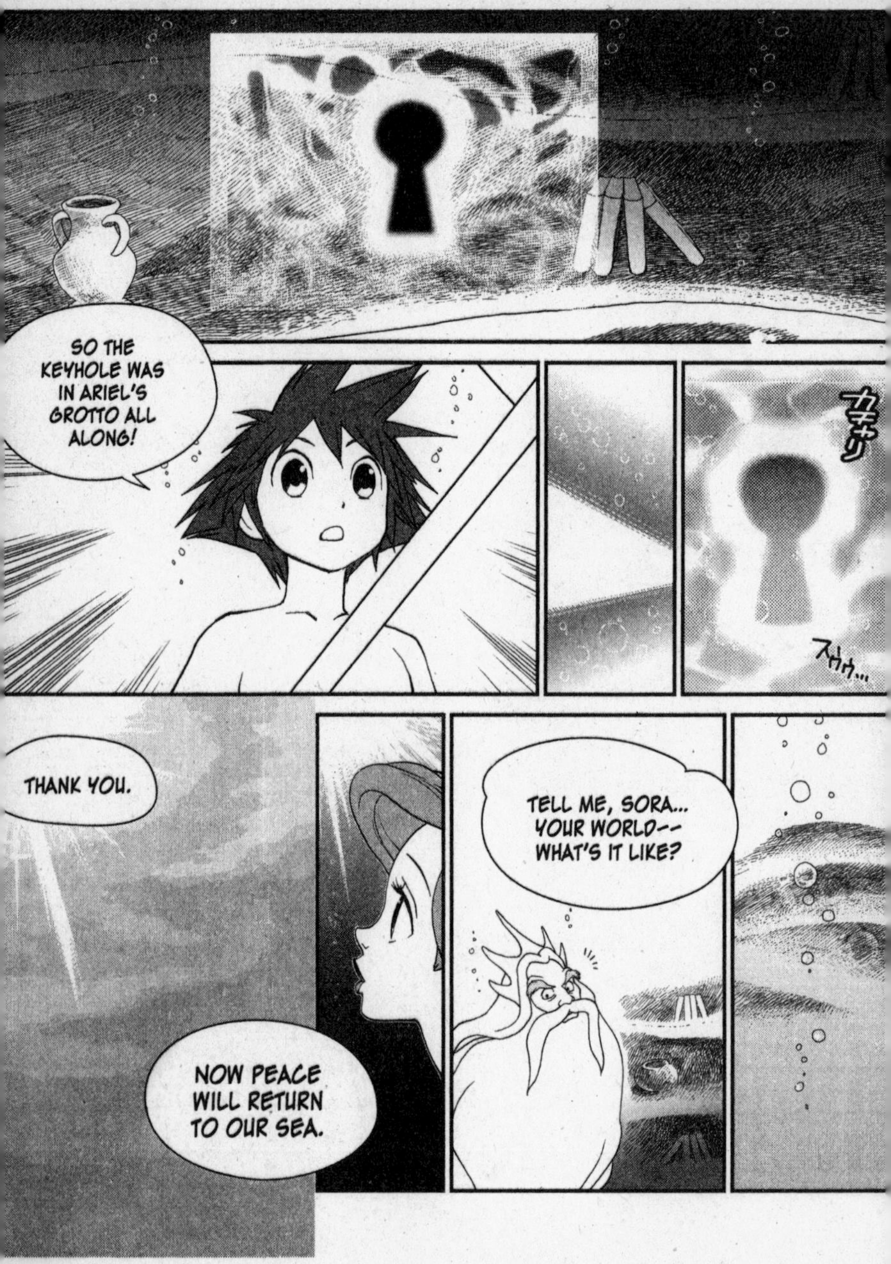
SO THE KEYHOLE WAS IN ARIEL'S GROTTO ALL ALONG!
カチャリ
スゥゥ…
THANK YOU.
NOW PEACE WILL RETURN TO OUR SEA.
TELL ME, SORA... YOUR WORLD-- WHAT'S IT LIKE?

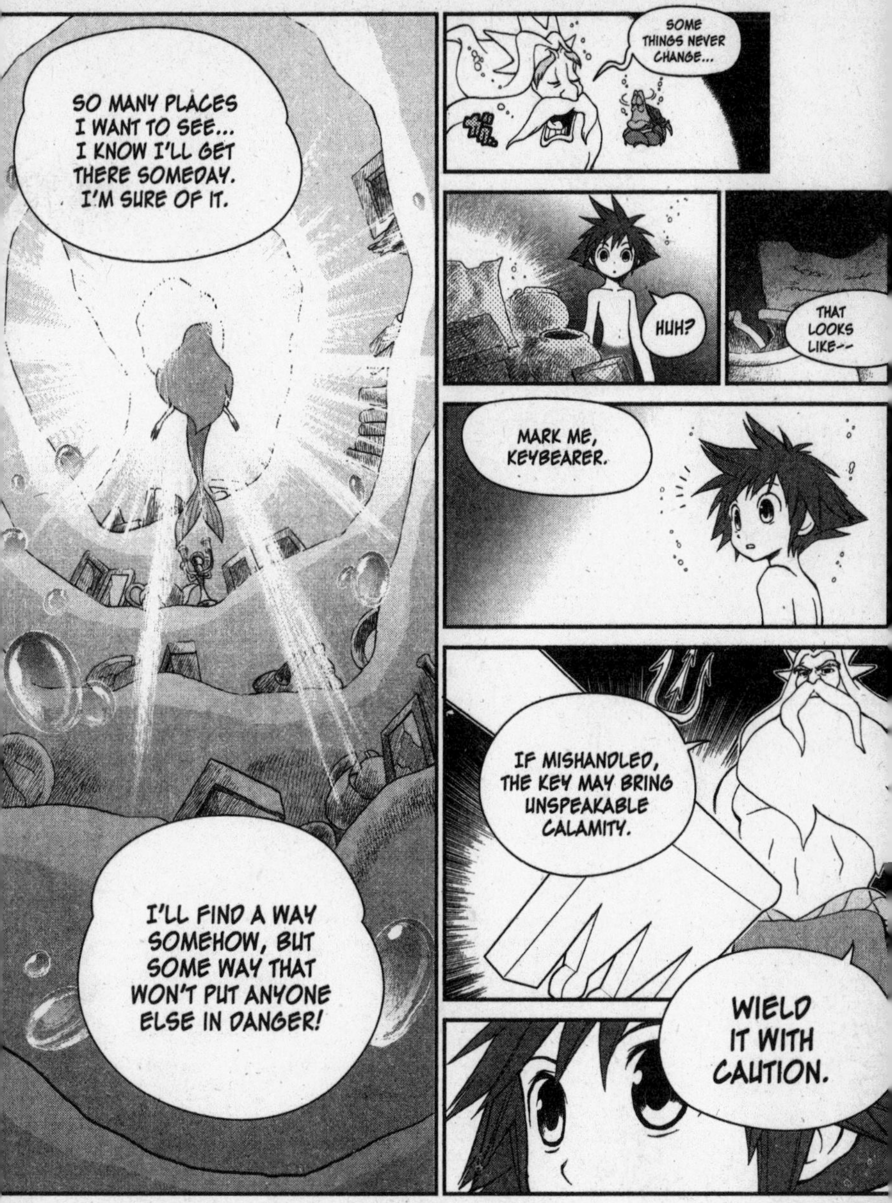
SO MANY PLACES I WANT TO SEE... I KNOW I'LL GET THERE SOMEDAY. I'M SURE OF IT.
I'LL FIND A WAY SOMEHOW, BUT SOME WAY THAT WON'T PUT ANYONE ELSE IN DANGER!
SOME THINGS NEVER CHANGE...
HUH?
THAT LOOKS LIKE--
MARK ME, KEYBEARER.
IF MISHANDLED, THE KEY MAY BRING UNSPEAKABLE CALAMITY.
WIELD IT WITH CAUTION.

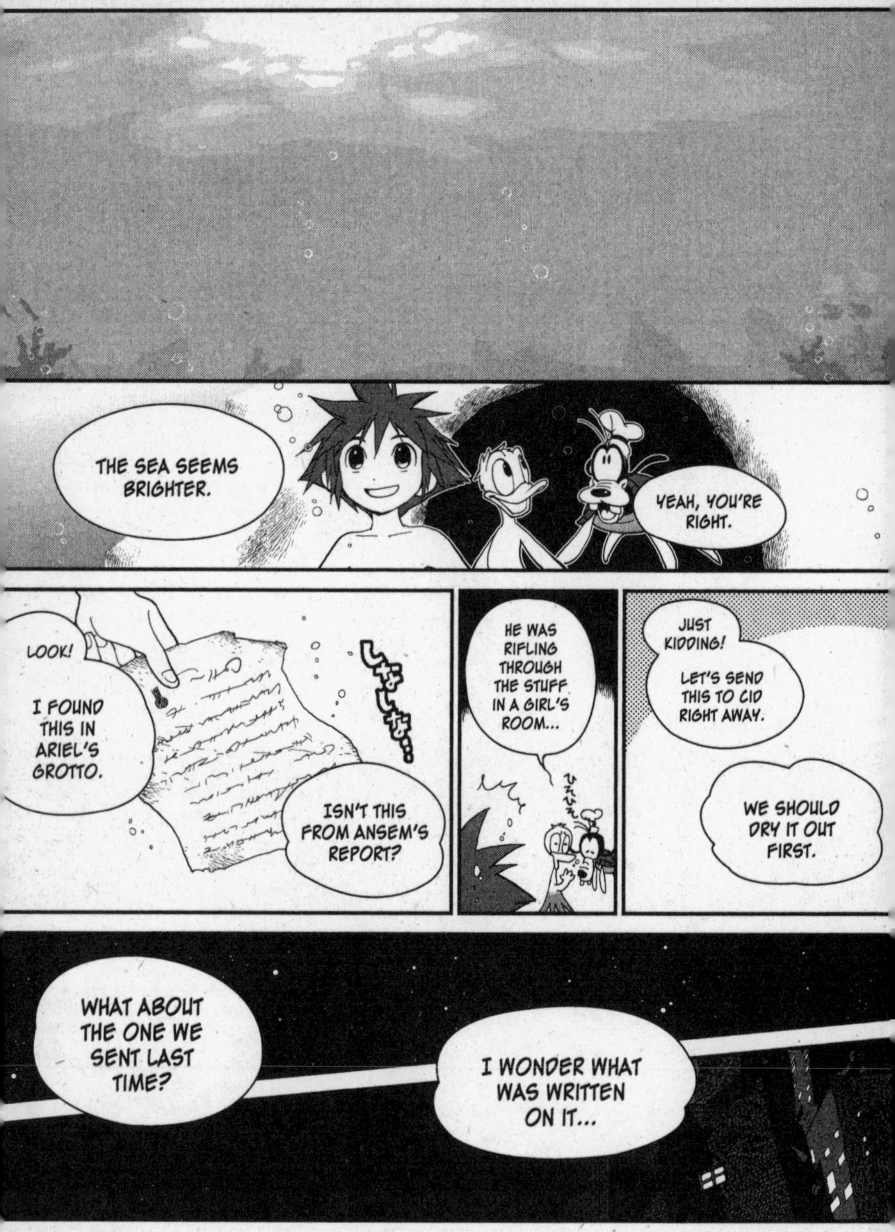
THE SEA SEEMS BRIGHTER.
YEAH, YOU'RE RIGHT.
LOOK!
I FOUND THIS IN ARIEL'S GROTTO.
しなしな…
ISN'T THIS FROM ANSEM'S REPORT?
HE WAS RIFLING THROUGH THE STUFF IN A GIRL'S ROOM...
JUST KIDDING!
LET'S SEND THIS TO CID RIGHT AWAY.
WE SHOULD DRY IT OUT FIRST.
WHAT ABOUT THE ONE WE SENT LAST TIME?
I WONDER WHAT WAS WRITTEN ON IT...

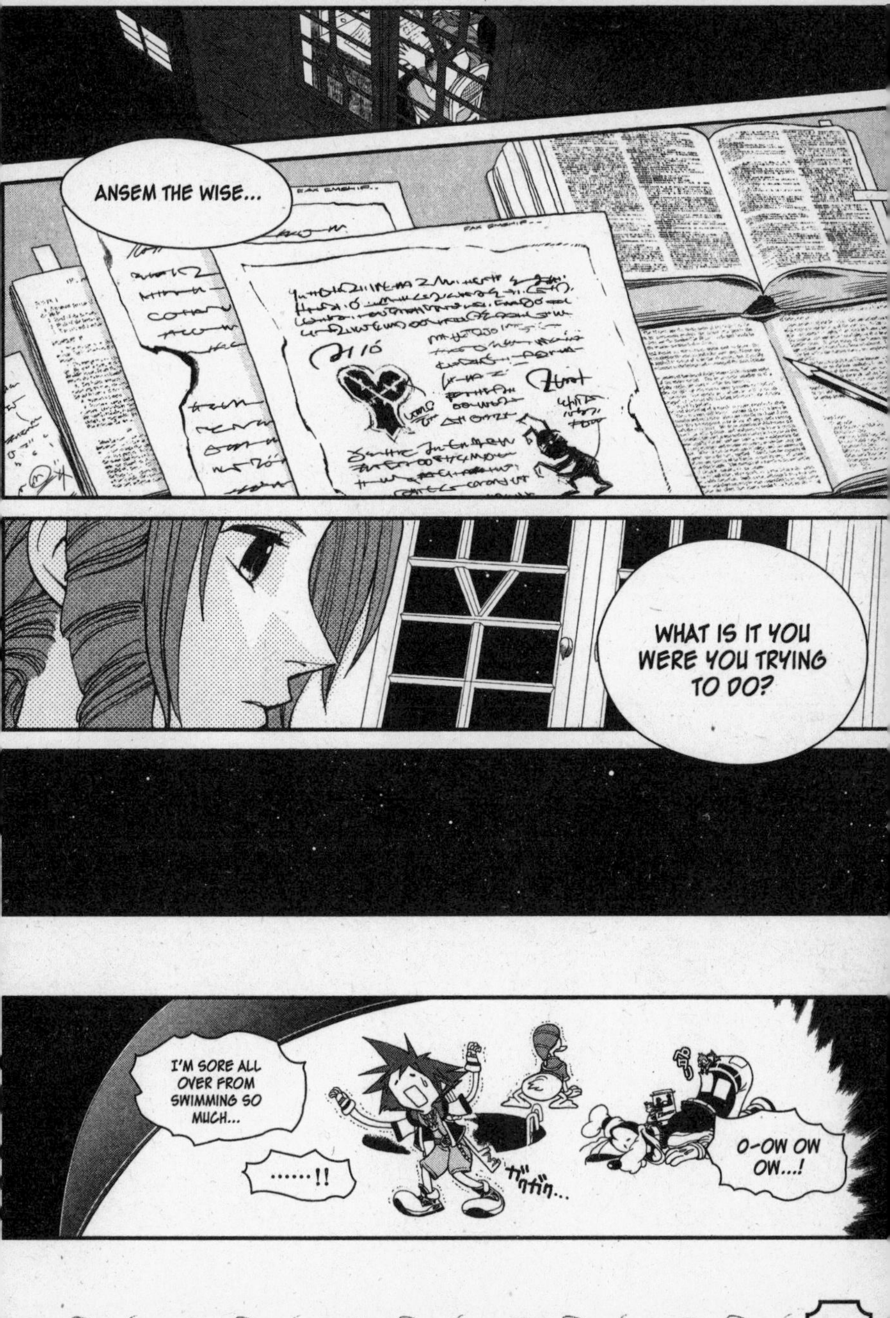
ANSEM THE WISE...
WHAT IS IT YOU WERE YOU TRYING TO DO?
I'M SORE ALL OVER FROM SWIMMING SO MUCH...
......!!
O-OW OW OW...!

# Episode 32

## A Scientist's Notes

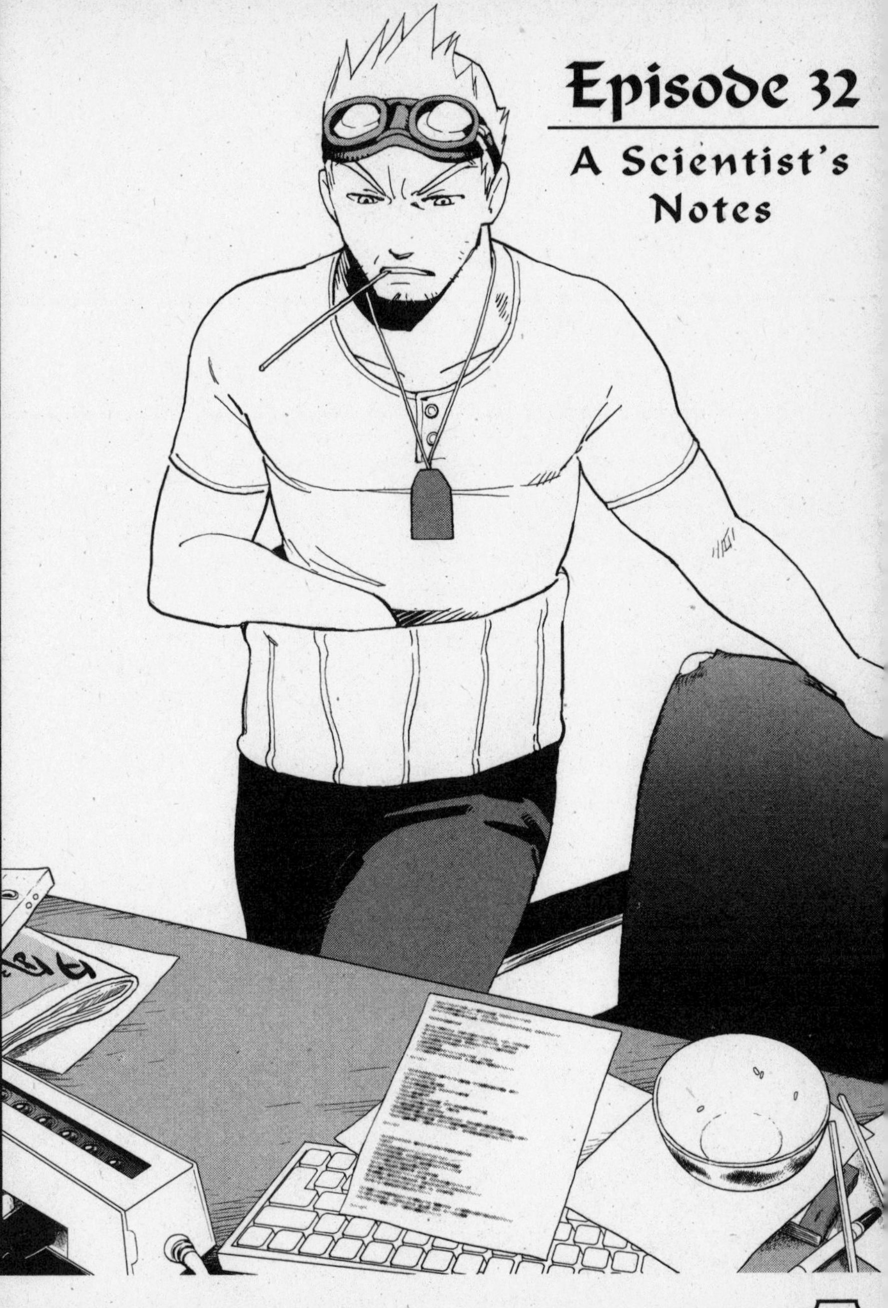

OKAY, IT'S DRY!

TRANS-MITTING...

YOU SURE USING A HAIRDRYER IS ALL RIGHT?

A-HYUCK.

Good job! Another mystery solved.

SO WHAT'S WRITTEN IN THE REPORT?

Oh yeah.

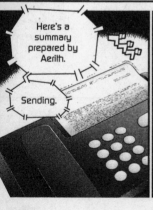

Here's a summary prepared by Aerith.

Sending.

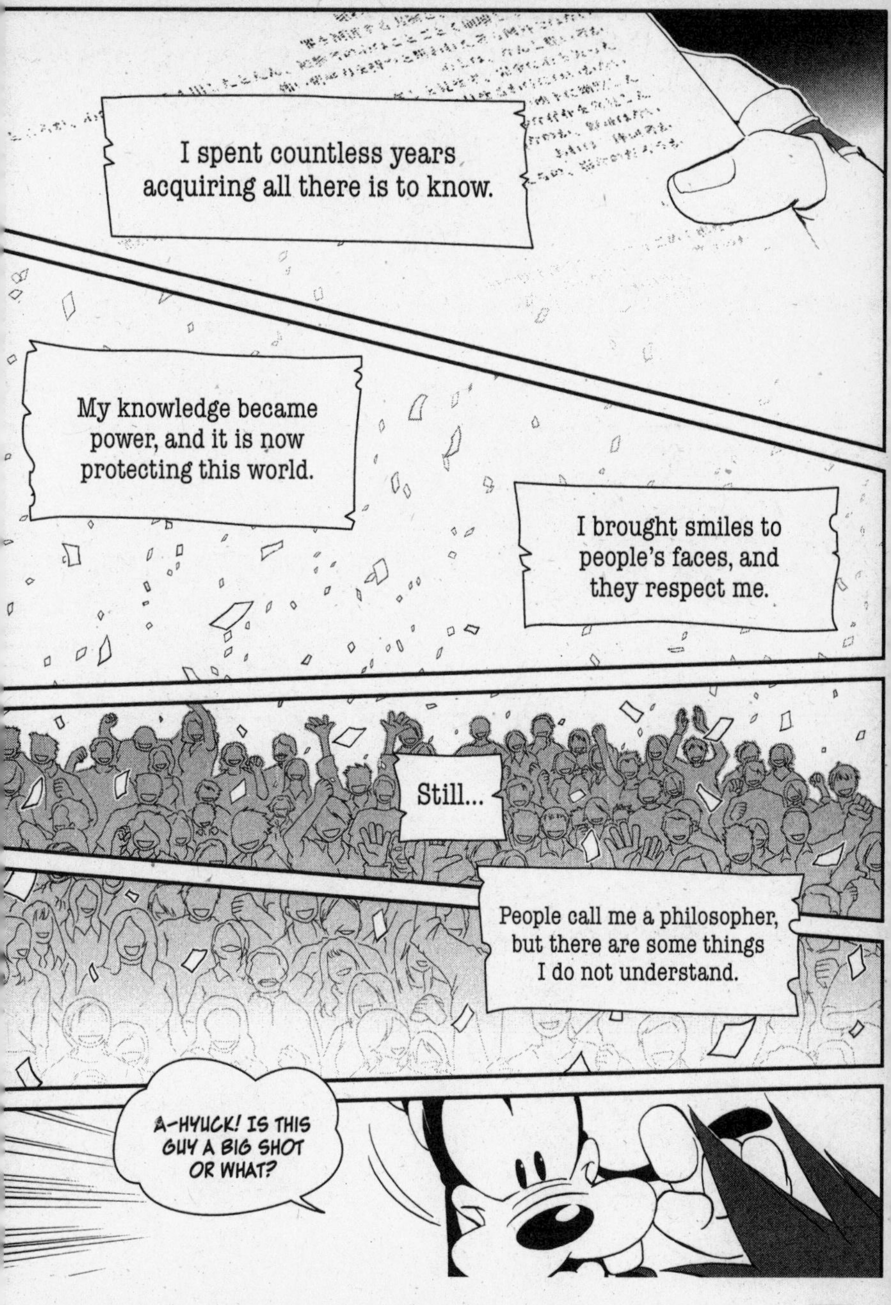
I spent countless years acquiring all there is to know.
My knowledge became power, and it is now protecting this world.
I brought smiles to people's faces, and they respect me.
Still...
People call me a philosopher, but there are some things I do not understand.
A-HYUCK! IS THIS GUY A BIG SHOT OR WHAT?

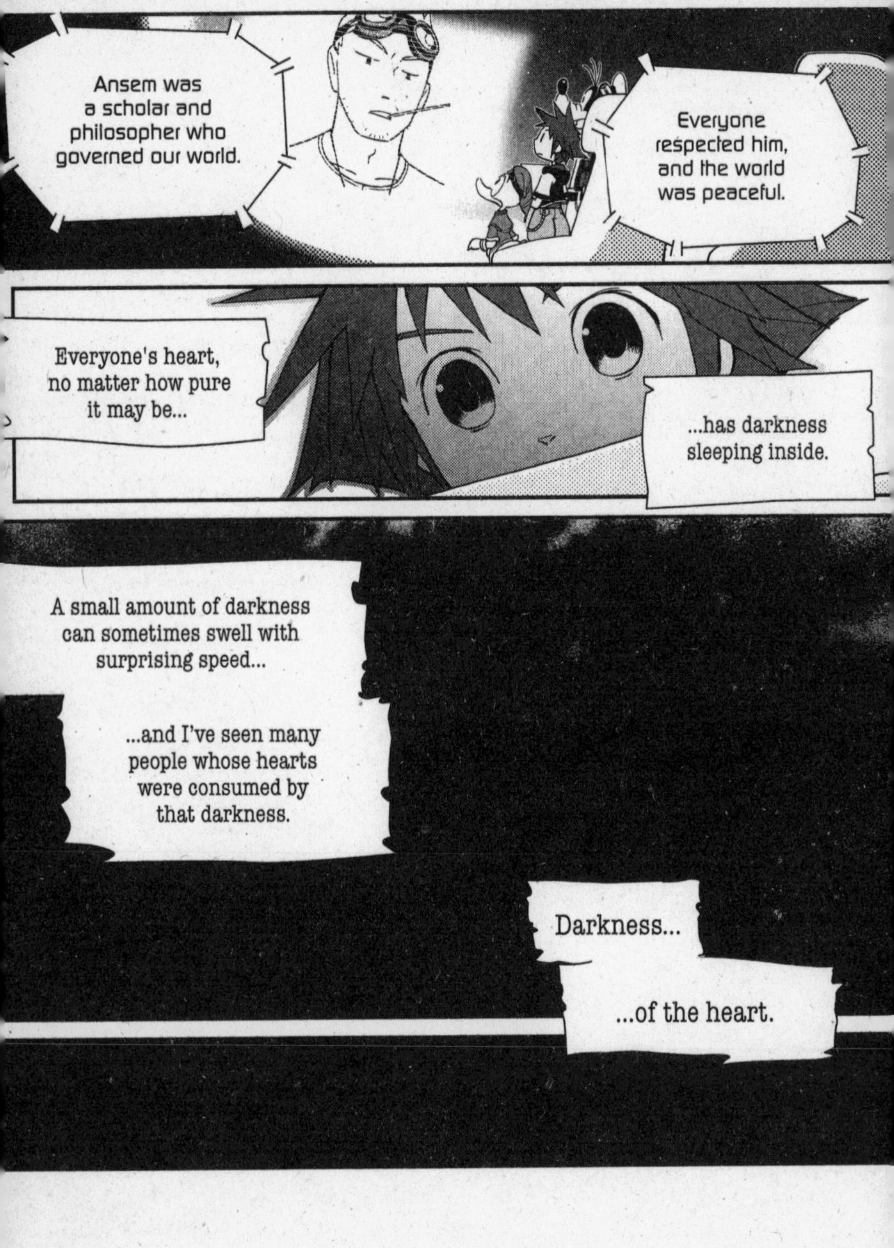

Ansem was a scholar and philosopher who governed our world.
Everyone respected him, and the world was peaceful.
Everyone's heart, no matter how pure it may be...
...has darkness sleeping inside.
A small amount of darkness can sometimes swell with surprising speed...
...and I've seen many people whose hearts were consumed by that darkness.
Darkness...
...of the heart.

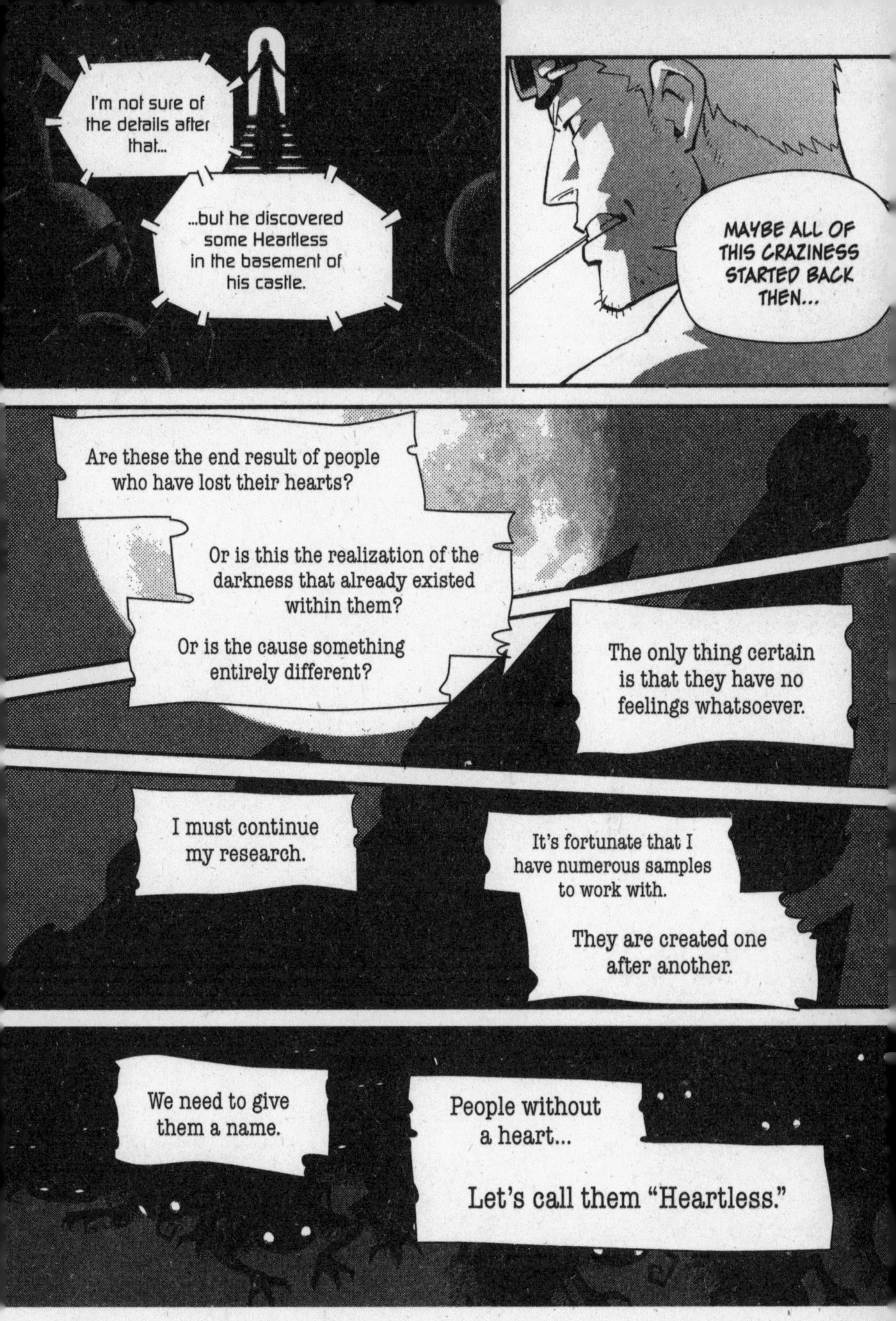

I'm not sure of the details after that...
...but he discovered some Heartless in the basement of his castle.
MAYBE ALL OF THIS CRAZINESS STARTED BACK THEN...
Are these the end result of people who have lost their hearts?
Or is this the realization of the darkness that already existed within them?
Or is the cause something entirely different?
The only thing certain is that they have no feelings whatsoever.
I must continue my research.
It's fortunate that I have numerous samples to work with.
They are created one after another.
We need to give them a name.
People without a heart...
Let's call them "Heartless."

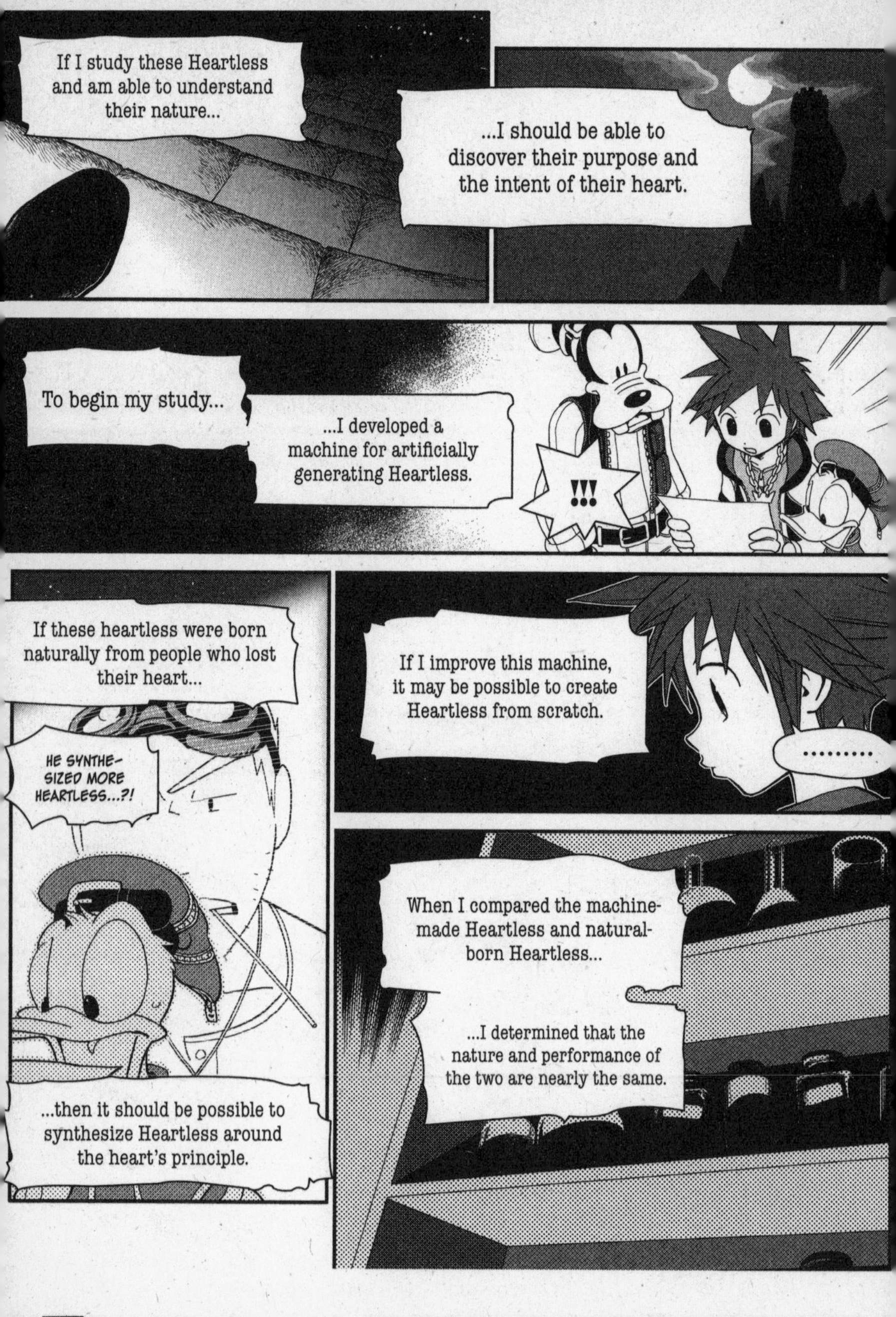

If I study these Heartless and am able to understand their nature...
...I should be able to discover their purpose and the intent of their heart.
To begin my study...
...I developed a machine for artificially generating Heartless.
!!!
If these heartless were born naturally from people who lost their heart...
HE SYNTHESIZED MORE HEARTLESS...?!
...then it should be possible to synthesize Heartless around the heart's principle.
If I improve this machine, it may be possible to create Heartless from scratch.
.........
When I compared the machine-made Heartless and natural-born Heartless...
...I determined that the nature and performance of the two are nearly the same.

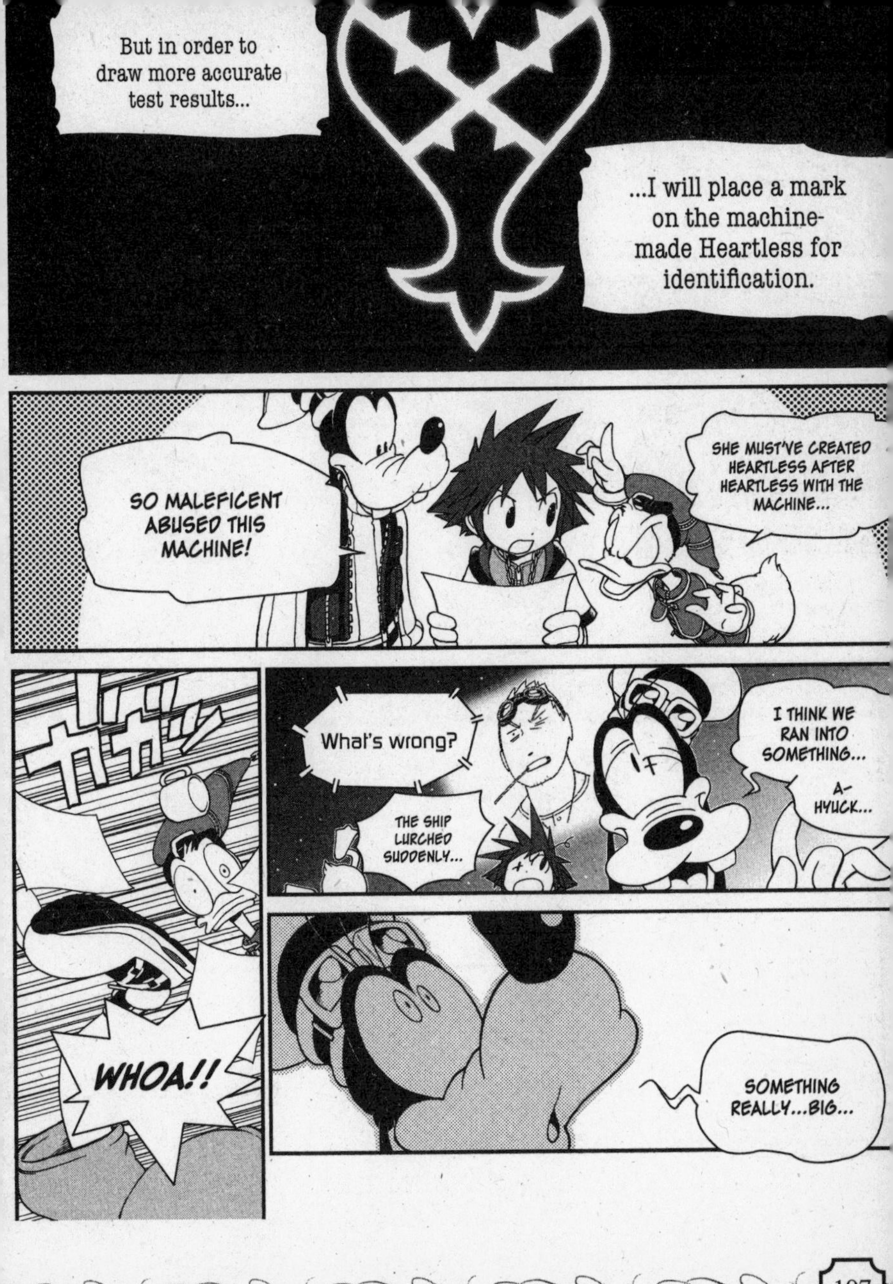
But in order to draw more accurate test results...
...I will place a mark on the machine-made Heartless for identification.
SO MALEFICENT ABUSED THIS MACHINE!
SHE MUST'VE CREATED HEARTLESS AFTER HEARTLESS WITH THE MACHINE...
WHOA!!
What's wrong?
THE SHIP LURCHED SUDDENLY...
I THINK WE RAN INTO SOMETHING...
A-HYUCK...
SOMETHING REALLY...BIG...

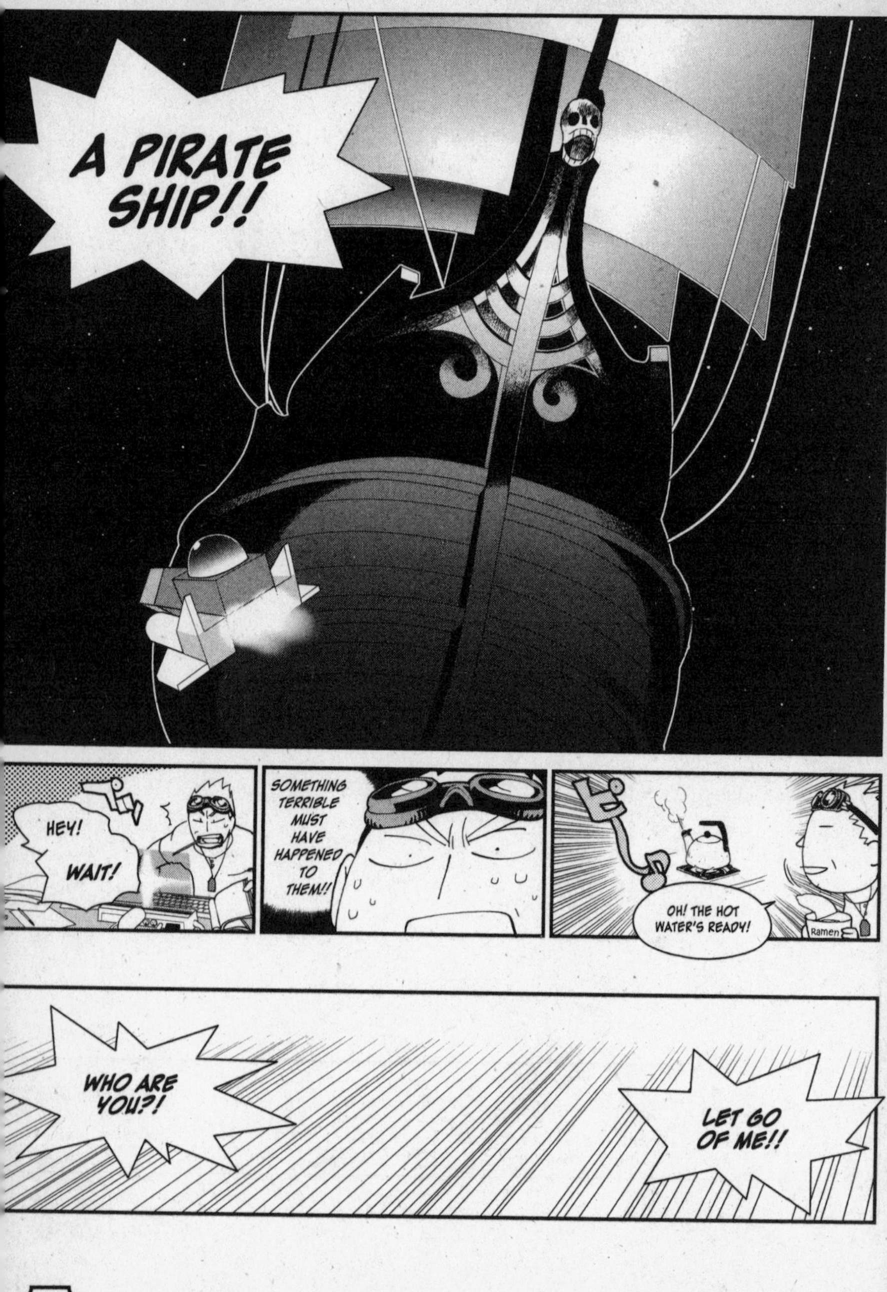
A PIRATE SHIP!!
HEY!
WAIT!
SOMETHING TERRIBLE MUST HAVE HAPPENED TO THEM!!
OH! THE HOT WATER'S READY!
Ramen
WHO ARE YOU?!
LET GO OF ME!!

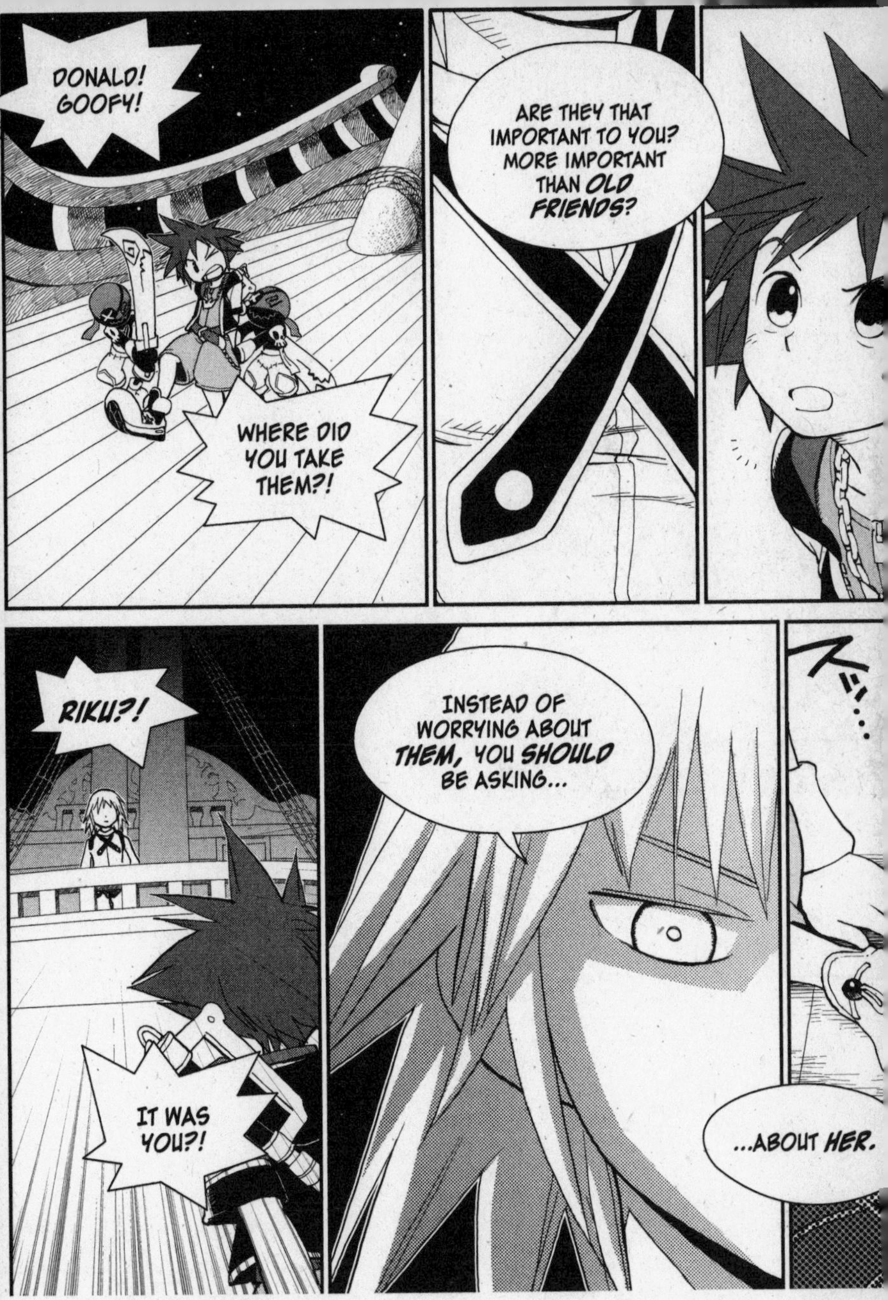
DONALD! GOOFY!
WHERE DID YOU TAKE THEM?!
ARE THEY THAT IMPORTANT TO YOU? MORE IMPORTANT THAN *OLD FRIENDS?*
*RIKU?!*
IT WAS YOU?!
INSTEAD OF WORRYING ABOUT *THEM,* YOU *SHOULD* BE ASKING...
スッ…
...ABOUT *HER.*

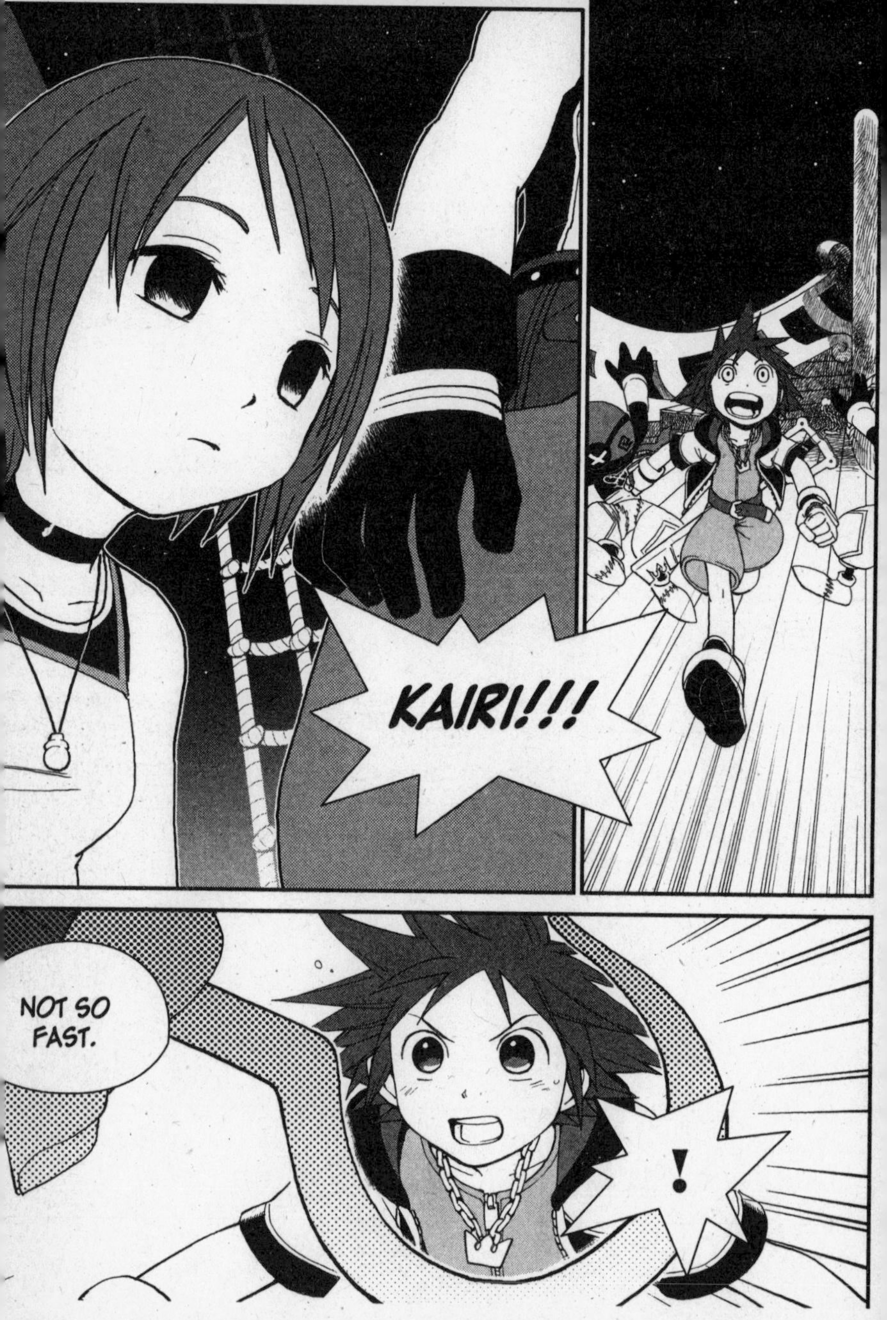
KAIRI!!!
NOT SO FAST.
!

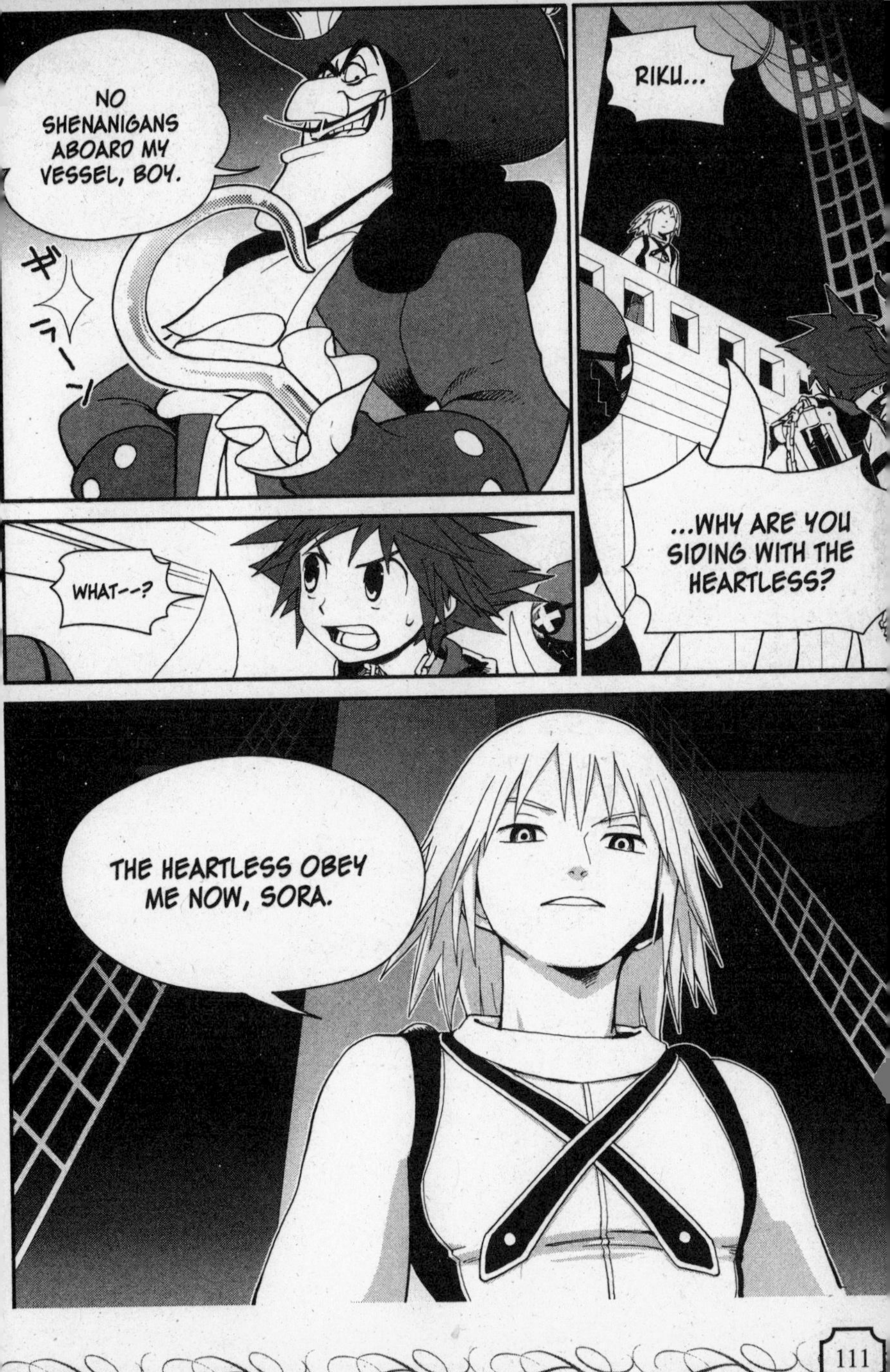
NO SHENANIGANS ABOARD MY VESSEL, BOY.
ギラーン
WHAT--?
RIKU...
...WHY ARE YOU SIDING WITH THE HEARTLESS?
THE HEARTLESS OBEY ME NOW, SORA.

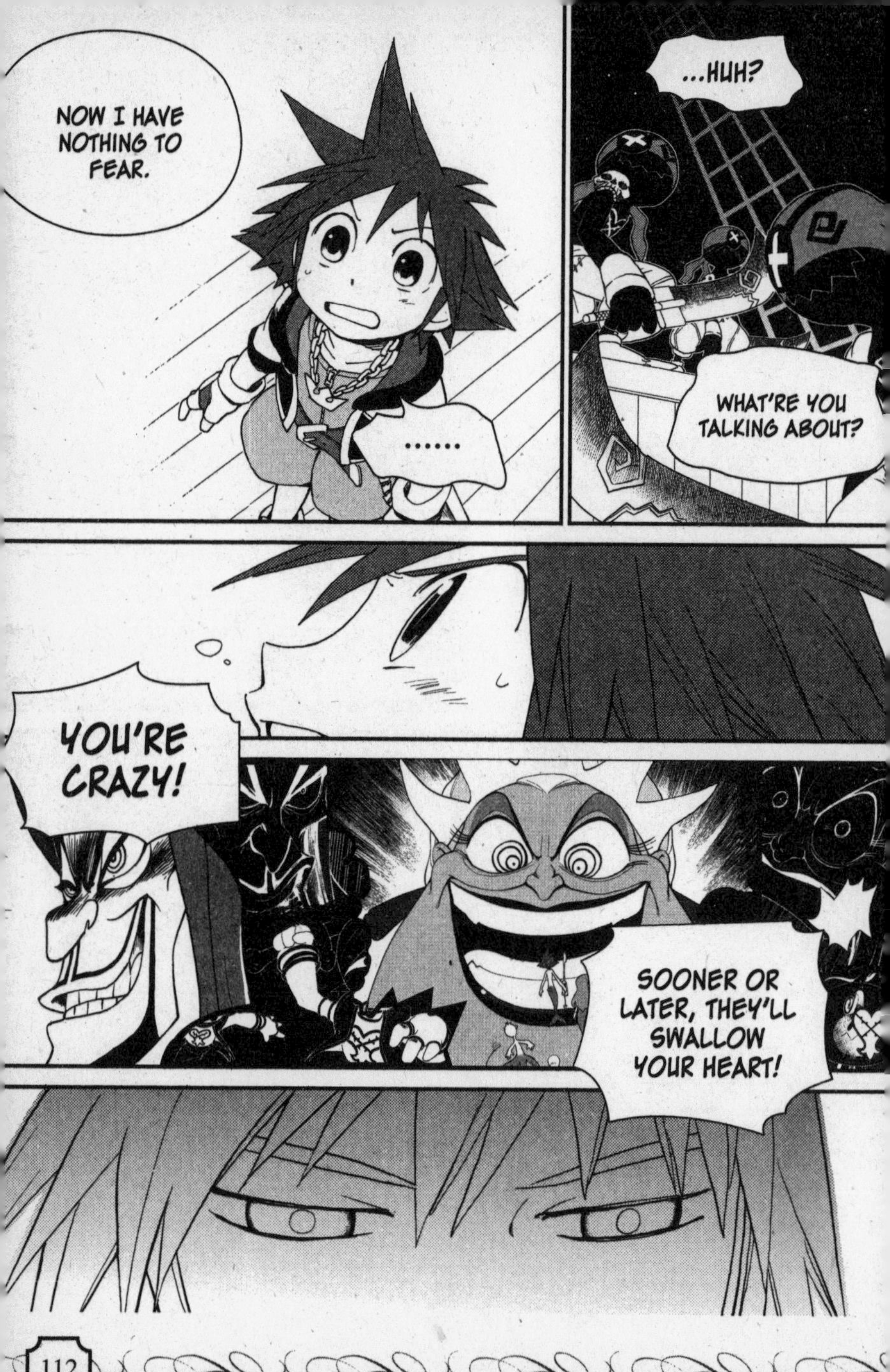
NOW I HAVE NOTHING TO FEAR.
......
...HUH?
WHAT'RE YOU TALKING ABOUT?
YOU'RE CRAZY!
SOONER OR LATER, THEY'LL SWALLOW YOUR HEART!

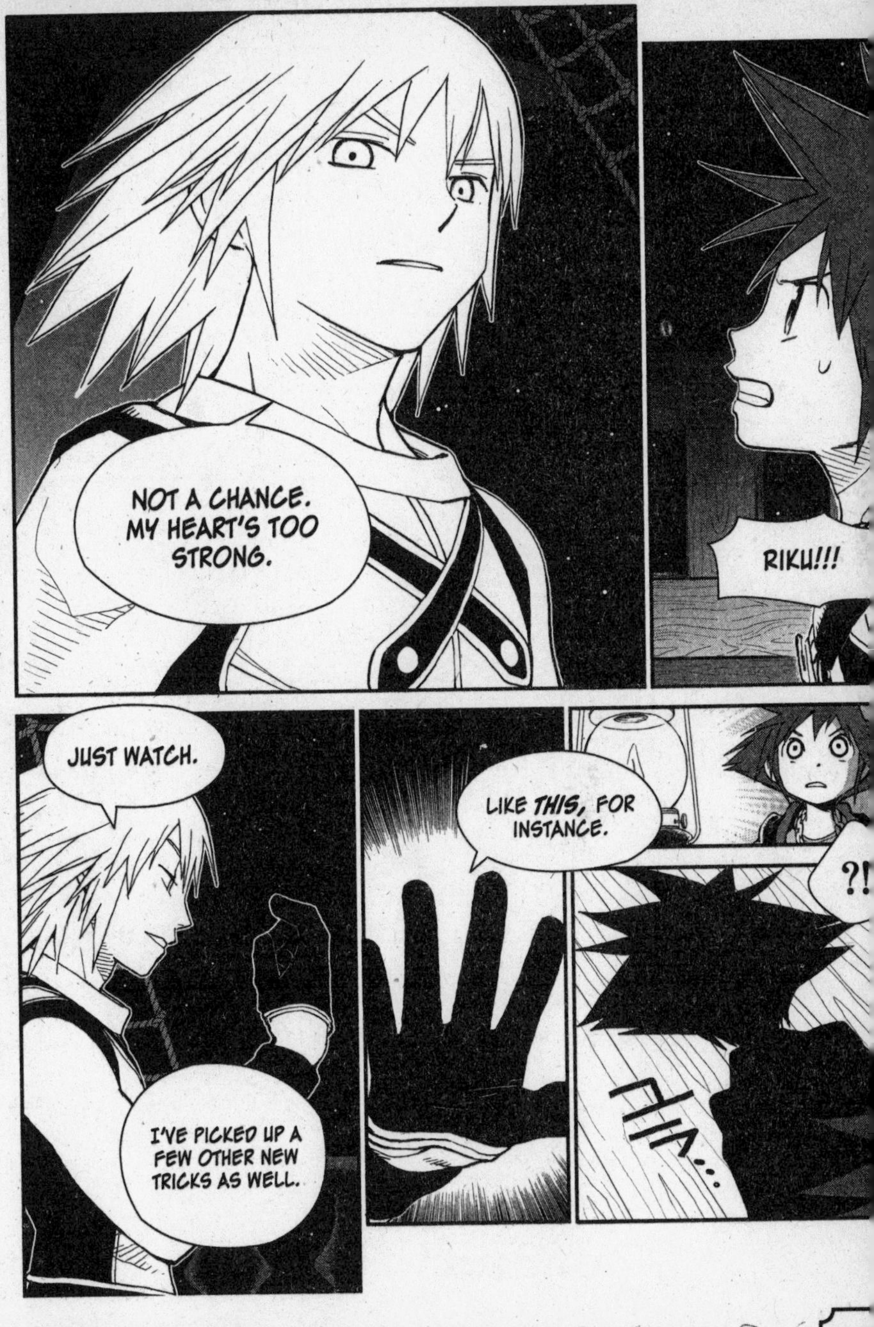
NOT A CHANCE. MY HEART'S TOO STRONG.
RIKU!!!
JUST WATCH.
I'VE PICKED UP A FEW OTHER NEW TRICKS AS WELL.
LIKE *THIS,* FOR INSTANCE.
?!

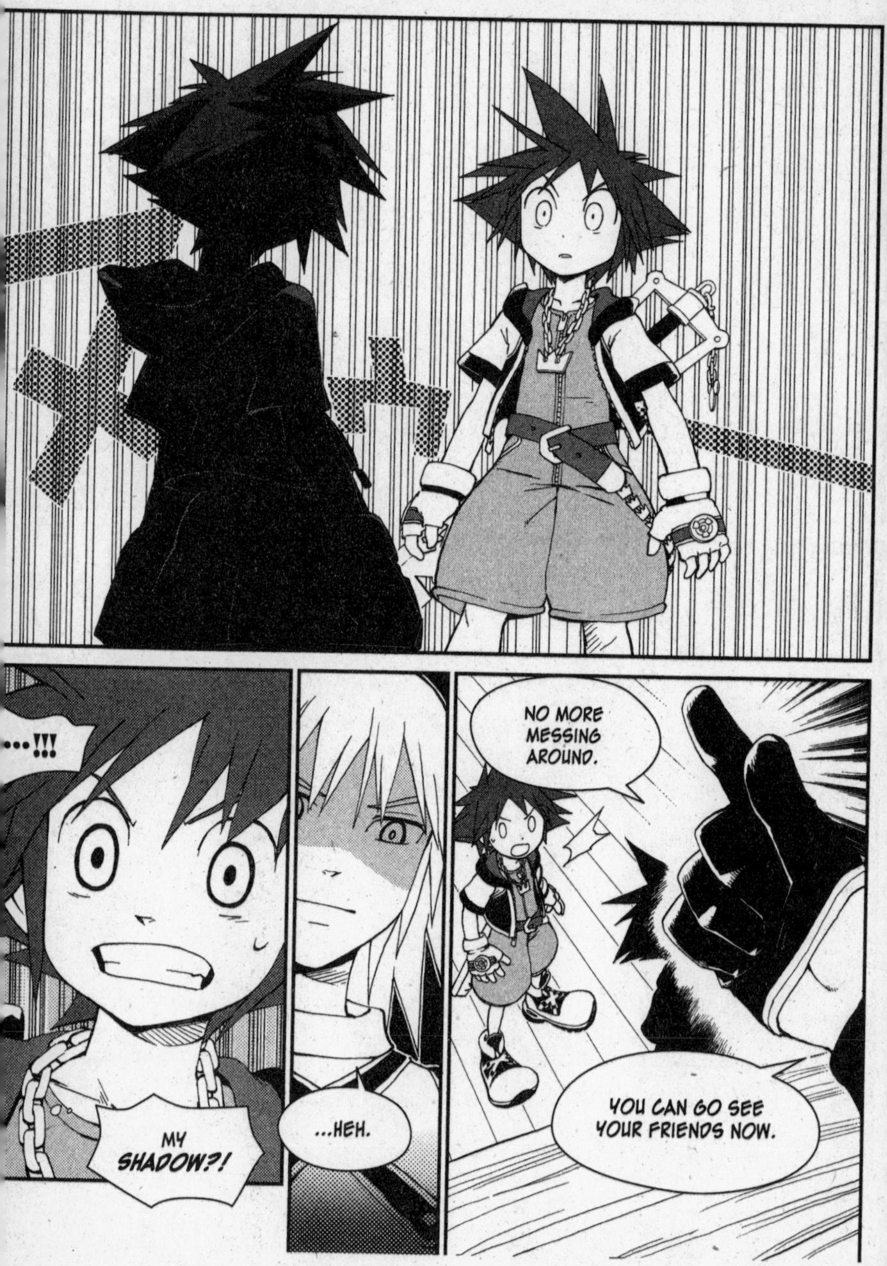
...!!!
MY SHADOW?!
...HEH.
NO MORE MESSING AROUND.
YOU CAN GO SEE YOUR FRIENDS NOW.

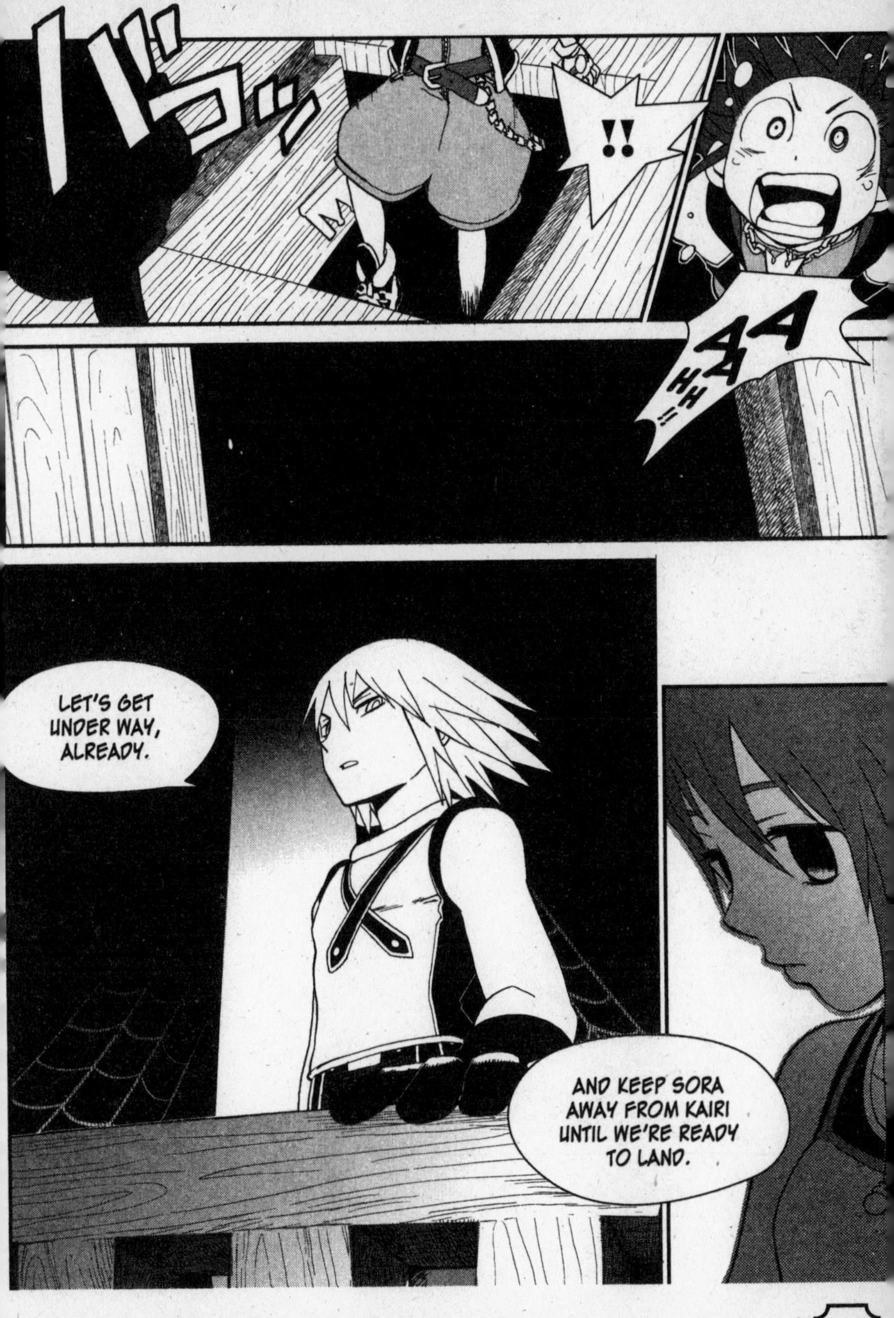

バッ
!!
AAAHH!!
LET'S GET UNDER WAY, ALREADY.
AND KEEP SORA AWAY FROM KAIRI UNTIL WE'RE READY TO LAND.

# Episode 33

## Pirate Ship

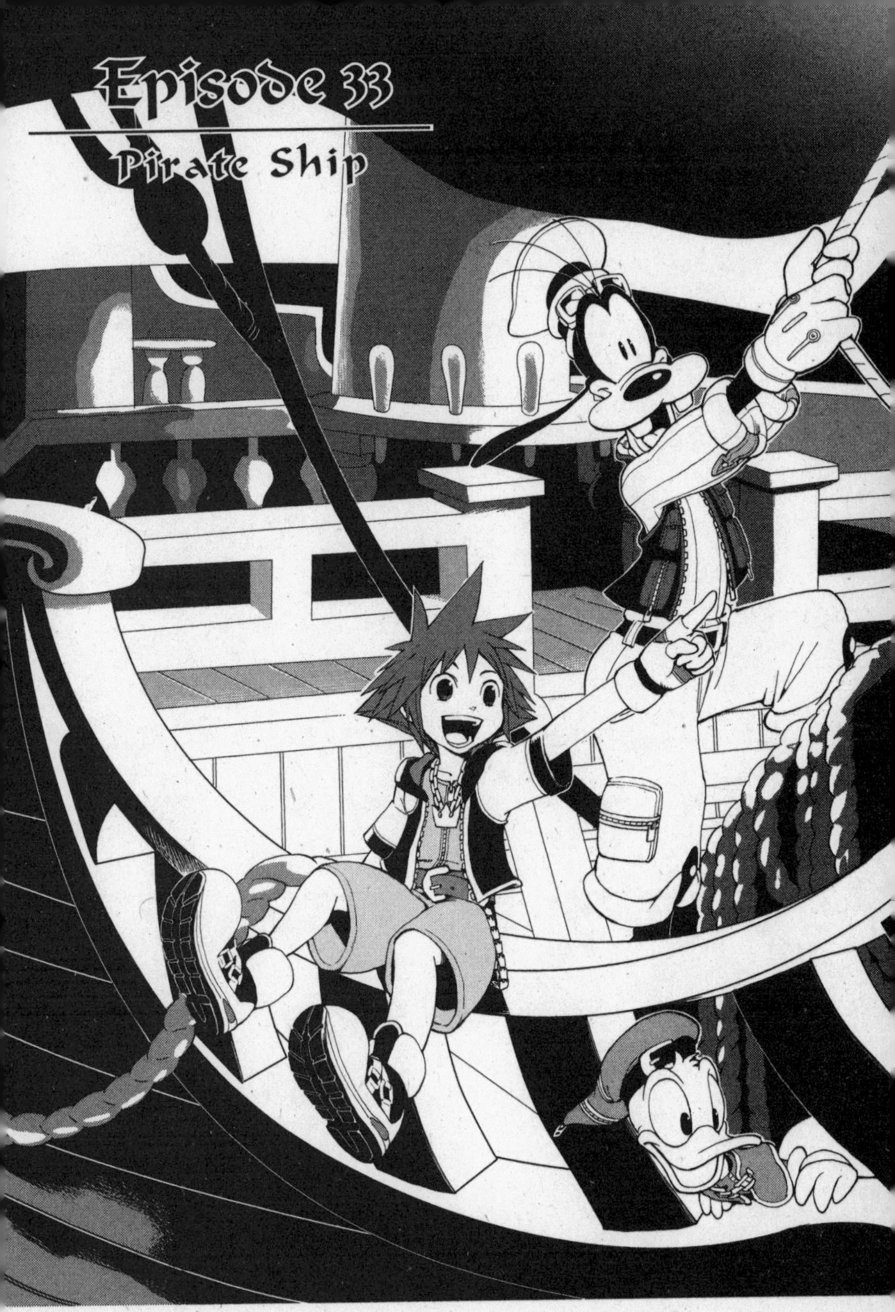

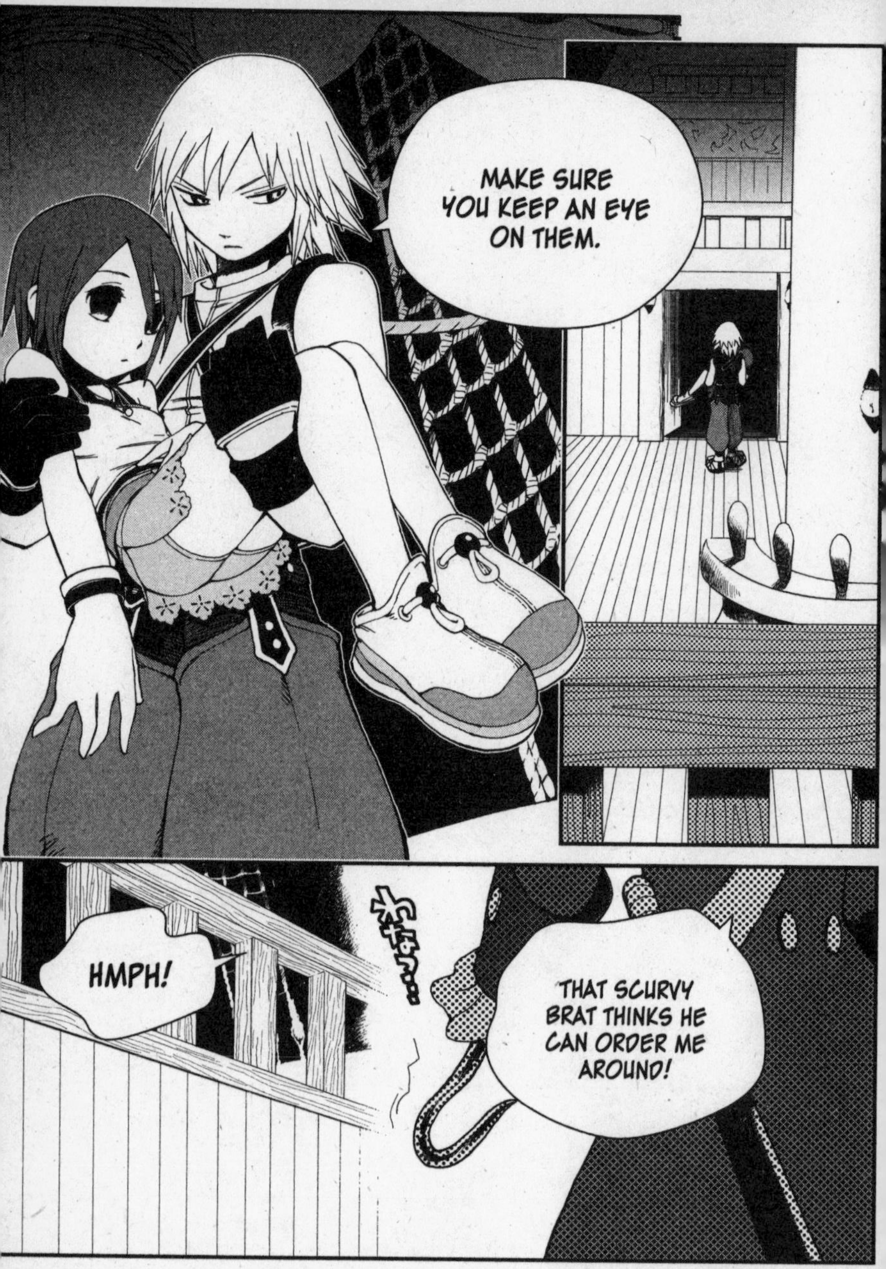
MAKE SURE YOU KEEP AN EYE ON THEM.
HMPH!
THAT SCURVY BRAT THINKS HE CAN ORDER ME AROUND!

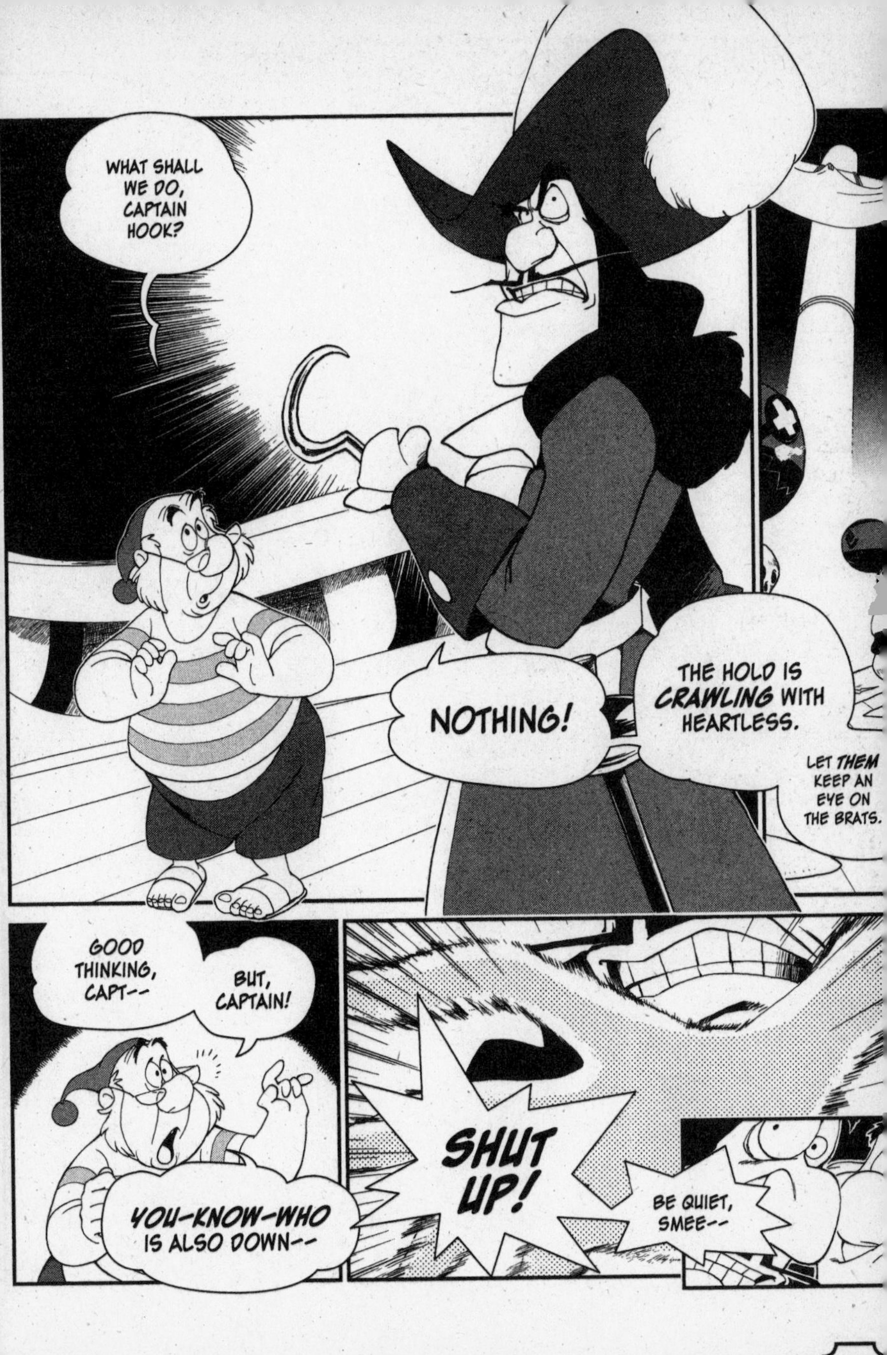
WHAT SHALL WE DO, CAPTAIN HOOK?
NOTHING!
THE HOLD IS *CRAWLING* WITH HEARTLESS.
LET *THEM* KEEP AN EYE ON THE BRATS.
GOOD THINKING, CAPT--
BUT, CAPTAIN!
*YOU-KNOW-WHO* IS ALSO DOWN--
*SHUT UP!*
BE QUIET, SMEE--

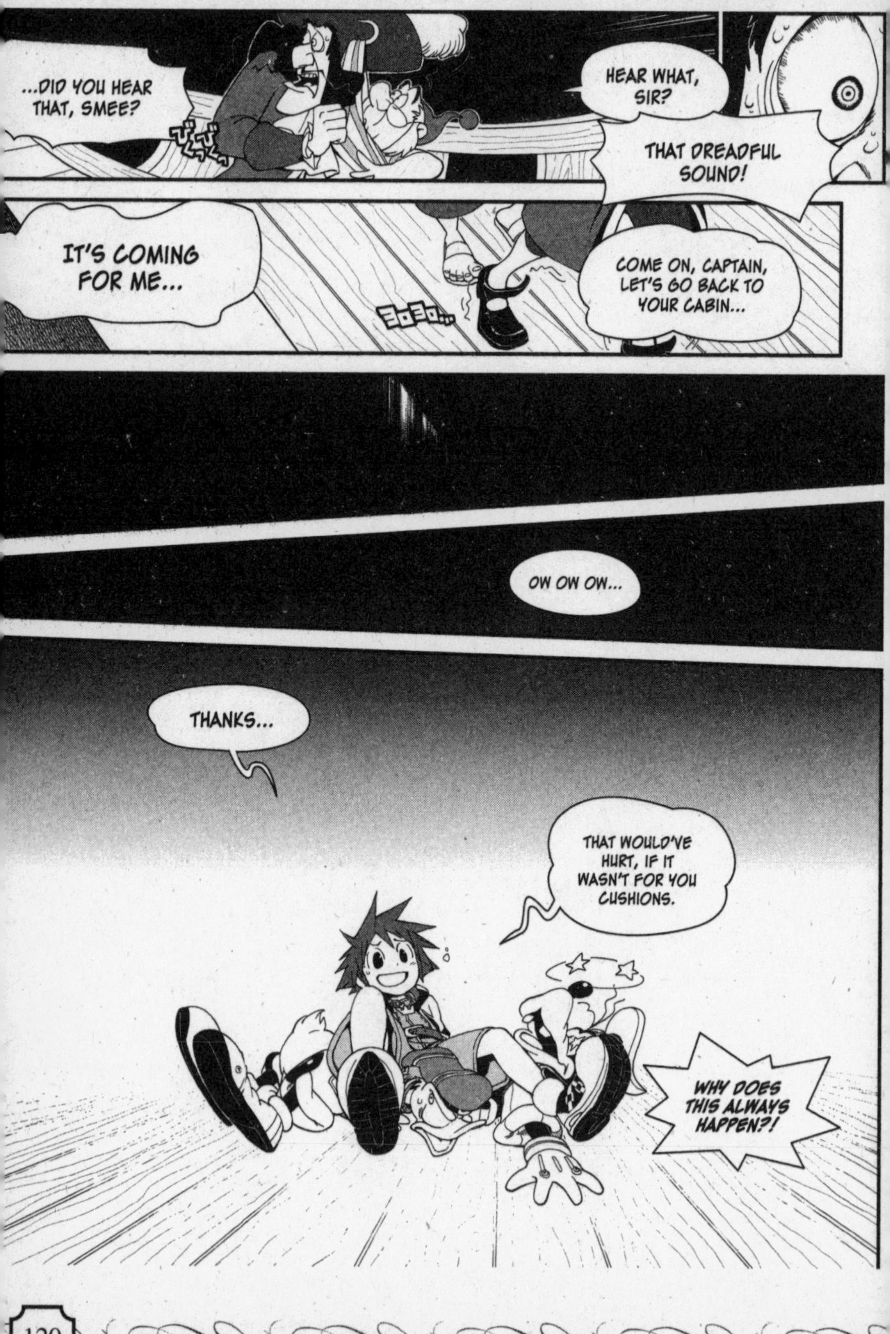
...DID YOU HEAR THAT, SMEE?
HEAR WHAT, SIR?
THAT DREADFUL SOUND!
IT'S COMING FOR ME...
COME ON, CAPTAIN, LET'S GO BACK TO YOUR CABIN...
OW OW OW...
THANKS...
THAT WOULD'VE HURT, IF IT WASN'T FOR YOU CUSHIONS.
WHY DOES THIS ALWAYS HAPPEN?!

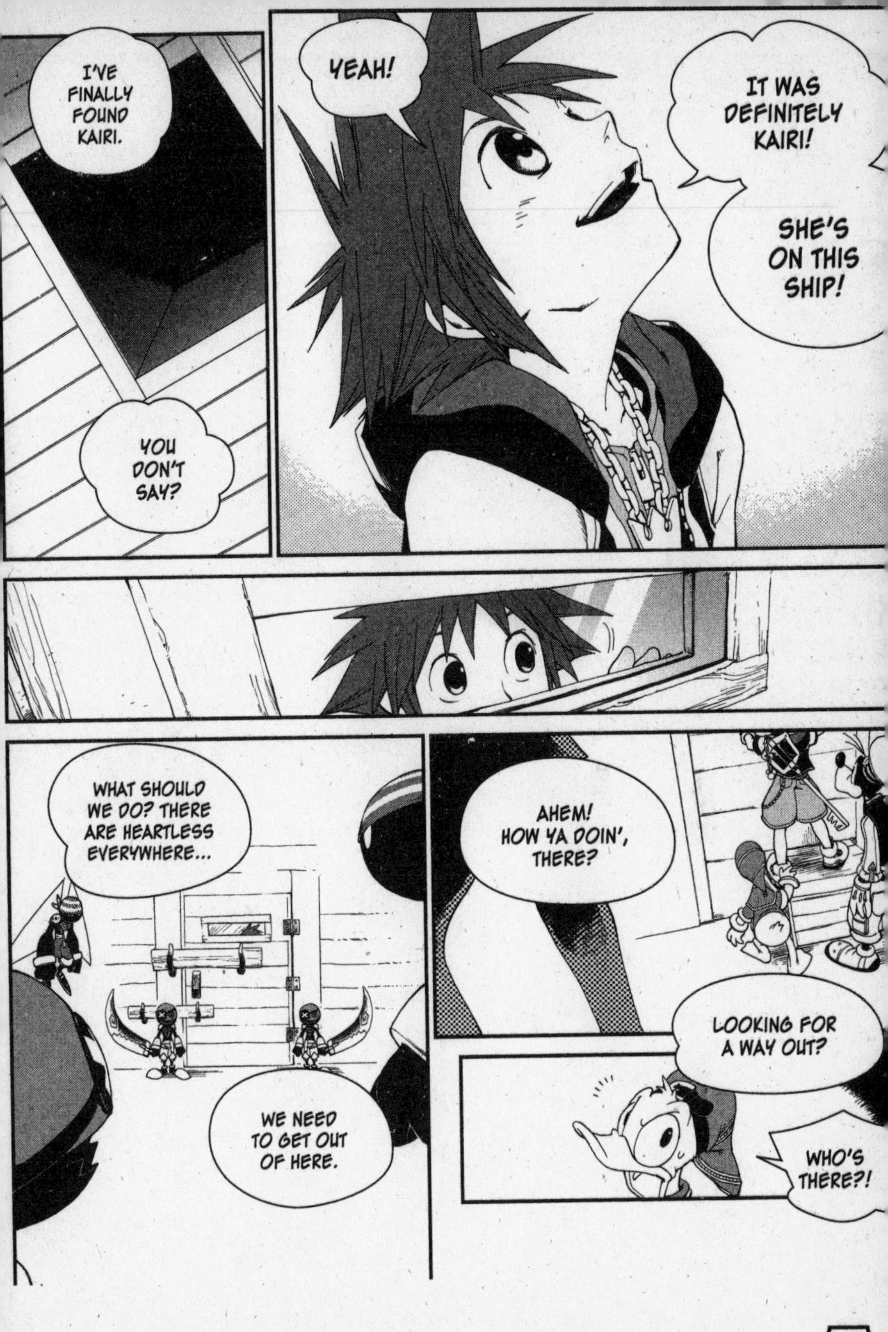
I'VE FINALLY FOUND KAIRI.
YOU DON'T SAY?
YEAH!
IT WAS DEFINITELY KAIRI!
SHE'S ON THIS SHIP!
WHAT SHOULD WE DO? THERE ARE HEARTLESS EVERYWHERE...
WE NEED TO GET OUT OF HERE.
AHEM! HOW YA DOIN', THERE?
LOOKING FOR A WAY OUT?
WHO'S THERE?!

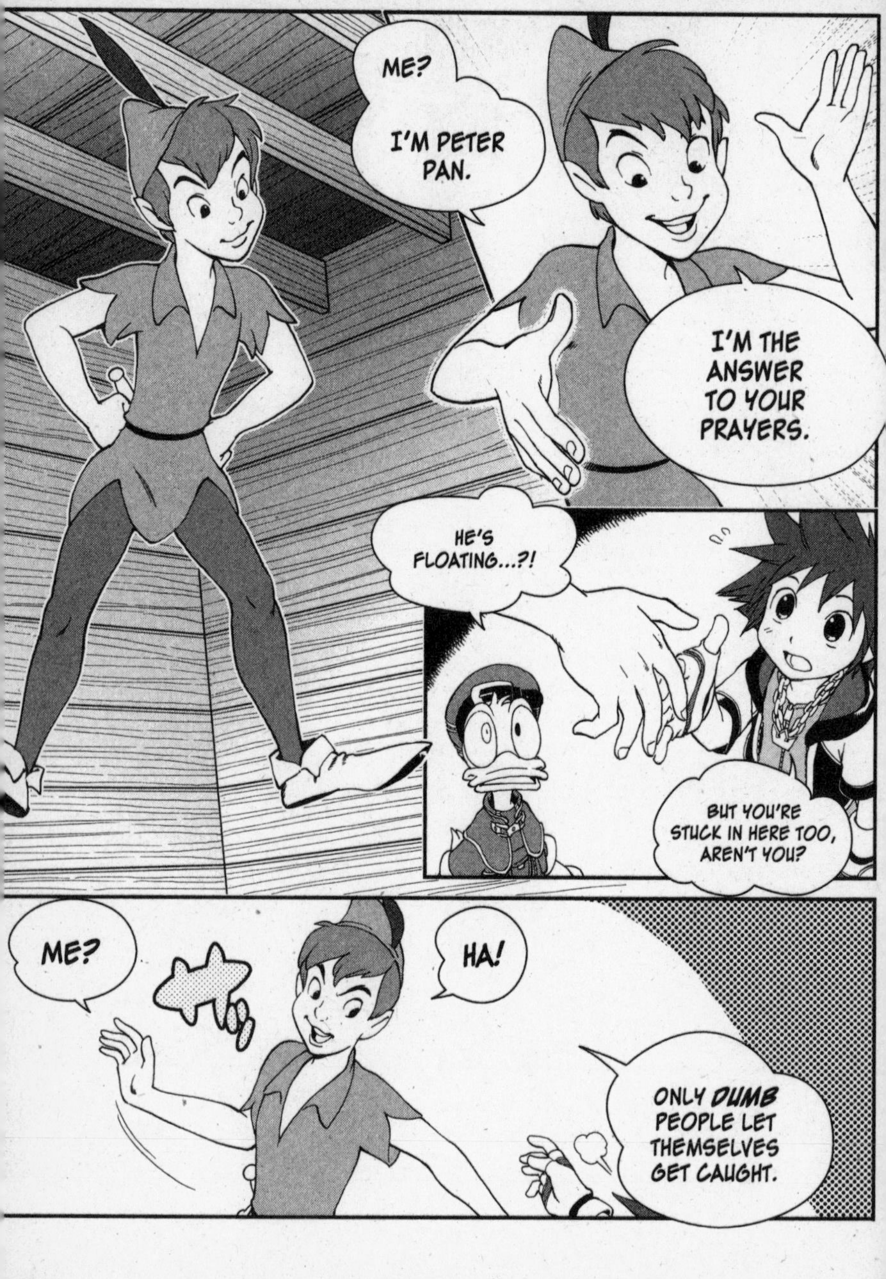
ME?
I'M PETER PAN.
I'M THE ANSWER TO YOUR PRAYERS.
HE'S FLOATING...?!
BUT YOU'RE STUCK IN HERE TOO, AREN'T YOU?
ME?
HA!
ONLY DUMB PEOPLE LET THEMSELVES GET CAUGHT.

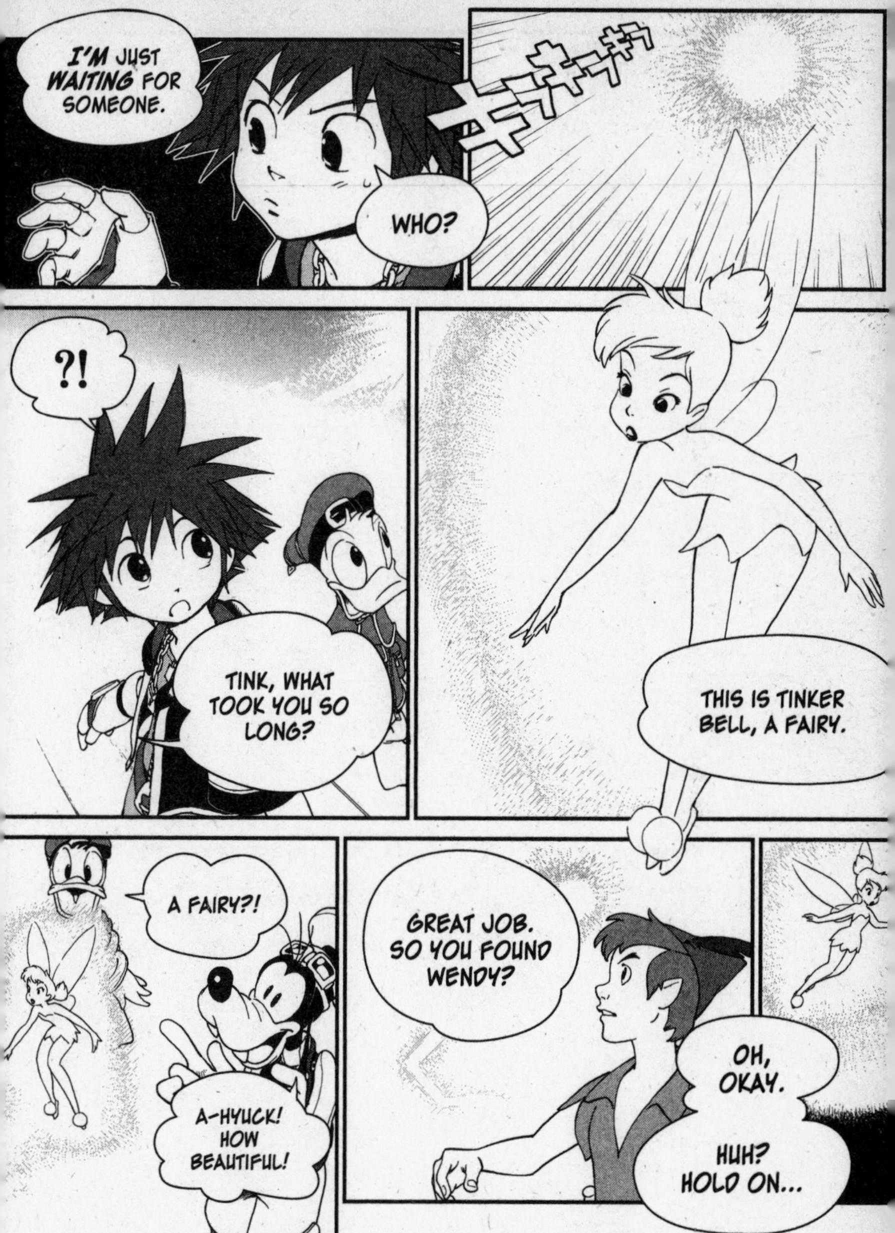
I'M JUST WAITING FOR SOMEONE.
WHO?
?!
TINK, WHAT TOOK YOU SO LONG?
THIS IS TINKER BELL, A FAIRY.
A FAIRY?!
A-HYUCK! HOW BEAUTIFUL!
GREAT JOB. SO YOU FOUND WENDY?
OH, OKAY.
HUH? HOLD ON...

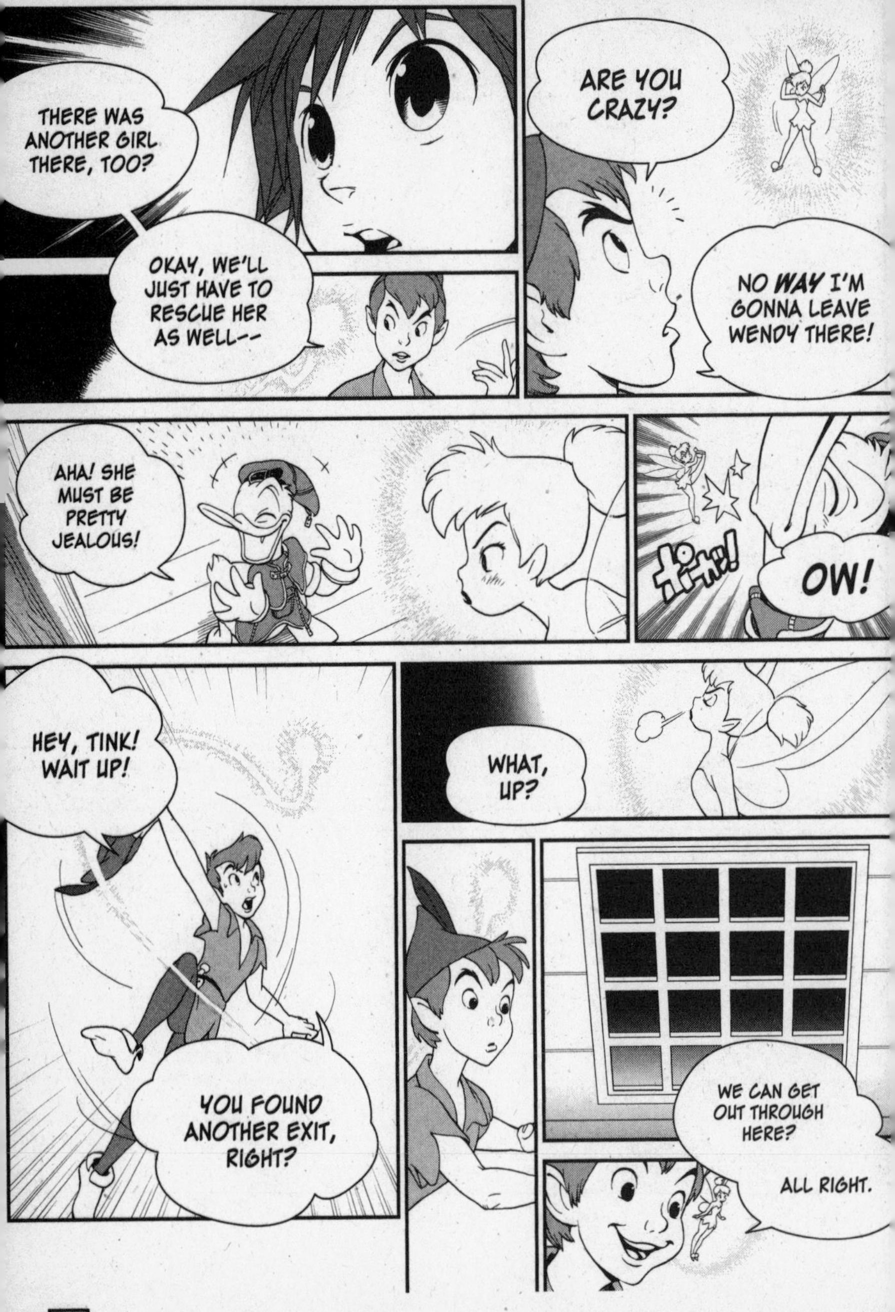
THERE WAS ANOTHER GIRL THERE, TOO?
OKAY, WE'LL JUST HAVE TO RESCUE HER AS WELL--
ARE YOU CRAZY?
NO *WAY* I'M GONNA LEAVE WENDY THERE!
AHA! SHE MUST BE PRETTY JEALOUS!
ポカッ!
OW!
HEY, TINK! WAIT UP!
YOU FOUND ANOTHER EXIT, RIGHT?
WHAT, UP?
WE CAN GET OUT THROUGH HERE?
ALL RIGHT.

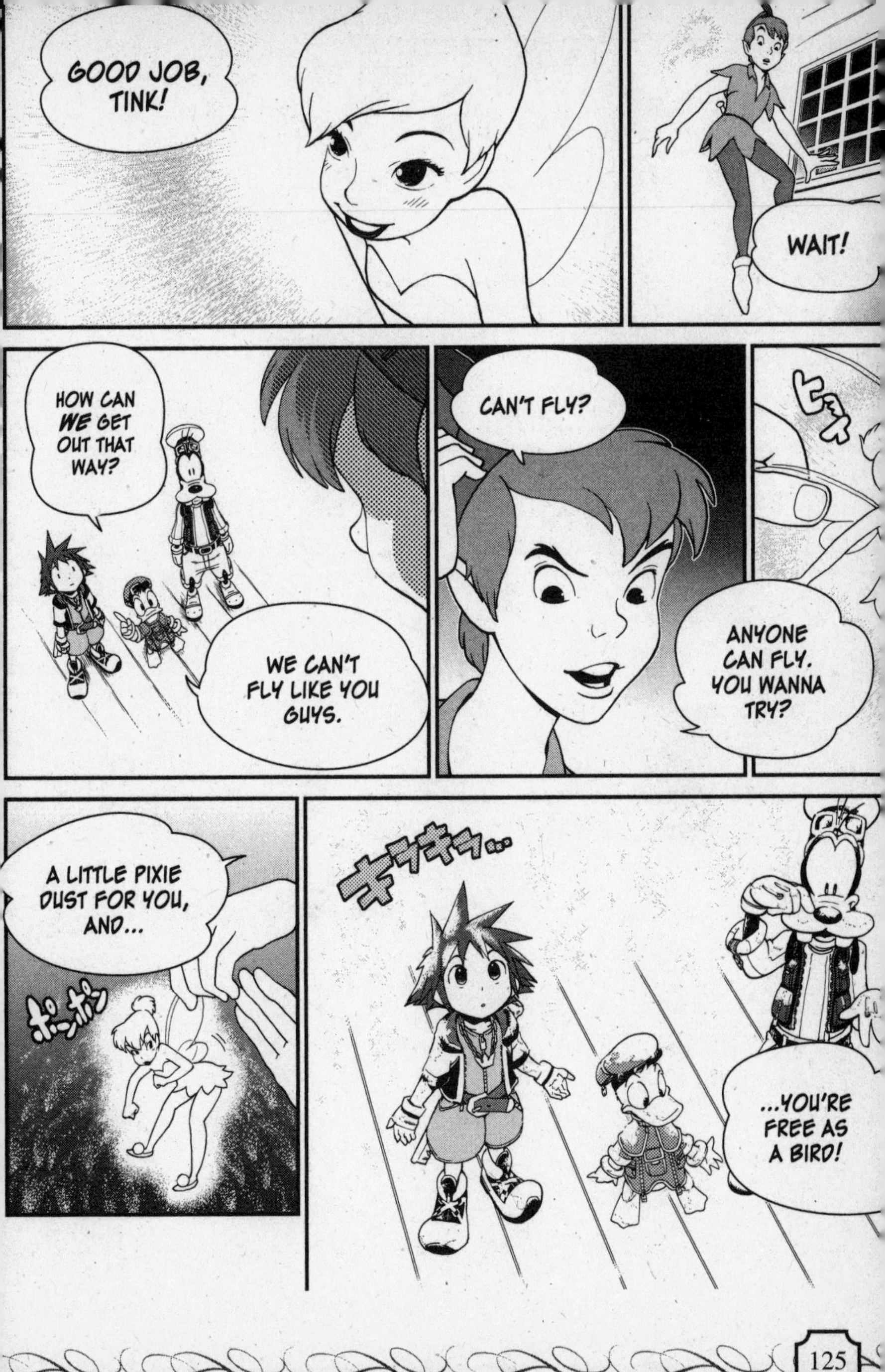
GOOD JOB, TINK!
WAIT!
HOW CAN *WE* GET OUT THAT WAY?
WE CAN'T FLY LIKE YOU GUYS.
CAN'T FLY?
ANYONE CAN FLY. YOU WANNA TRY?
A LITTLE PIXIE DUST FOR YOU, AND...
ポンポン
...YOU'RE FREE AS A BIRD!

COME ON, TRY FLYING!

IT CAN'T BE THAT EASY...

FLY!!

!!

ALL RIGHT...

HERE, GRAB THIS ROPE.

NOW YOU GIVE US THE ROPE...

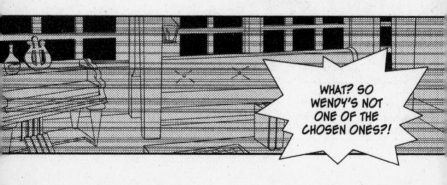

WHAT? SO WENDY'S NOT ONE OF THE CHOSEN ONES?!

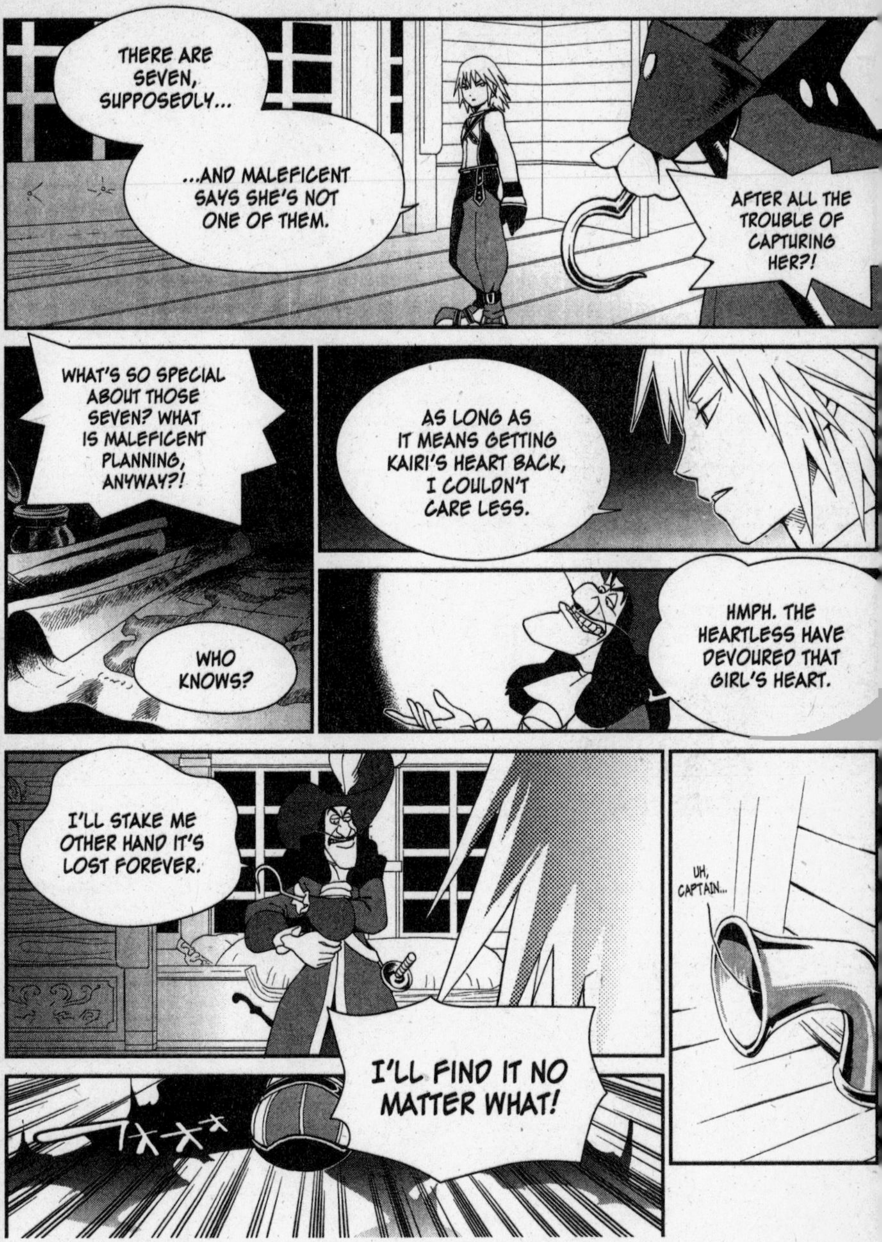
THERE ARE SEVEN, SUPPOSEDLY...
...AND MALEFICENT SAYS SHE'S NOT ONE OF THEM.
AFTER ALL THE TROUBLE OF CAPTURING HER?!
WHAT'S SO SPECIAL ABOUT THOSE SEVEN? WHAT IS MALEFICENT PLANNING, ANYWAY?!
WHO KNOWS?
AS LONG AS IT MEANS GETTING KAIRI'S HEART BACK, I COULDN'T CARE LESS.
HMPH. THE HEARTLESS HAVE DEVOURED THAT GIRL'S HEART.
I'LL STAKE ME OTHER HAND IT'S LOST FOREVER.
I'LL FIND IT NO MATTER WHAT!
UH, CAPTAIN...

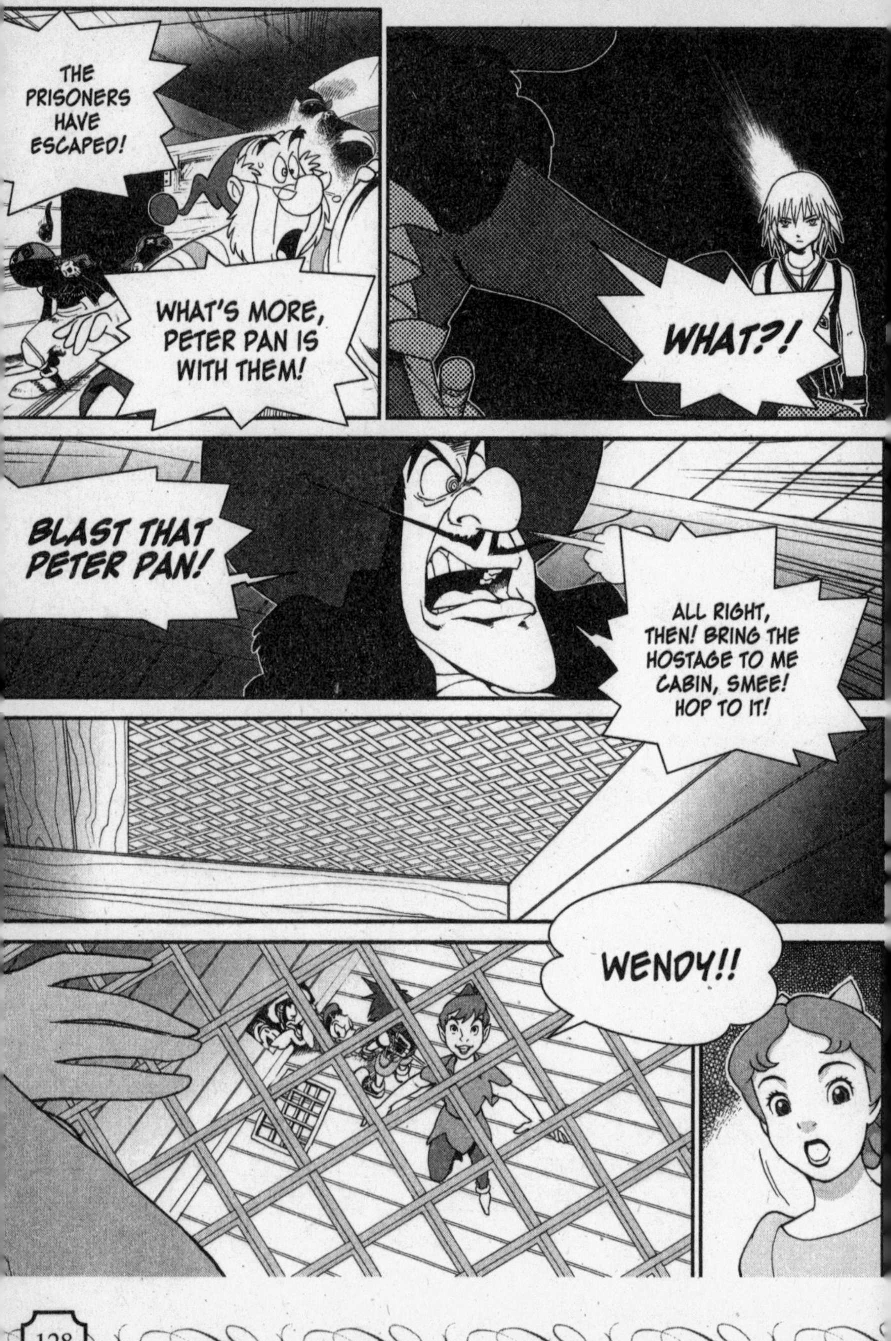
THE PRISONERS HAVE ESCAPED!
WHAT'S MORE, PETER PAN IS WITH THEM!
WHAT?!
BLAST THAT PETER PAN!
ALL RIGHT, THEN! BRING THE HOSTAGE TO ME CABIN, SMEE! HOP TO IT!
WENDY!!

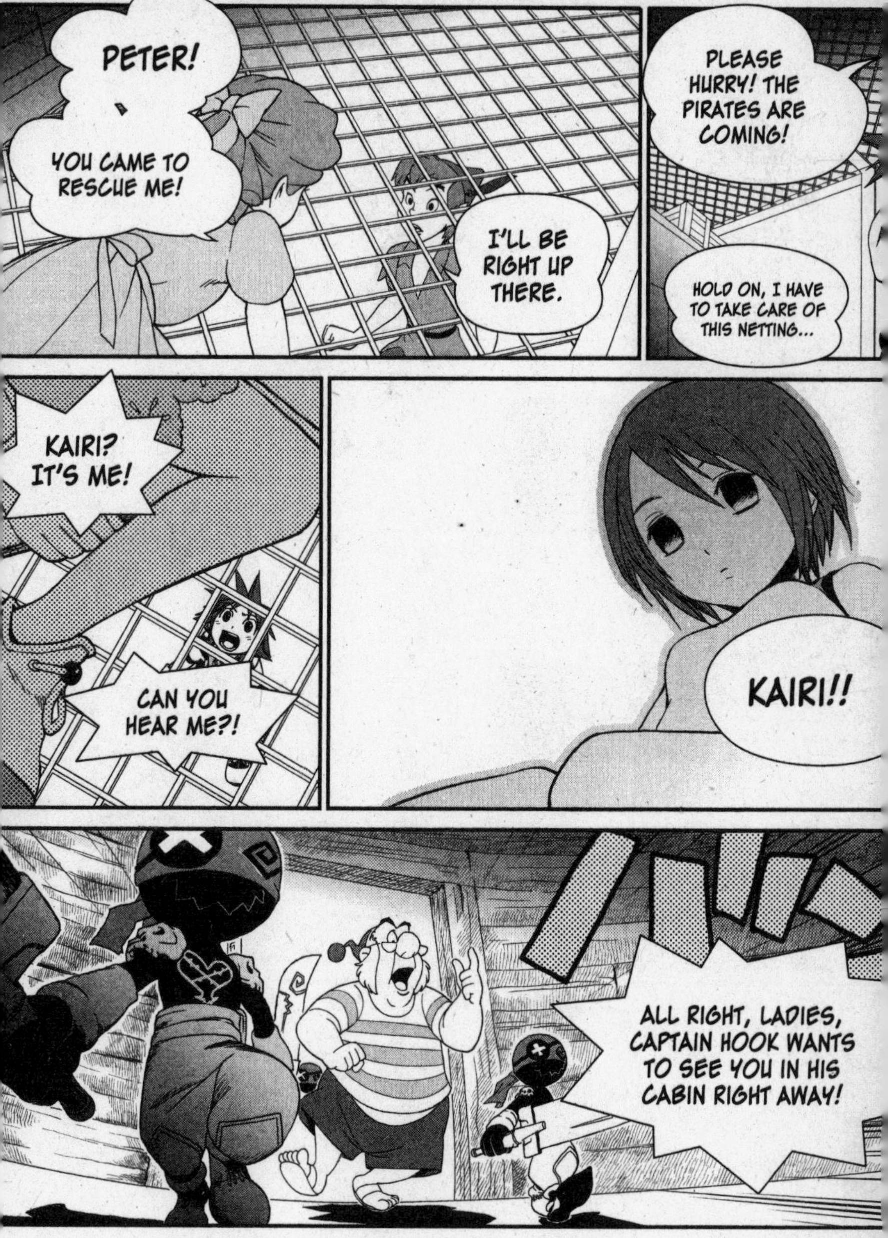
PETER!
YOU CAME TO RESCUE ME!
I'LL BE RIGHT UP THERE.
PLEASE HURRY! THE PIRATES ARE COMING!
HOLD ON, I HAVE TO TAKE CARE OF THIS NETTING...
KAIRI? IT'S ME!
CAN YOU HEAR ME?!
KAIRI!!
ALL RIGHT, LADIES, CAPTAIN HOOK WANTS TO SEE YOU IN HIS CABIN RIGHT AWAY!

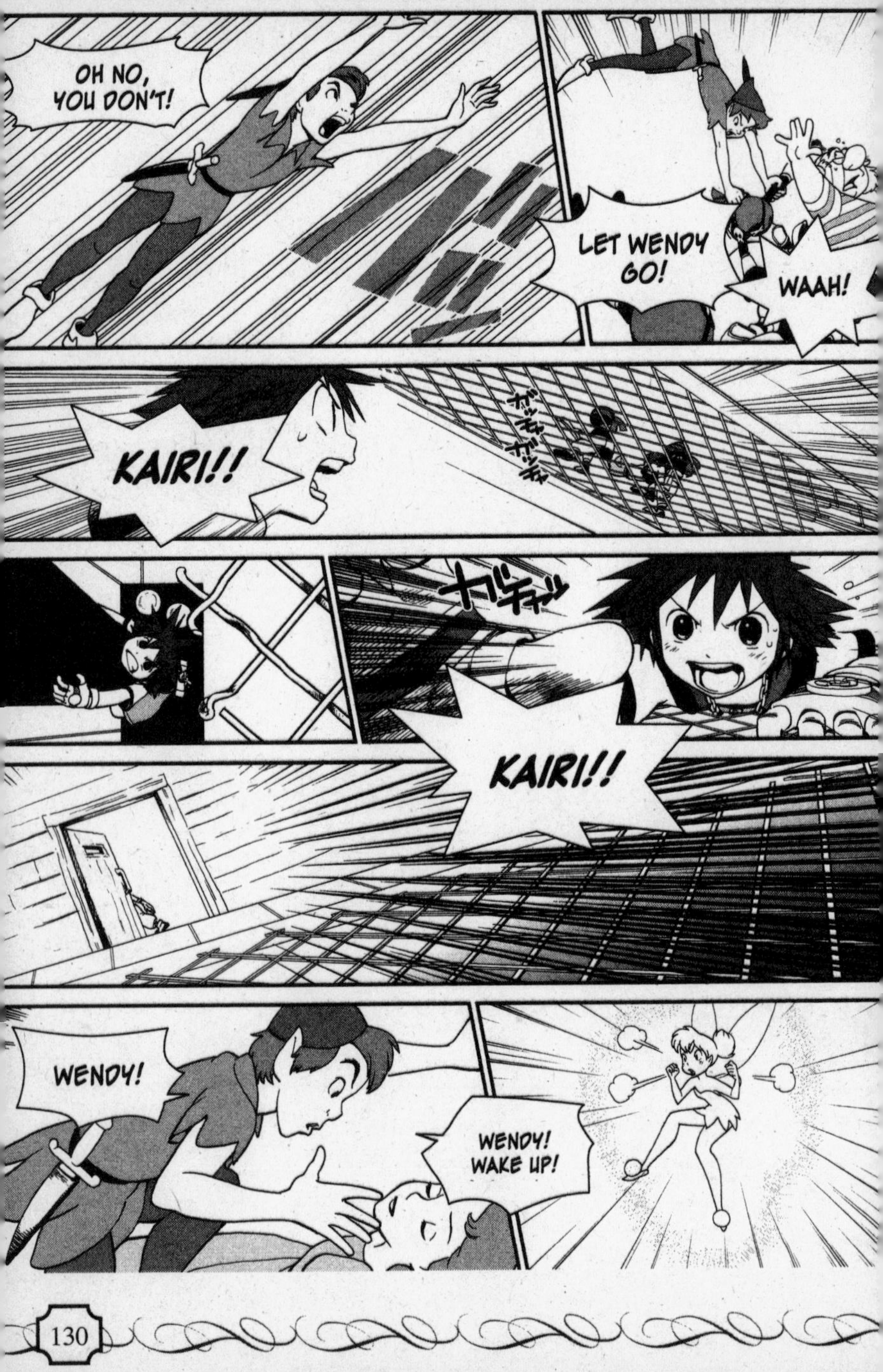

OH NO, YOU DON'T!
LET WENDY GO!
WAAH!
KAIRI!!
KAIRI!!
WENDY!
WENDY! WAKE UP!

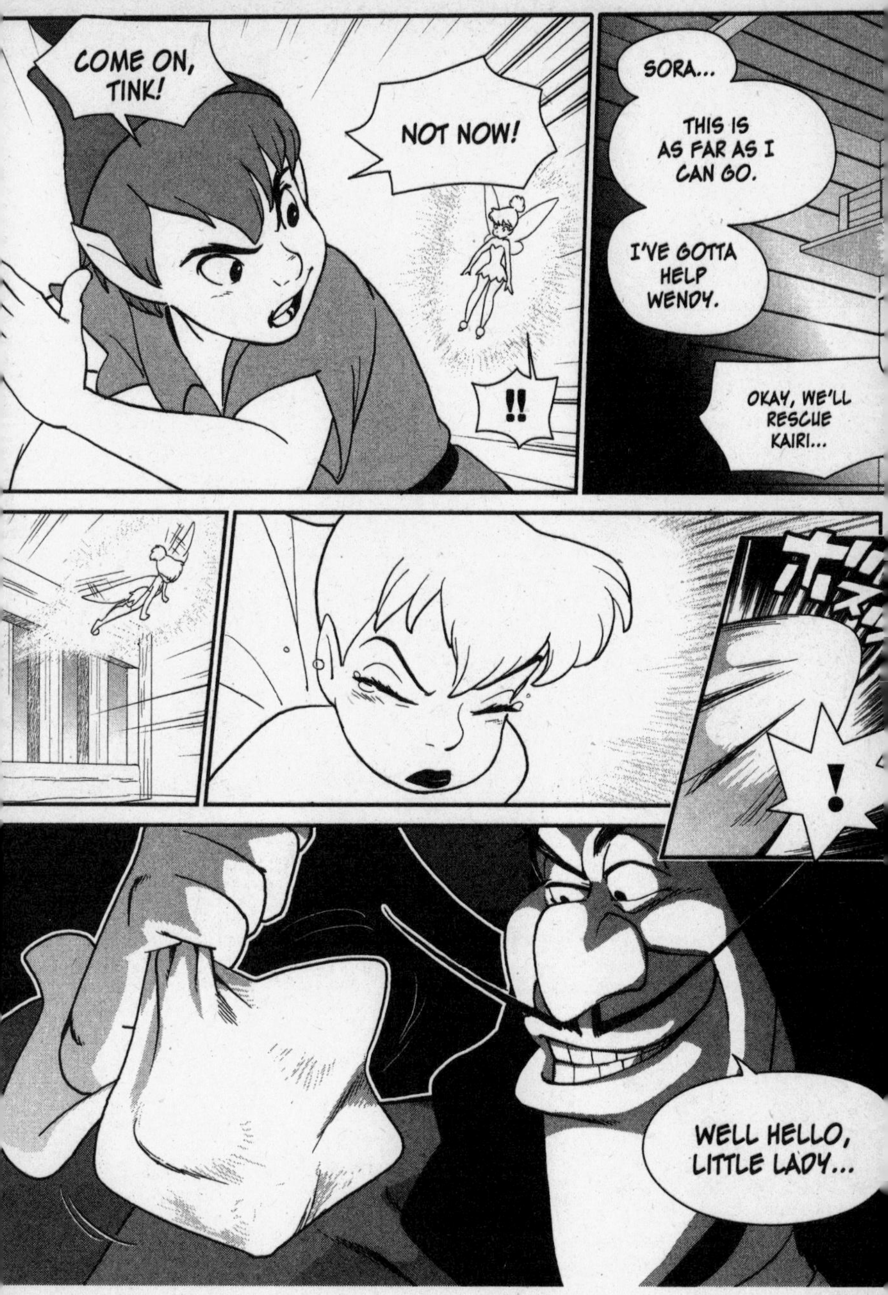
COME ON, TINK!
NOT NOW!
!!
SORA...
THIS IS AS FAR AS I CAN GO.
I'VE GOTTA HELP WENDY.
OKAY, WE'LL RESCUE KAIRI...
!
WELL HELLO, LITTLE LADY...

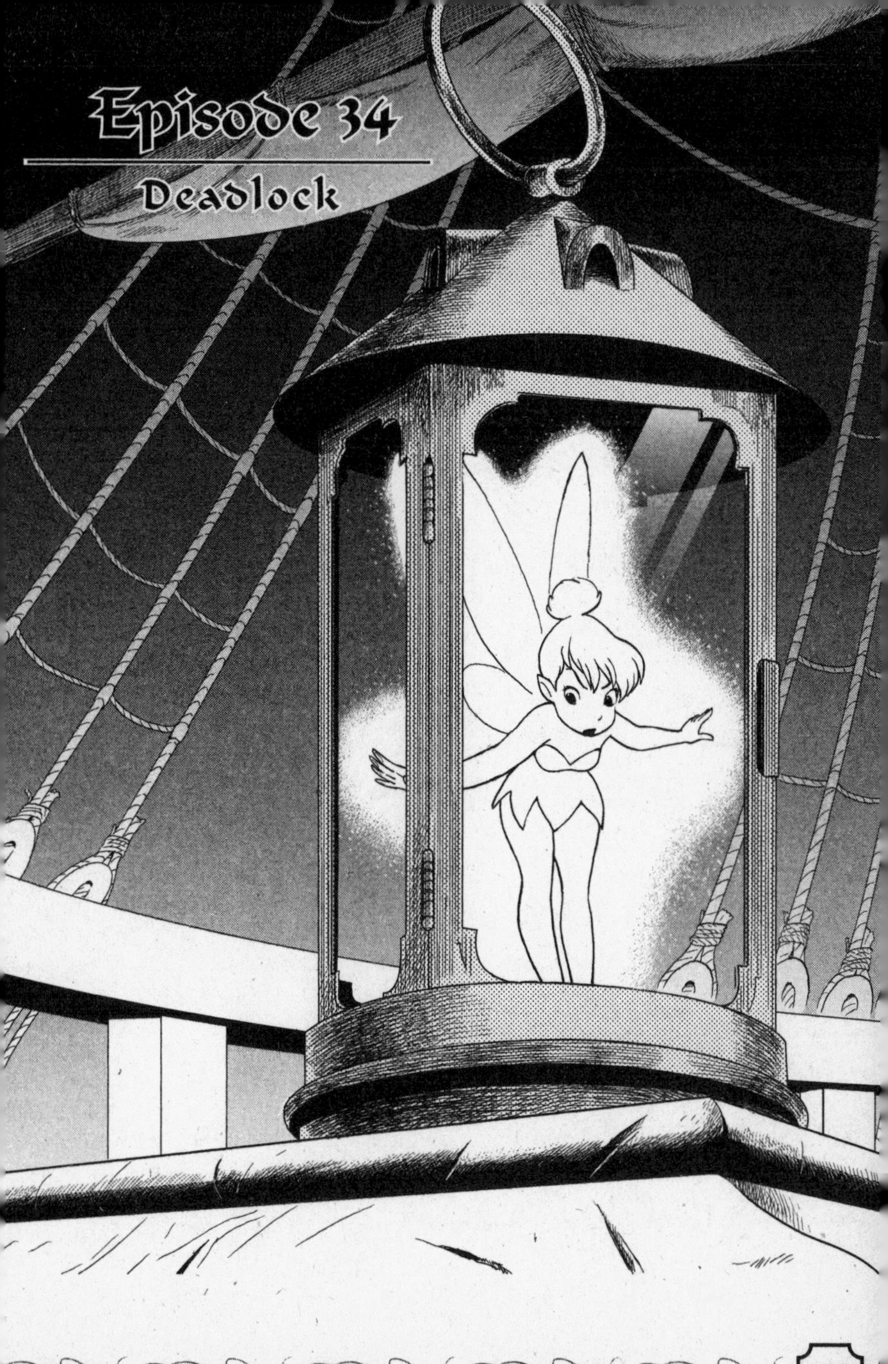
Episode 34
Deadlock

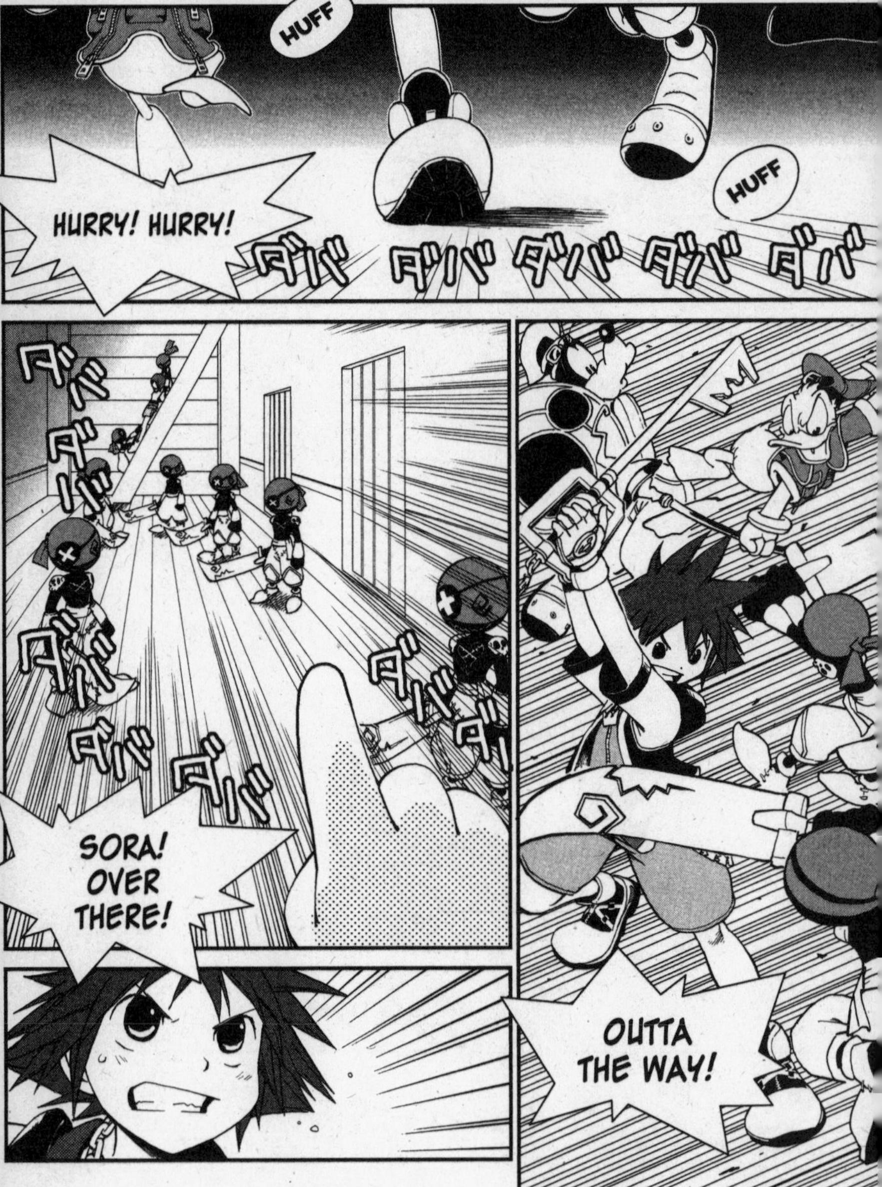
HUFF
HUFF
HURRY! HURRY!
ダバ ダバ ダバ ダバ ダバ
ダバダバ
ダバ
ダバダバ
ダバ
SORA! OVER THERE!
OUTTA THE WAY!

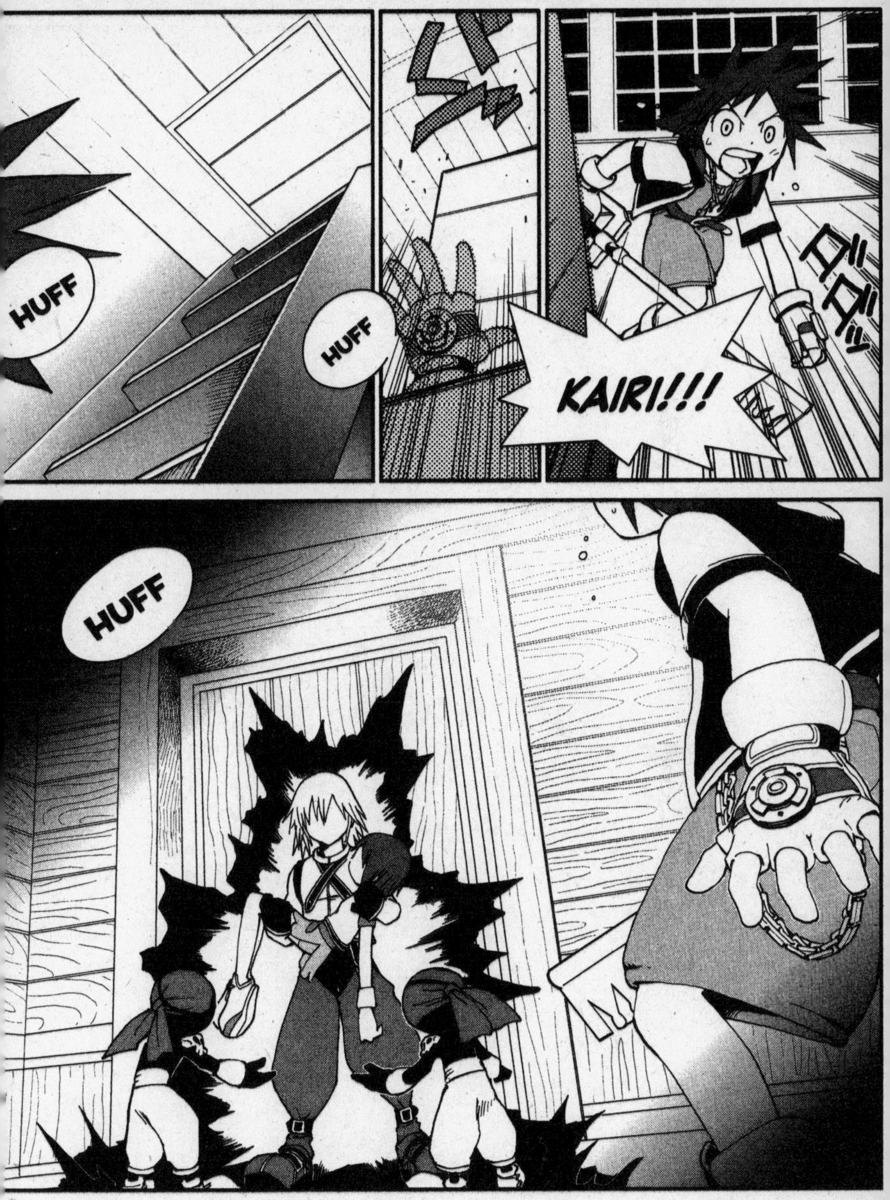
HUFF
HUFF
KAIRI!!!
HUFF

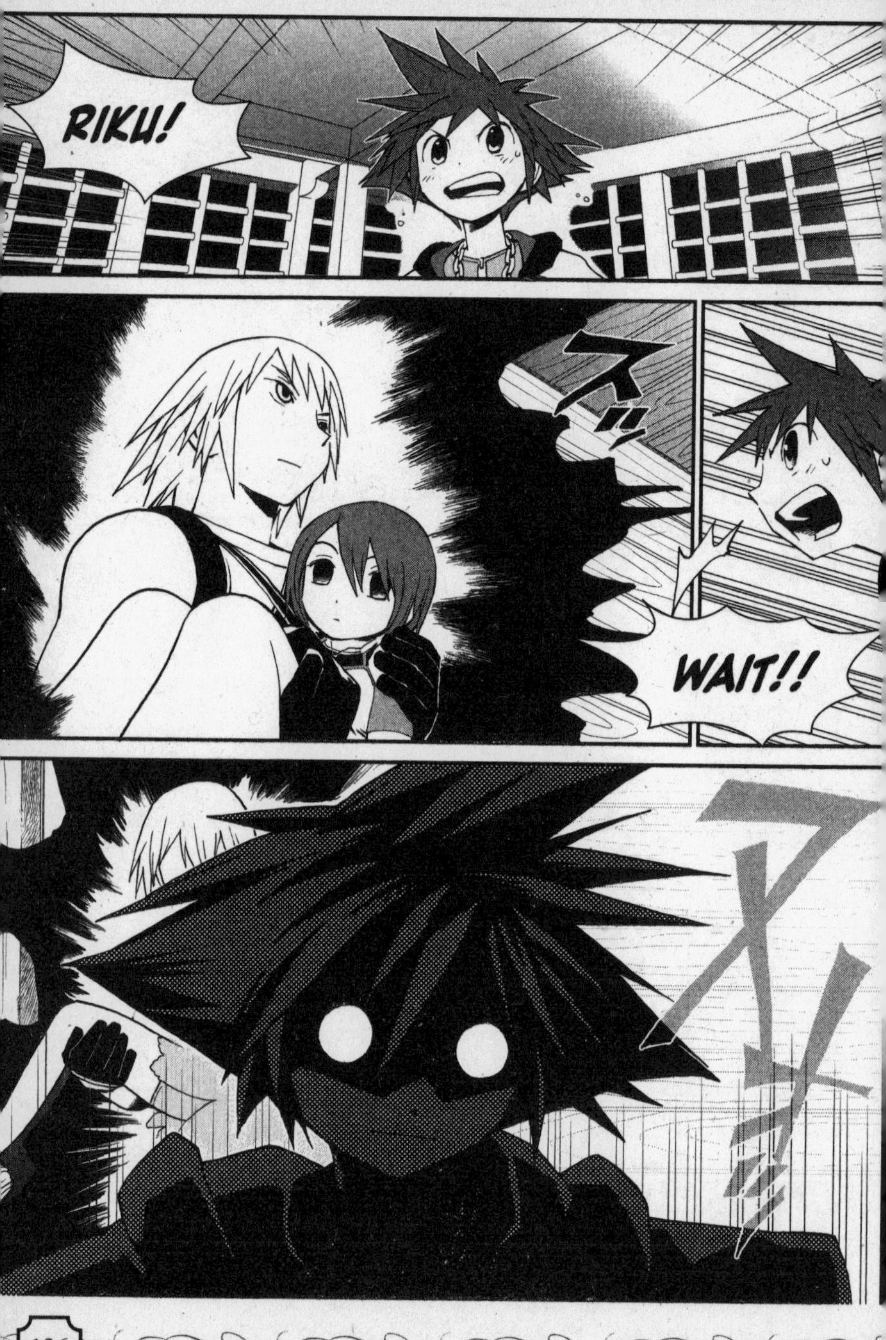
RIKU!
WAIT!!

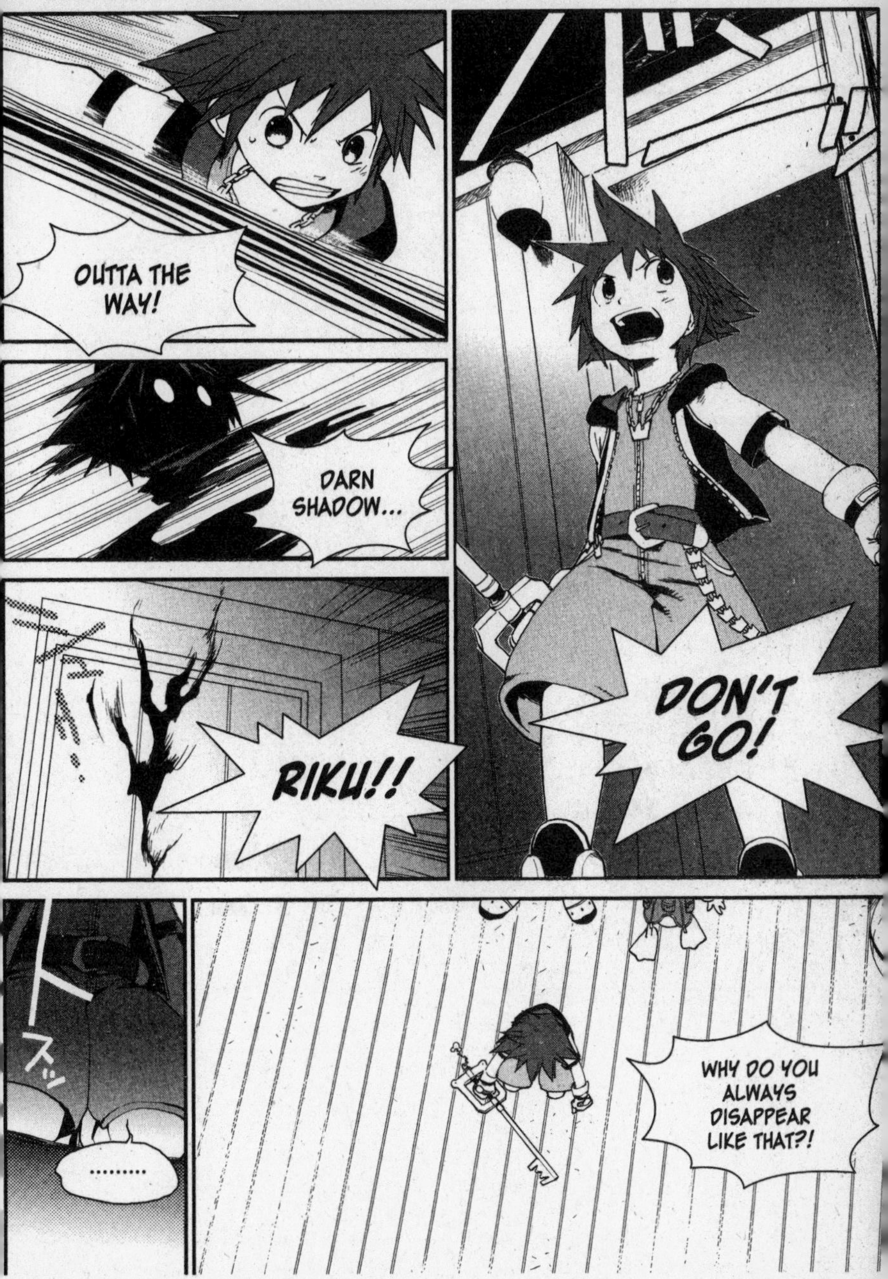
OUTTA THE WAY!
DARN SHADOW...
RIKU!!
DON'T GO!
..........
スッ
WHY DO YOU ALWAYS DISAPPEAR LIKE THAT?!

QUITE A CODFISH, THAT RIKU...

......

...RUNNING OFF WITH THAT GIRL WITHOUT EVEN SAYING GOODBYE.

RUN OFF WHERE? TELL ME, WHERE DID HE GO?!

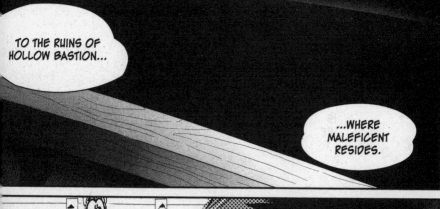

TO THE RUINS OF HOLLOW BASTION...

...WHERE MALEFICENT RESIDES.

MALEFICENT?!

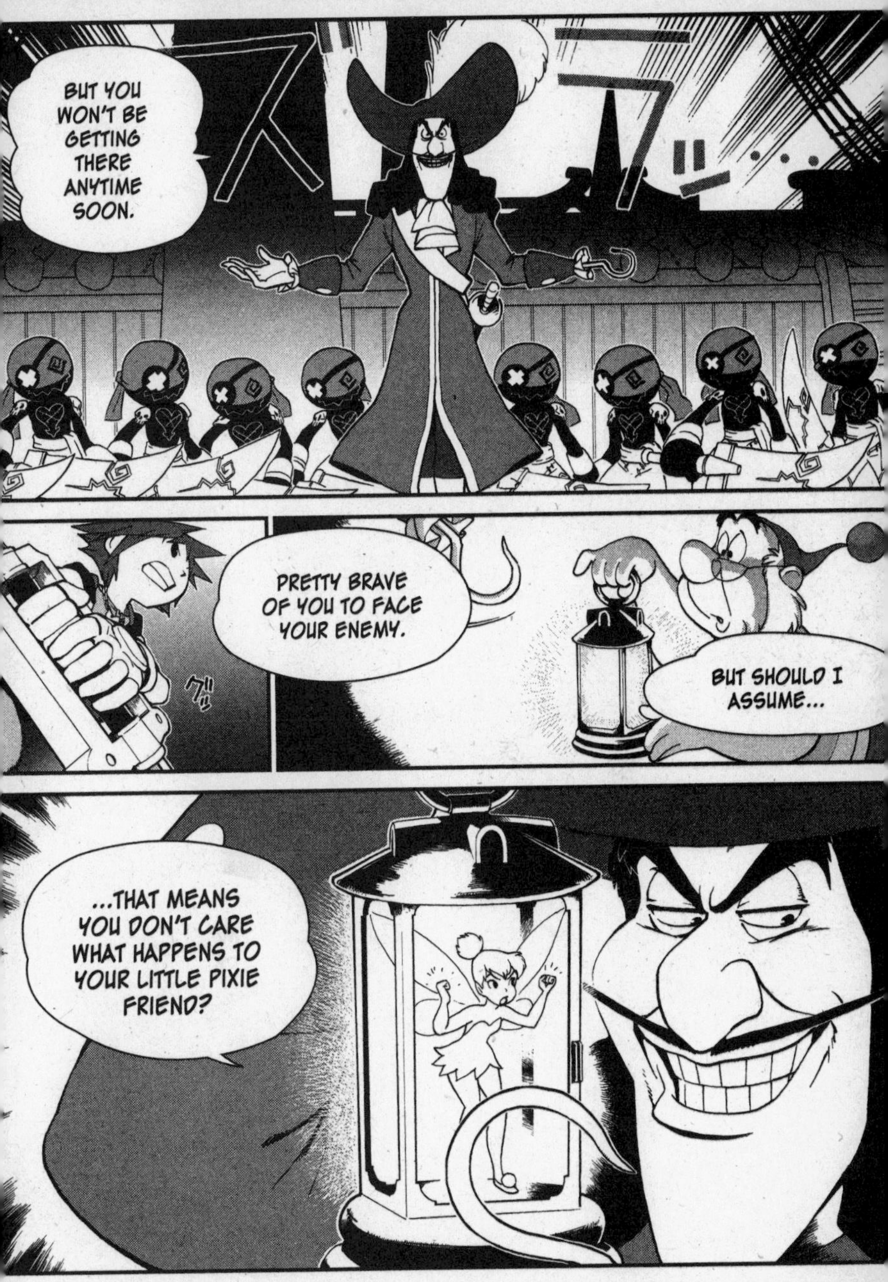
BUT YOU WON'T BE GETTING THERE ANYTIME SOON.
PRETTY BRAVE OF YOU TO FACE YOUR ENEMY.
BUT SHOULD I ASSUME...
...THAT MEANS YOU DON'T CARE WHAT HAPPENS TO YOUR LITTLE PIXIE FRIEND?

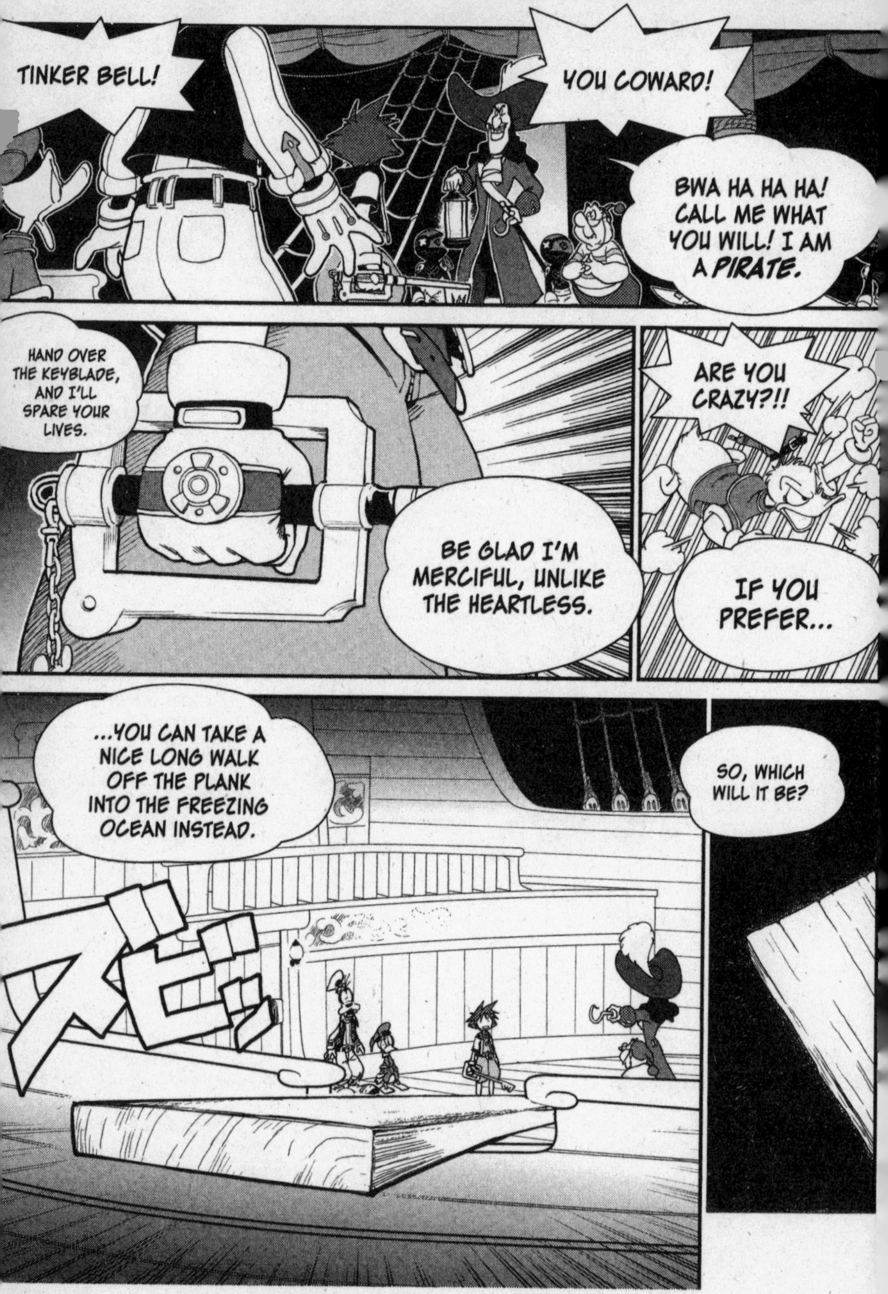
TINKER BELL!
YOU COWARD!
BWA HA HA HA! CALL ME WHAT YOU WILL! I AM A PIRATE.
HAND OVER THE KEYBLADE, AND I'LL SPARE YOUR LIVES.
BE GLAD I'M MERCIFUL, UNLIKE THE HEARTLESS.
ARE YOU CRAZY?!!
IF YOU PREFER...
...YOU CAN TAKE A NICE LONG WALK OFF THE PLANK INTO THE FREEZING OCEAN INSTEAD.
ズビッ
SO, WHICH WILL IT BE?

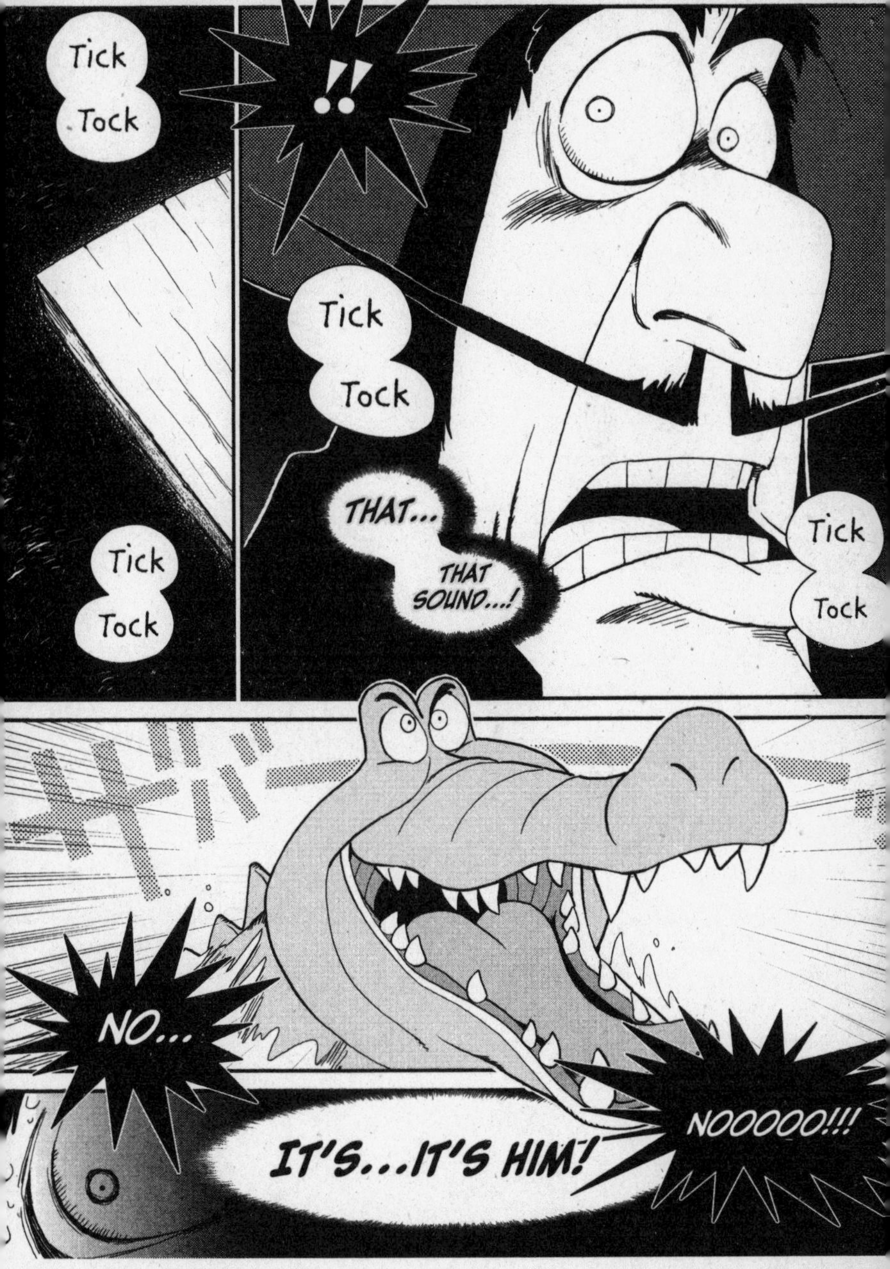
Tick
Tock
Tick
Tock
!!
Tick
Tock
THAT...
THAT SOUND...!
Tick
Tock
NO...
IT'S...IT'S HIM!
NOOOOO!!!

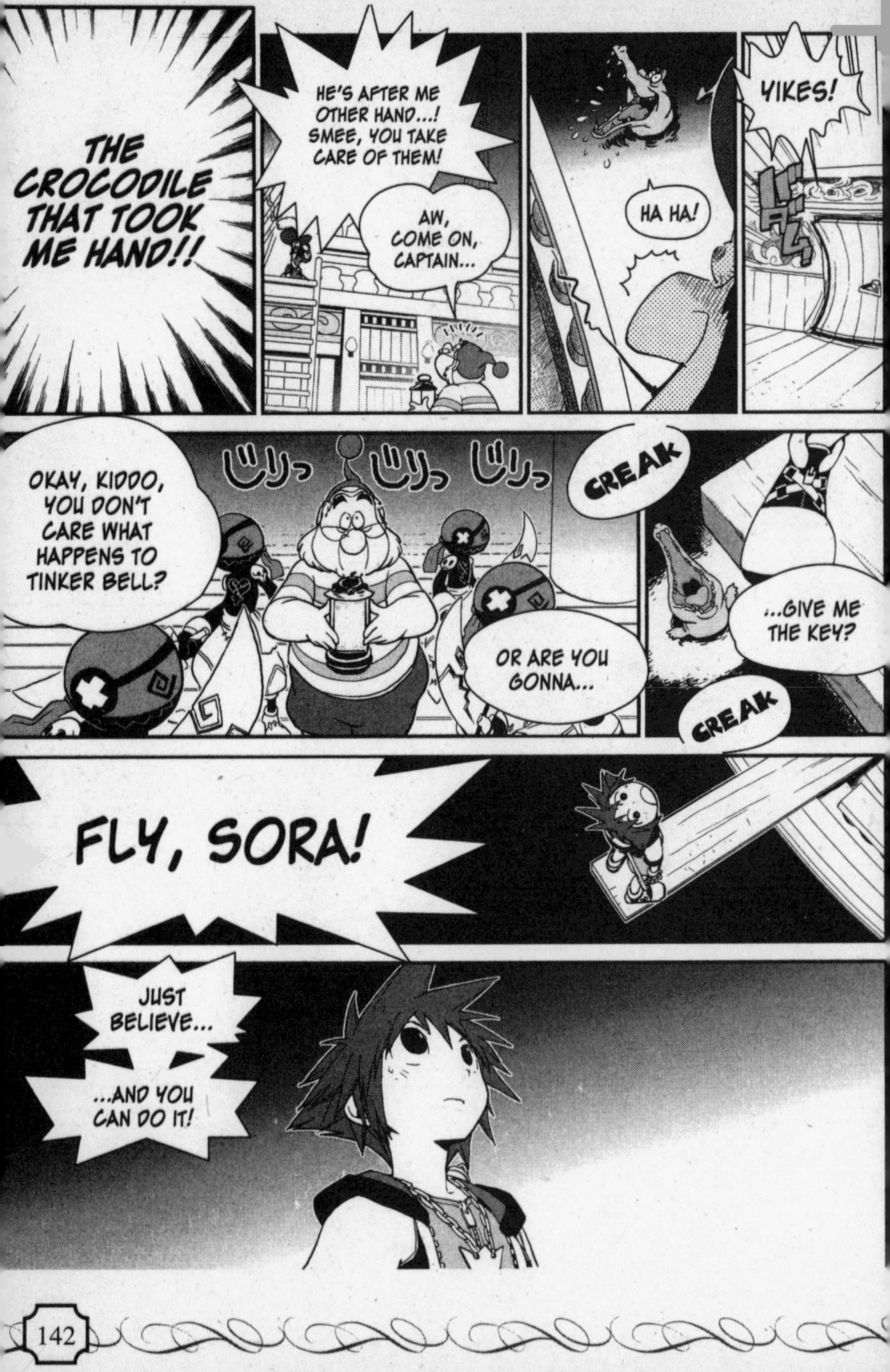
THE CROCODILE THAT TOOK ME HAND!!
HE'S AFTER ME OTHER HAND...! SMEE, YOU TAKE CARE OF THEM!
AW, COME ON, CAPTAIN...
HA HA!
YIKES!
OKAY, KIDDO, YOU DON'T CARE WHAT HAPPENS TO TINKER BELL?
じりっ じりっ じりっ
OR ARE YOU GONNA...
CREAK
...GIVE ME THE KEY?
CREAK
FLY, SORA!
JUST BELIEVE...
...AND YOU CAN DO IT!

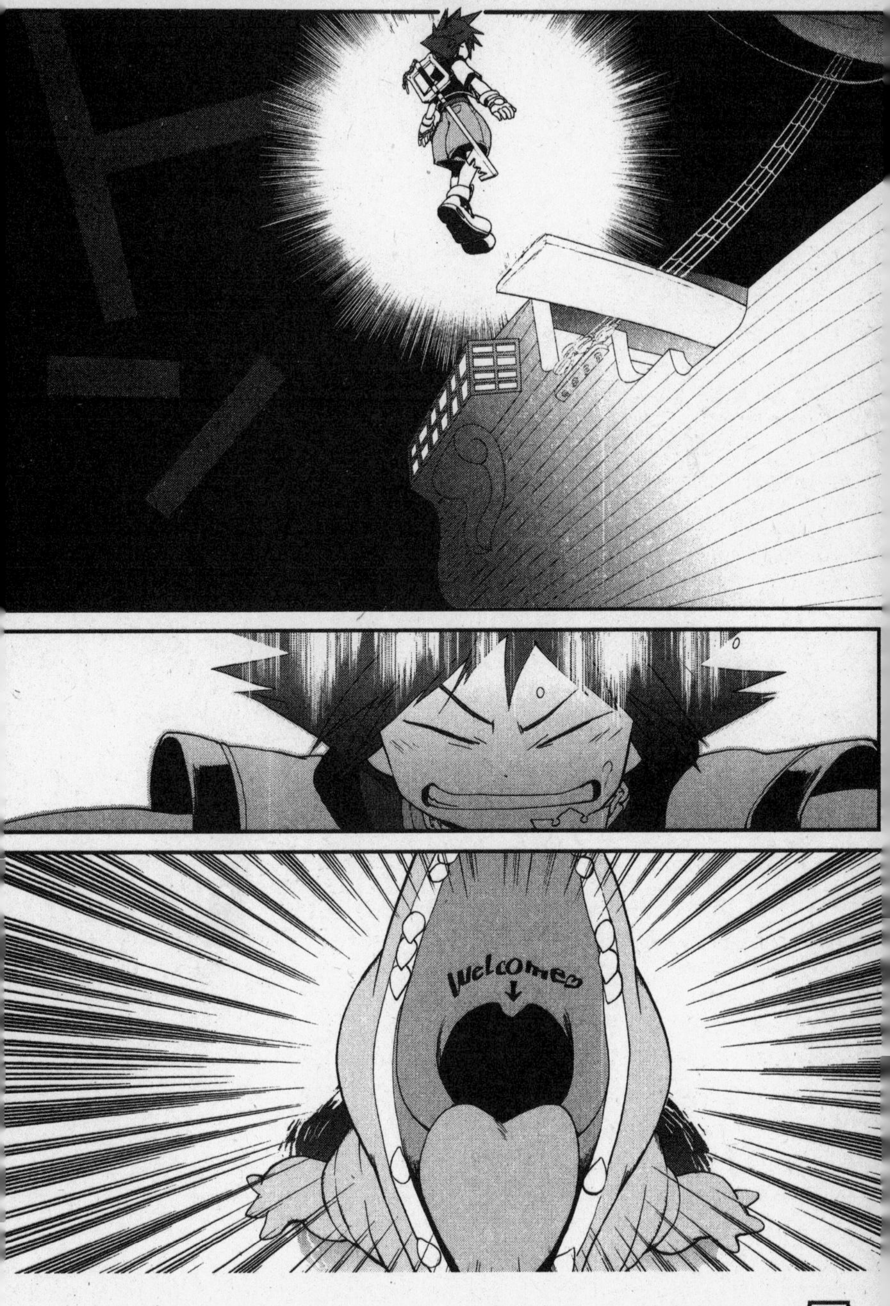
Welcome

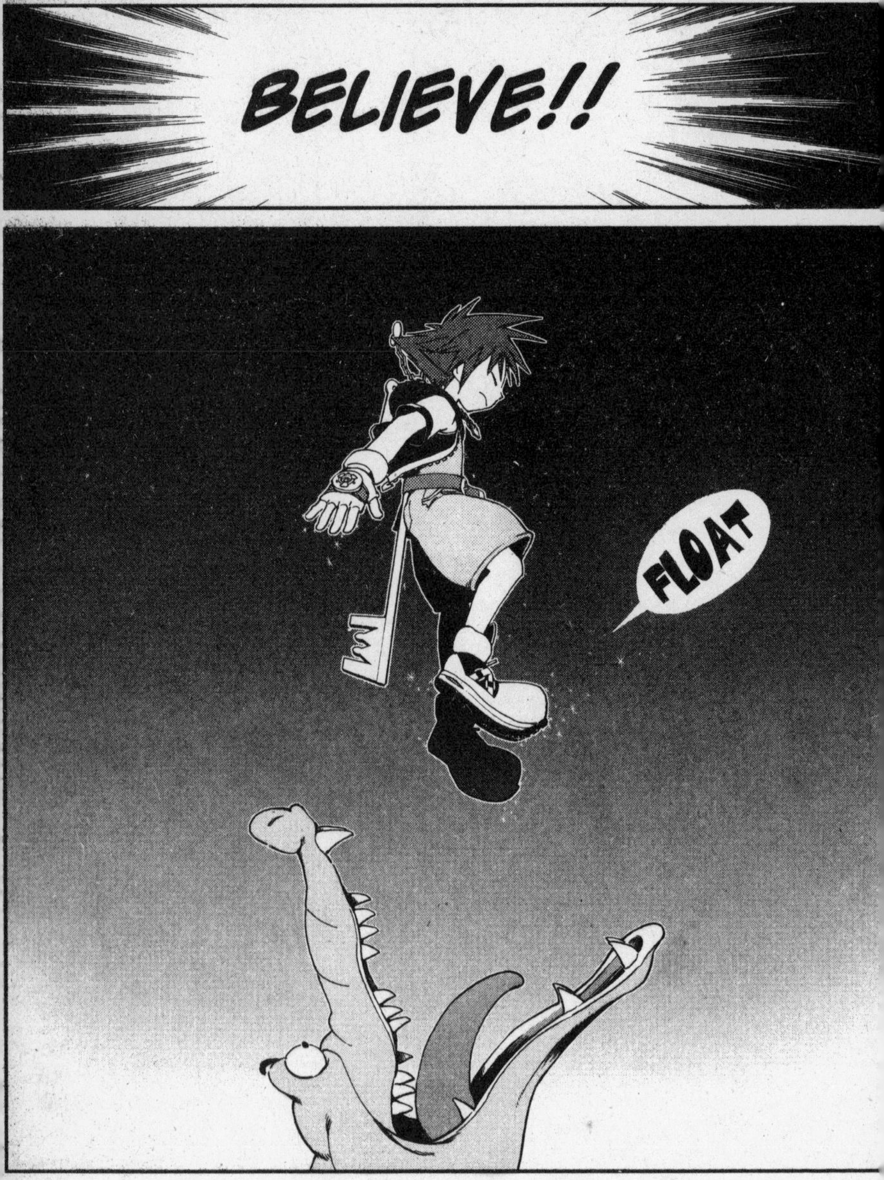
BELIEVE!!
FLOAT

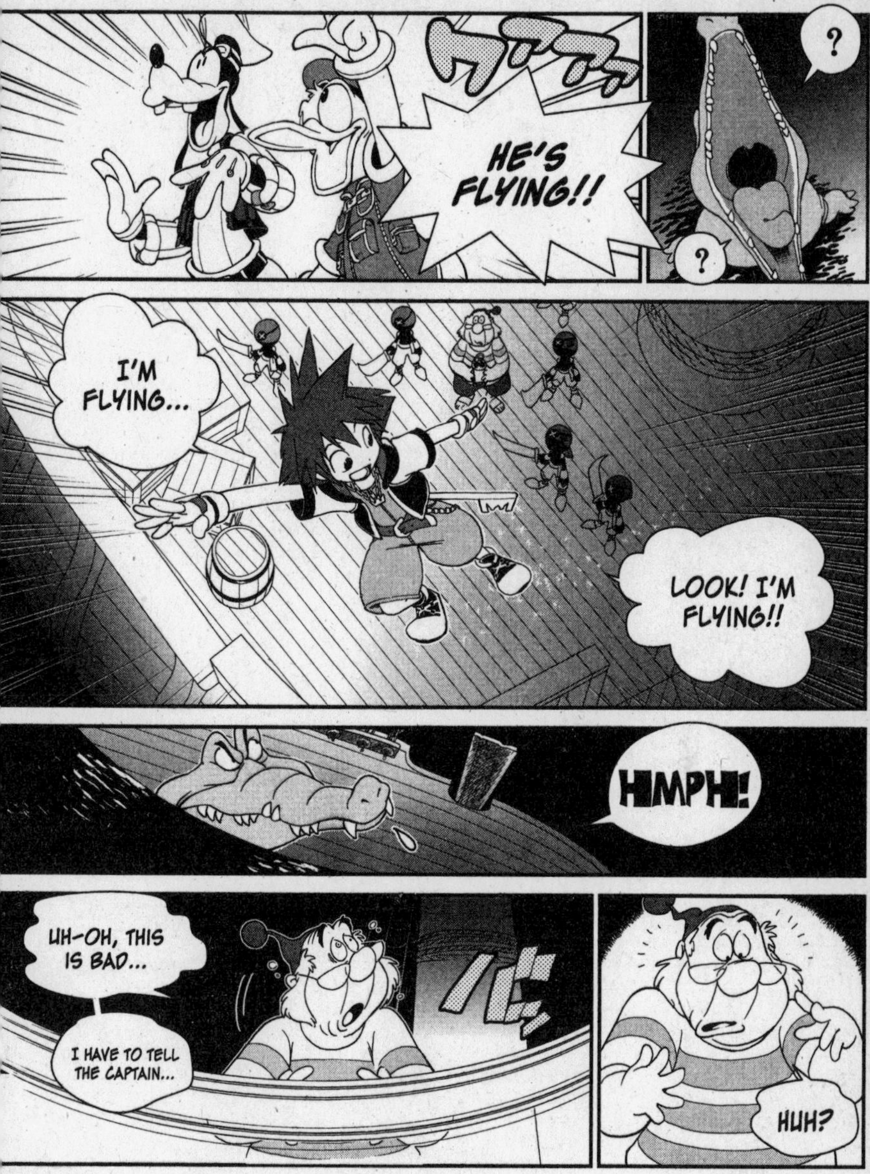
HE'S FLYING!!
?
?
I'M FLYING...
LOOK! I'M FLYING!!
HMPH!
UH-OH, THIS IS BAD...
I HAVE TO TELL THE CAPTAIN...
HUH?

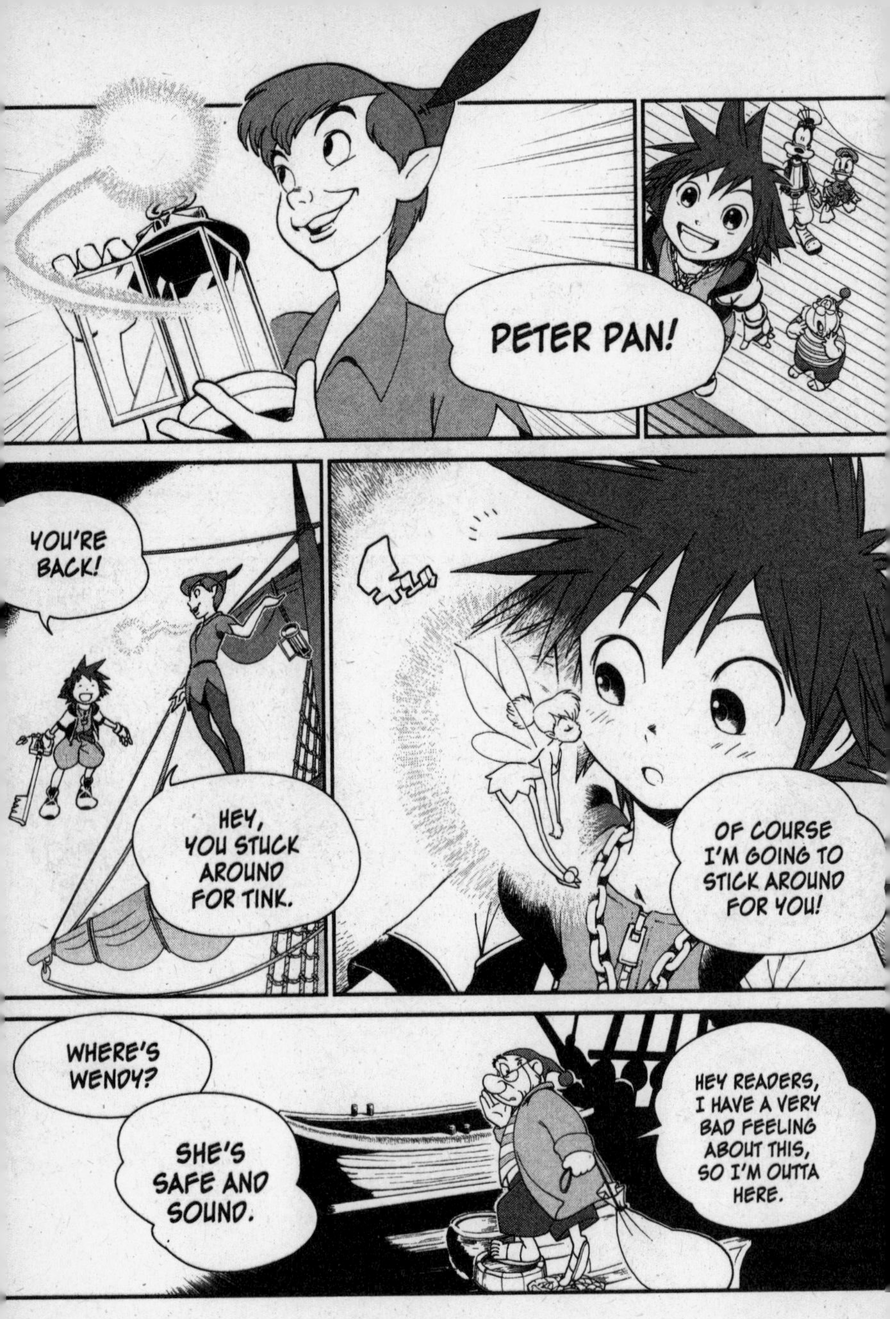
PETER PAN!
YOU'RE BACK!
HEY, YOU STUCK AROUND FOR TINK.
OF COURSE I'M GOING TO STICK AROUND FOR YOU!
WHERE'S WENDY?
SHE'S SAFE AND SOUND.
HEY READERS, I HAVE A VERY BAD FEELING ABOUT THIS, SO I'M OUTTA HERE.

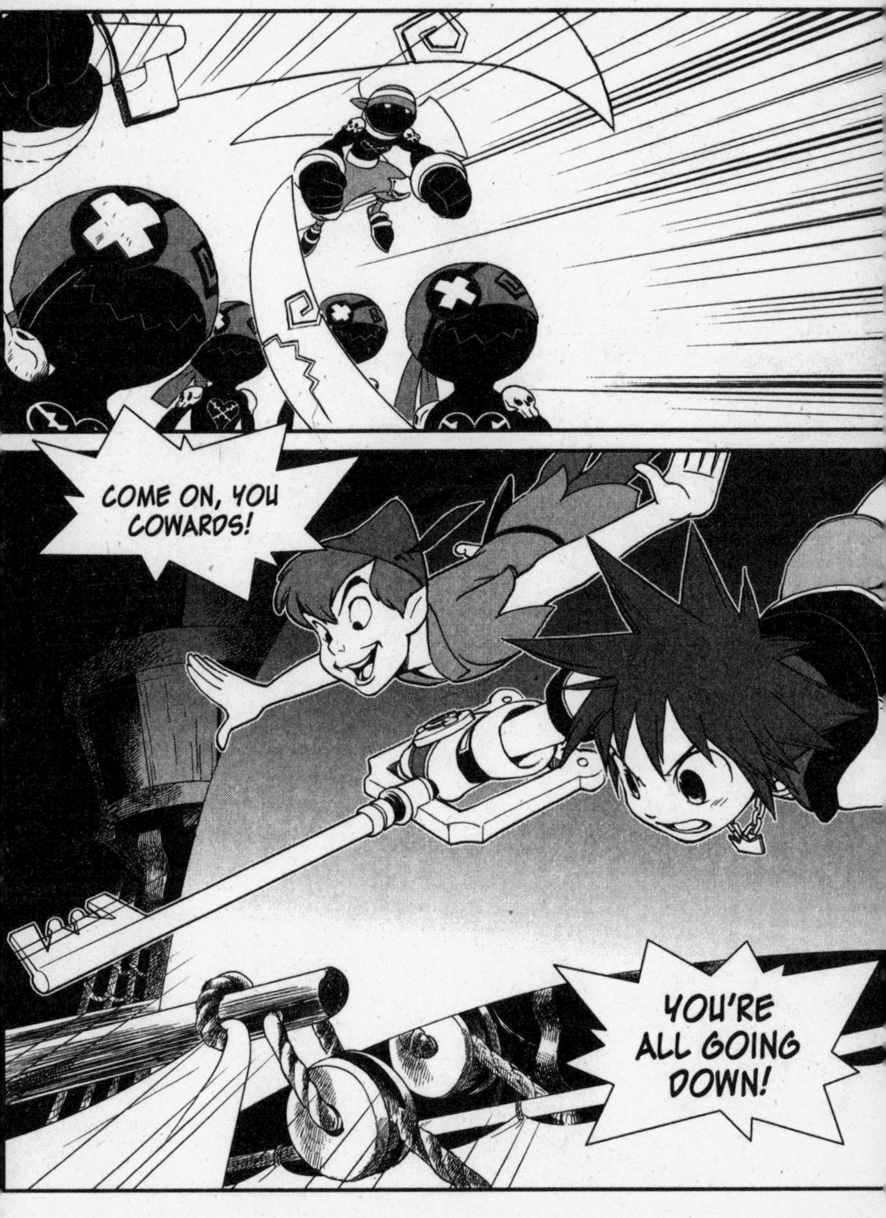
COME ON, YOU COWARDS!
YOU'RE ALL GOING DOWN!

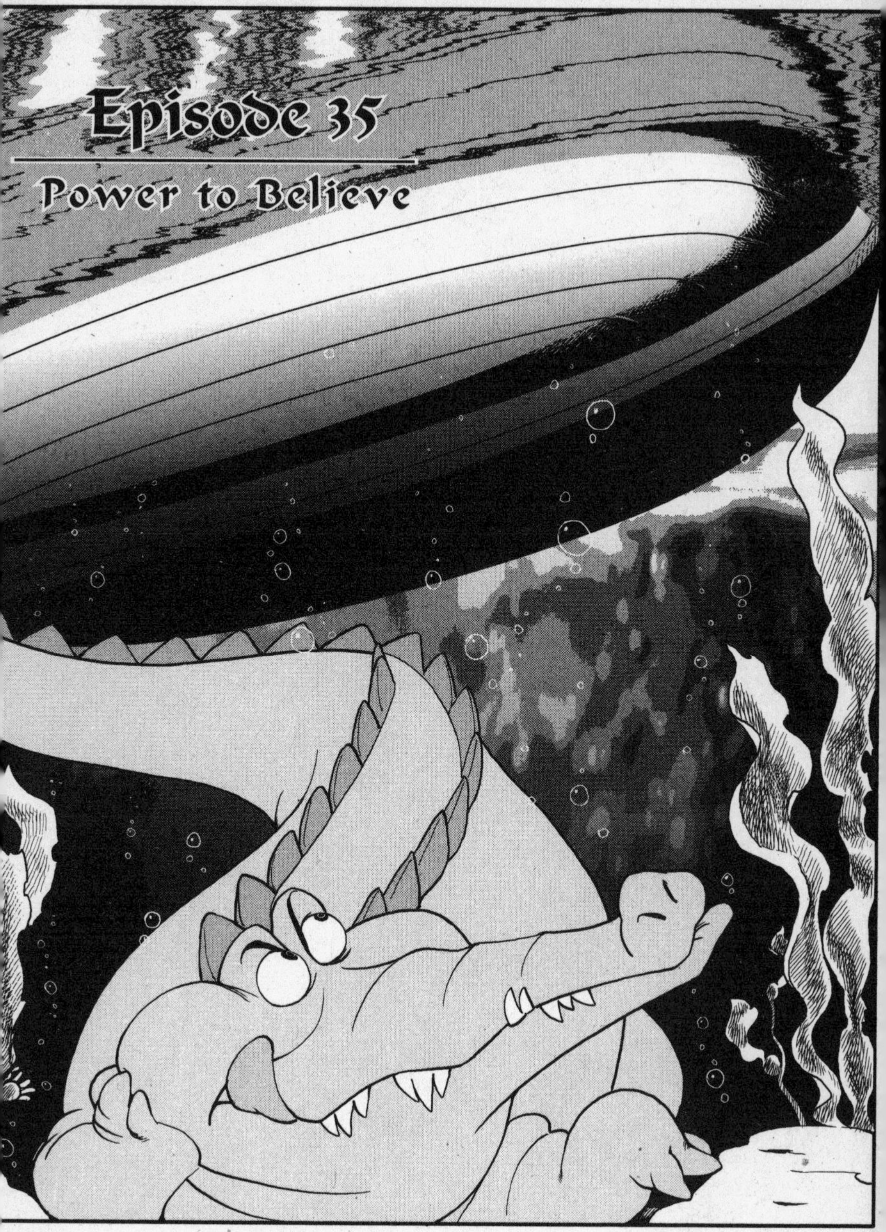
Episode 35
Power to Believe

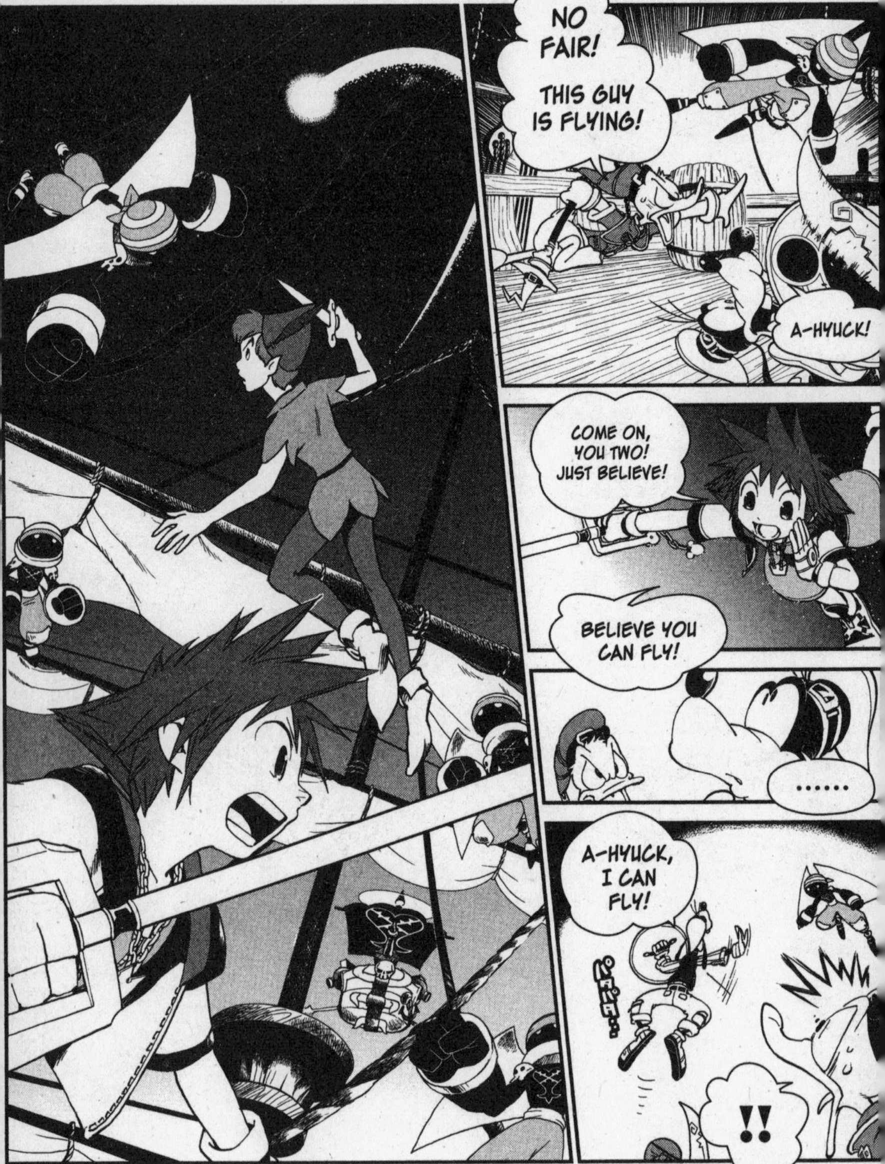
NO FAIR!
THIS GUY IS FLYING!
A-HYUCK!
COME ON, YOU TWO! JUST BELIEVE!
BELIEVE YOU CAN FLY!
......
A-HYUCK, I CAN FLY!
!!

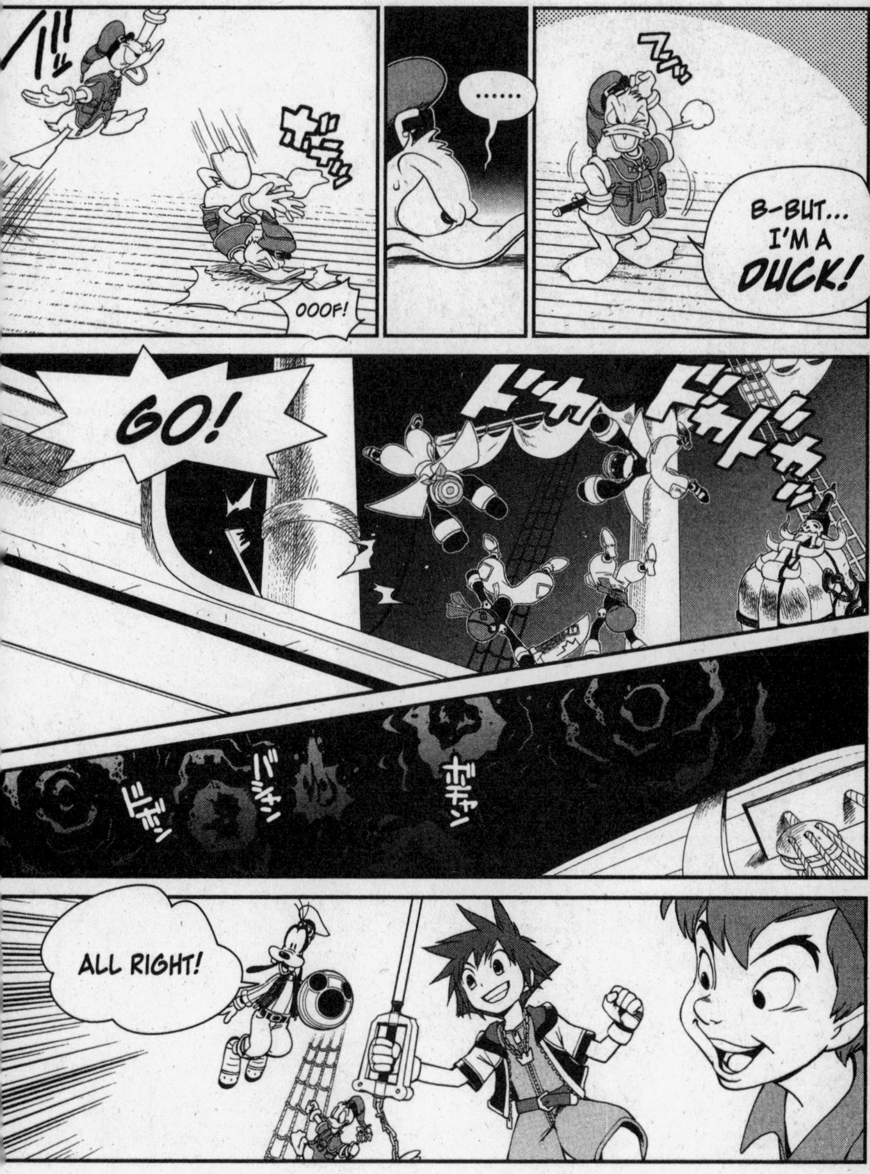

ブッ
ボテッ
OOOF!
.......
フンッ
B-BUT... I'M A DUCK!
GO!
ドカッ ドカドカッ
ジュボン
バシャン
ボチャン
ALL RIGHT!

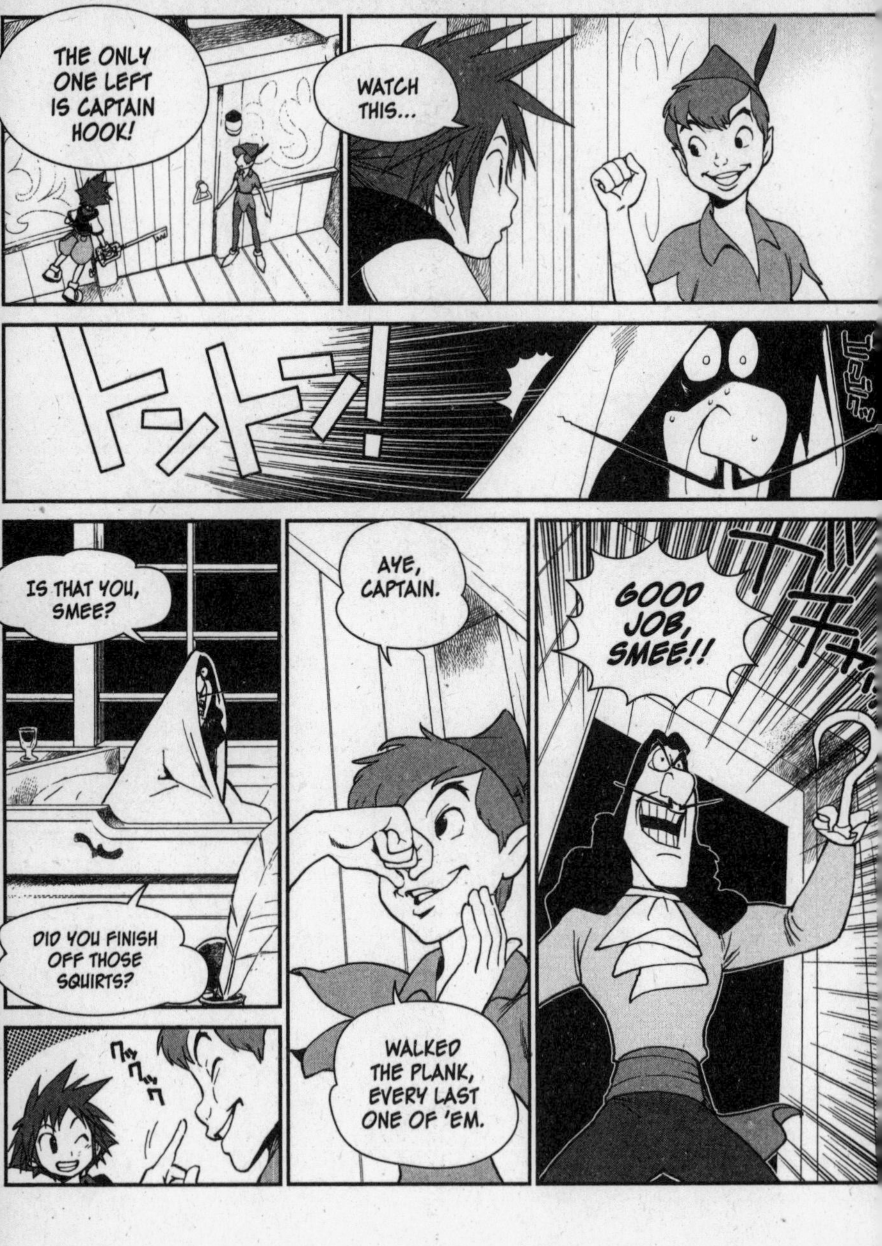
THE ONLY ONE LEFT IS CAPTAIN HOOK!
WATCH THIS...
トントン!
IS THAT YOU, SMEE?
DID YOU FINISH OFF THOSE SQUIRTS?
AYE, CAPTAIN.
WALKED THE PLANK, EVERY LAST ONE OF 'EM.
GOOD JOB, SMEE!!

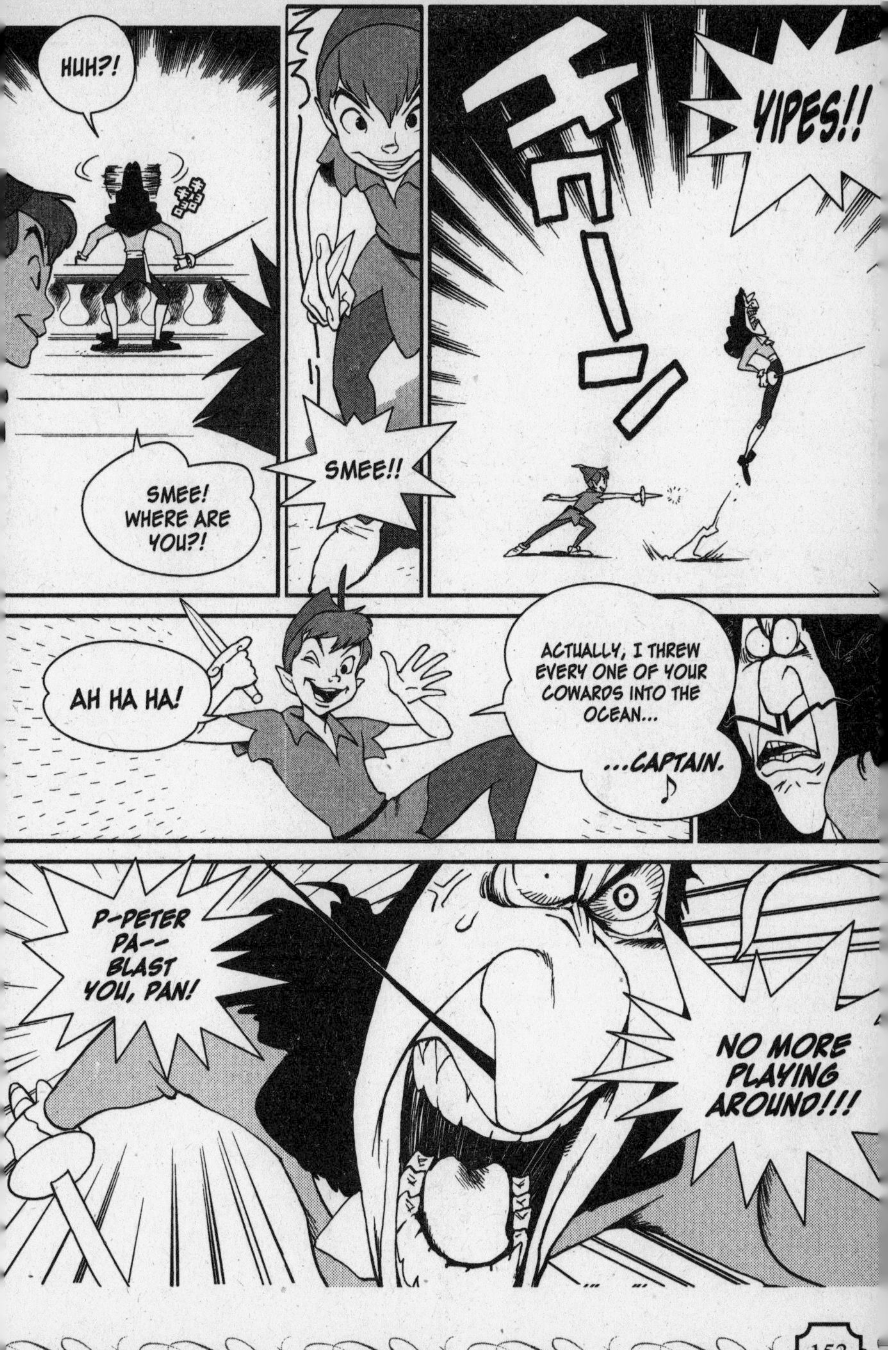
HUH?!
SMEE! WHERE ARE YOU?!
SMEE!!
YIPES!!
AH HA HA!
ACTUALLY, I THREW EVERY ONE OF YOUR COWARDS INTO THE OCEAN...
...CAPTAIN. ♪
P-PETER PA-- BLAST YOU, PAN!
NO MORE PLAYING AROUND!!!

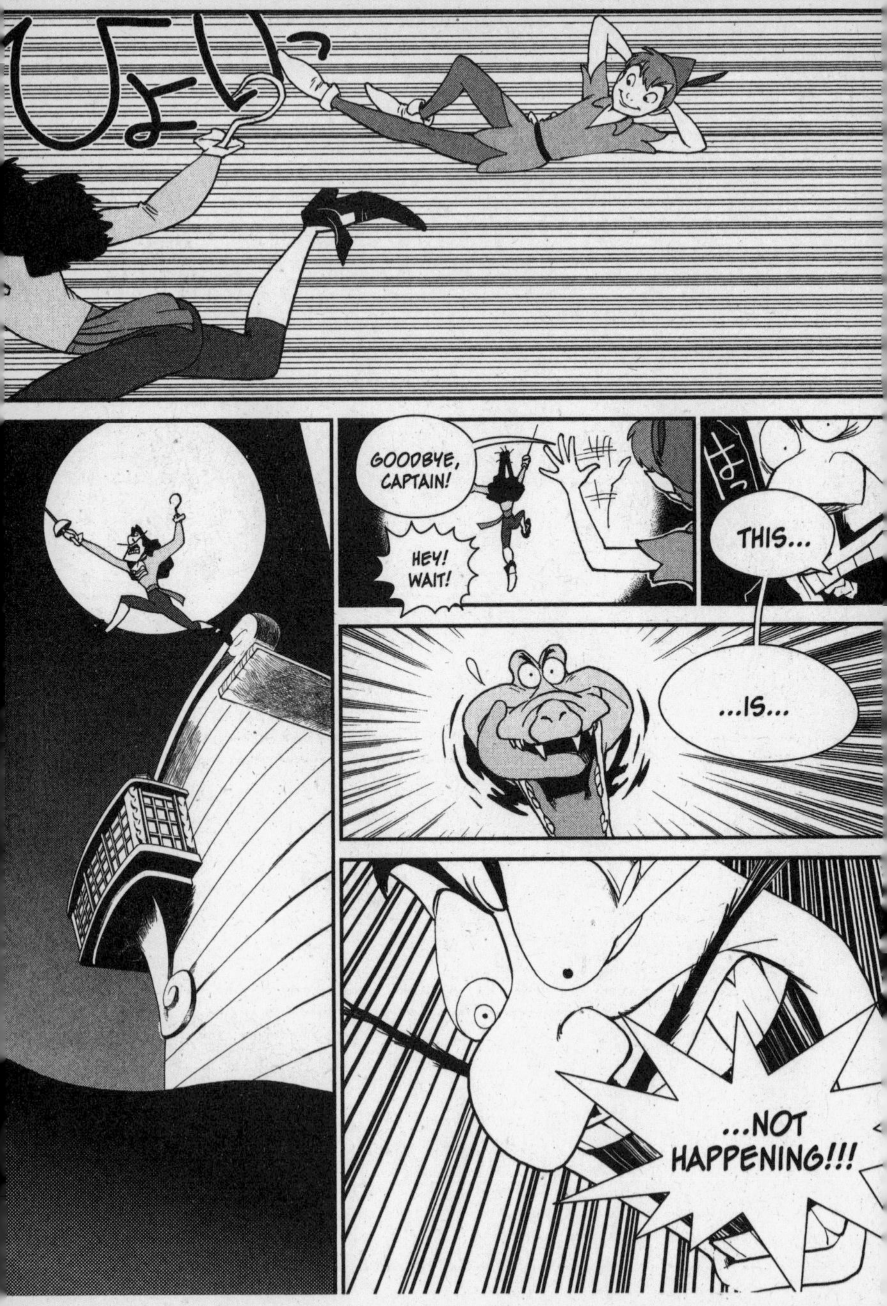
ひょいっ
GOODBYE, CAPTAIN!
HEY! WAIT!
THIS...
...IS...
...NOT HAPPENING!!!

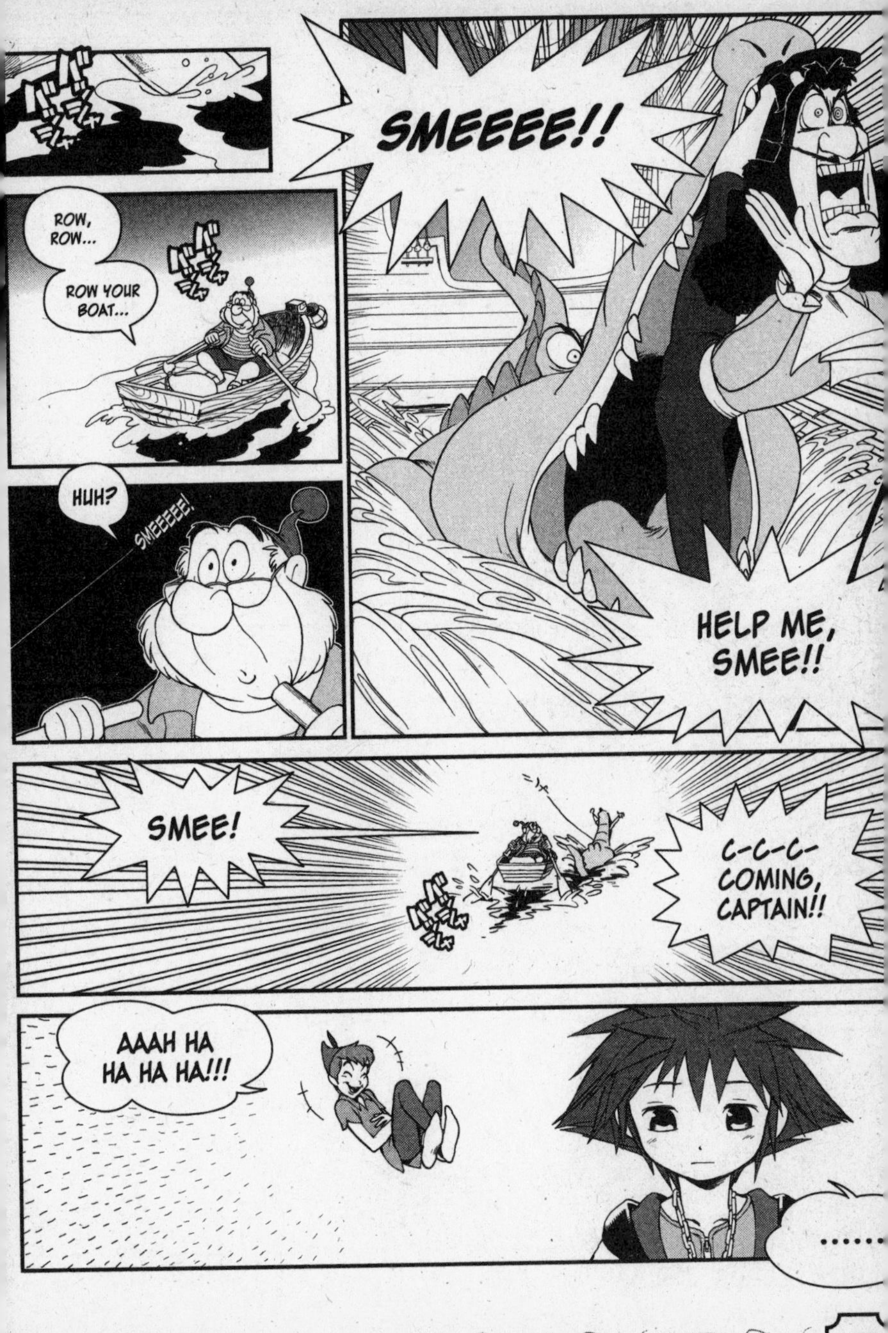
ROW, ROW...
ROW YOUR BOAT...
HUH?
SMEEEEE!
SMEEEE!!
HELP ME, SMEE!!
SMEE!
C-C-C-COMING, CAPTAIN!!
AAAH HA HA HA HA!!!
......

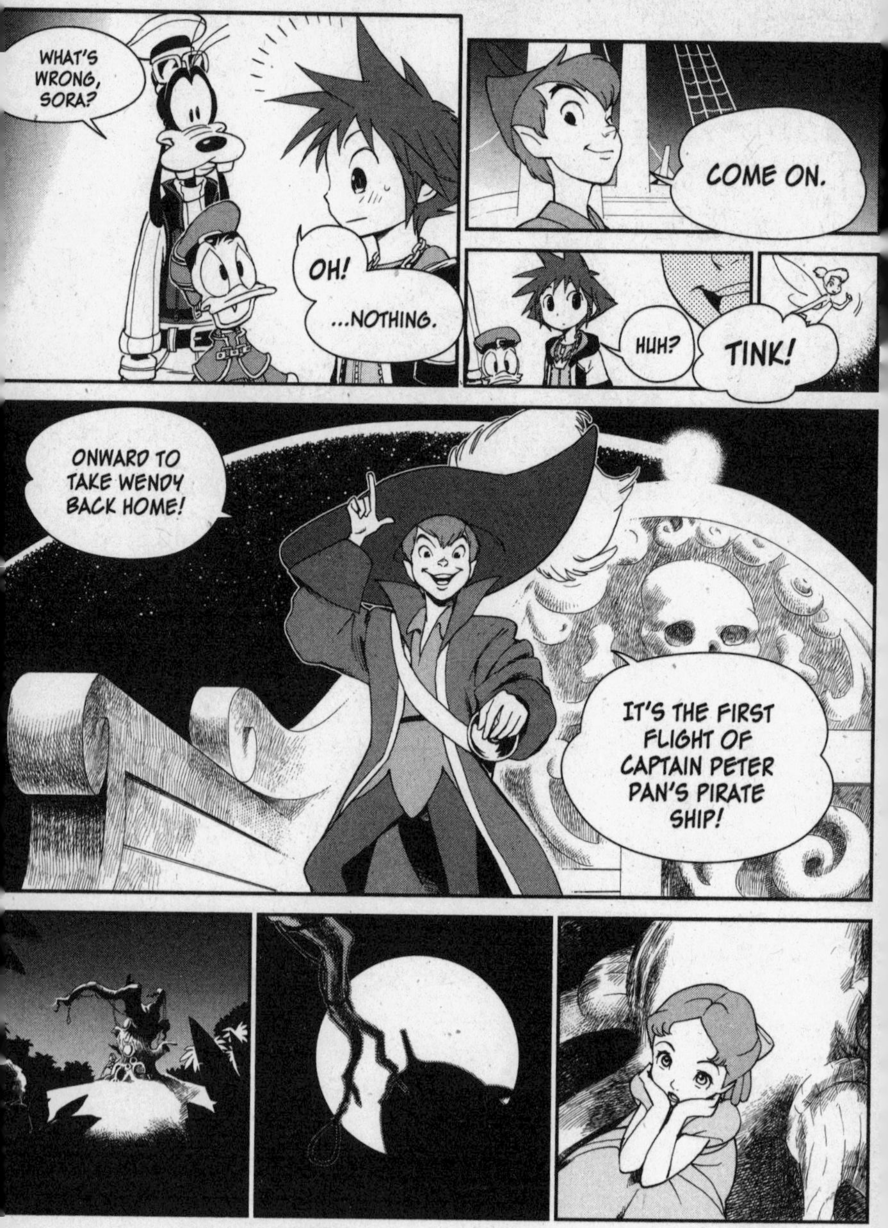
WHAT'S WRONG, SORA?
OH!
...NOTHING.
COME ON.
HUH?
TINK!
ONWARD TO TAKE WENDY BACK HOME!
IT'S THE FIRST FLIGHT OF CAPTAIN PETER PAN'S PIRATE SHIP!

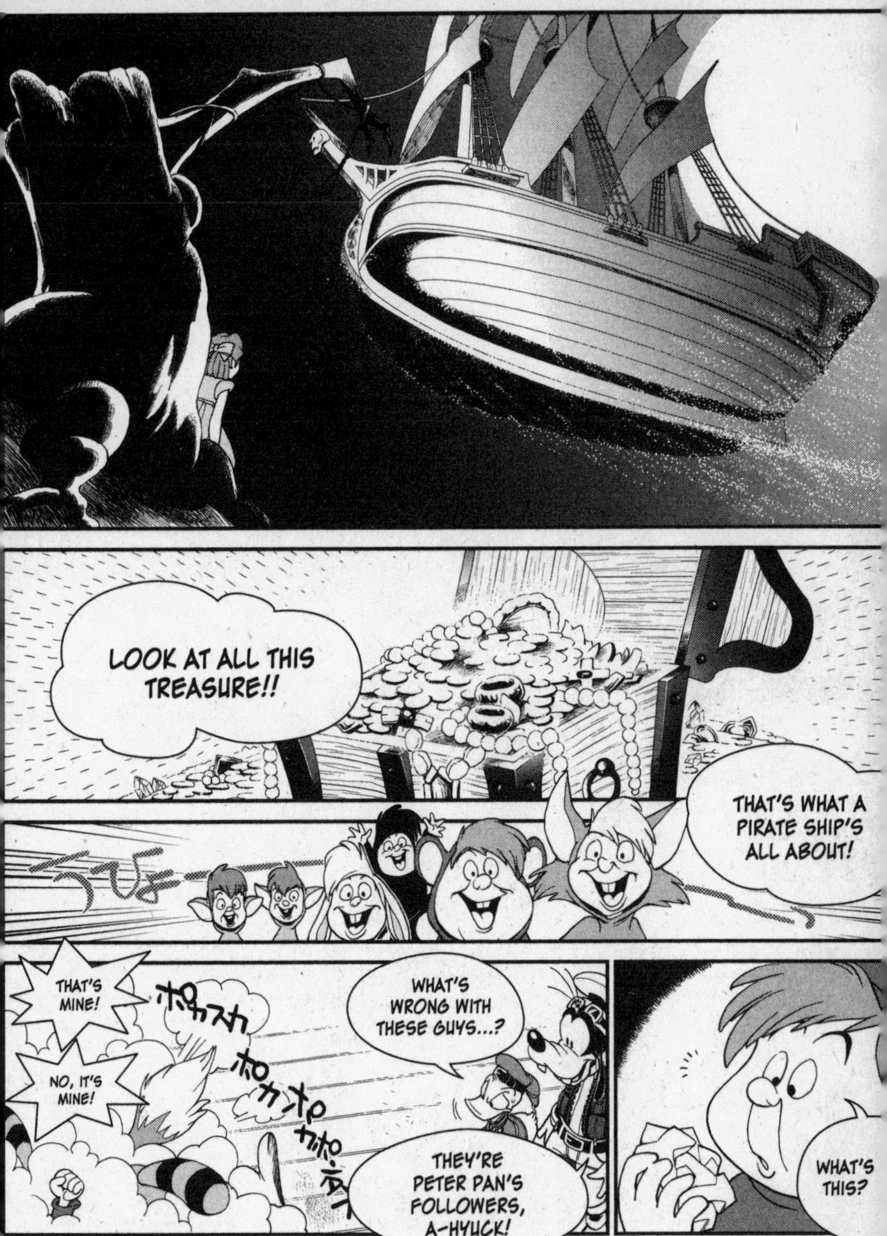
LOOK AT ALL THIS TREASURE!!
THAT'S WHAT A PIRATE SHIP'S ALL ABOUT!
THAT'S MINE!
NO, IT'S MINE!
WHAT'S WRONG WITH THESE GUYS...?
THEY'RE PETER PAN'S FOLLOWERS, A-HYUCK!
WHAT'S THIS?

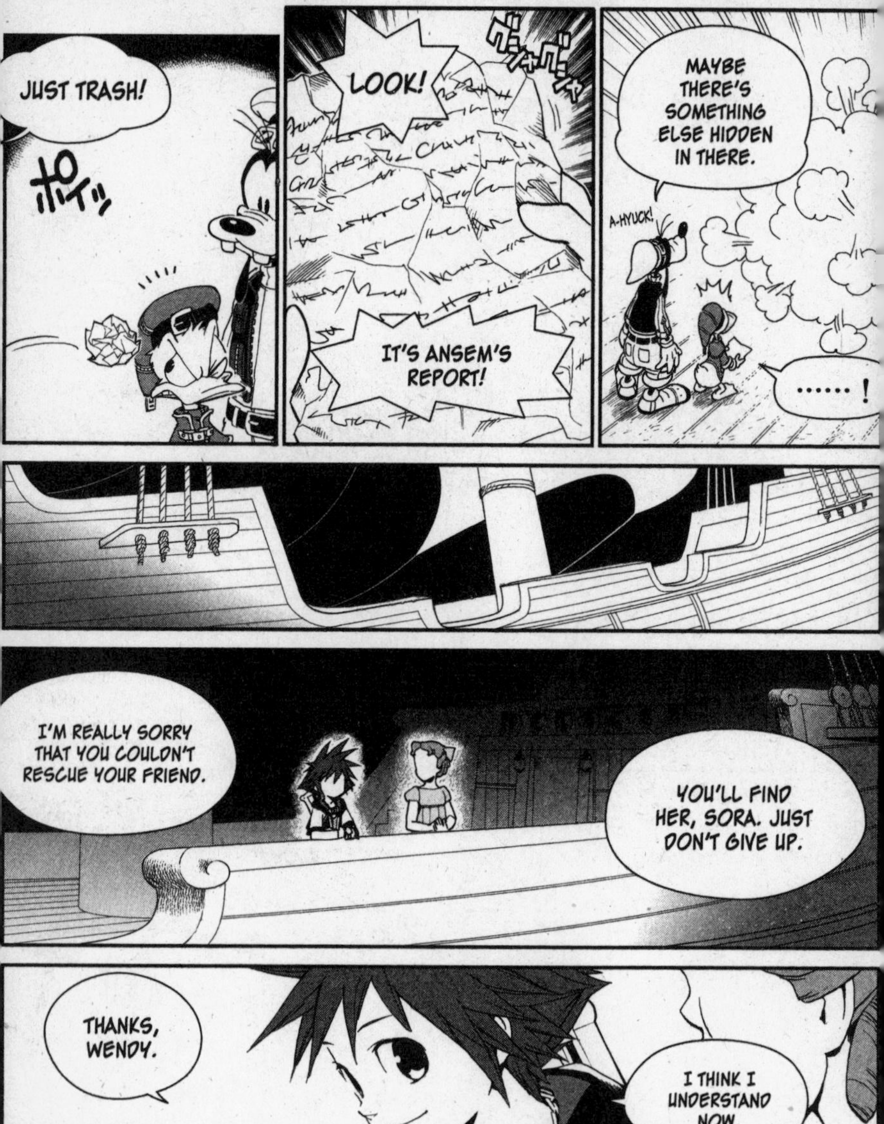
JUST TRASH!
LOOK!
IT'S ANSEM'S REPORT!
MAYBE THERE'S SOMETHING ELSE HIDDEN IN THERE.
A-HYUCK!
...... !
I'M REALLY SORRY THAT YOU COULDN'T RESCUE YOUR FRIEND.
YOU'LL FIND HER, SORA. JUST DON'T GIVE UP.
THANKS, WENDY.
I THINK I UNDERSTAND NOW.

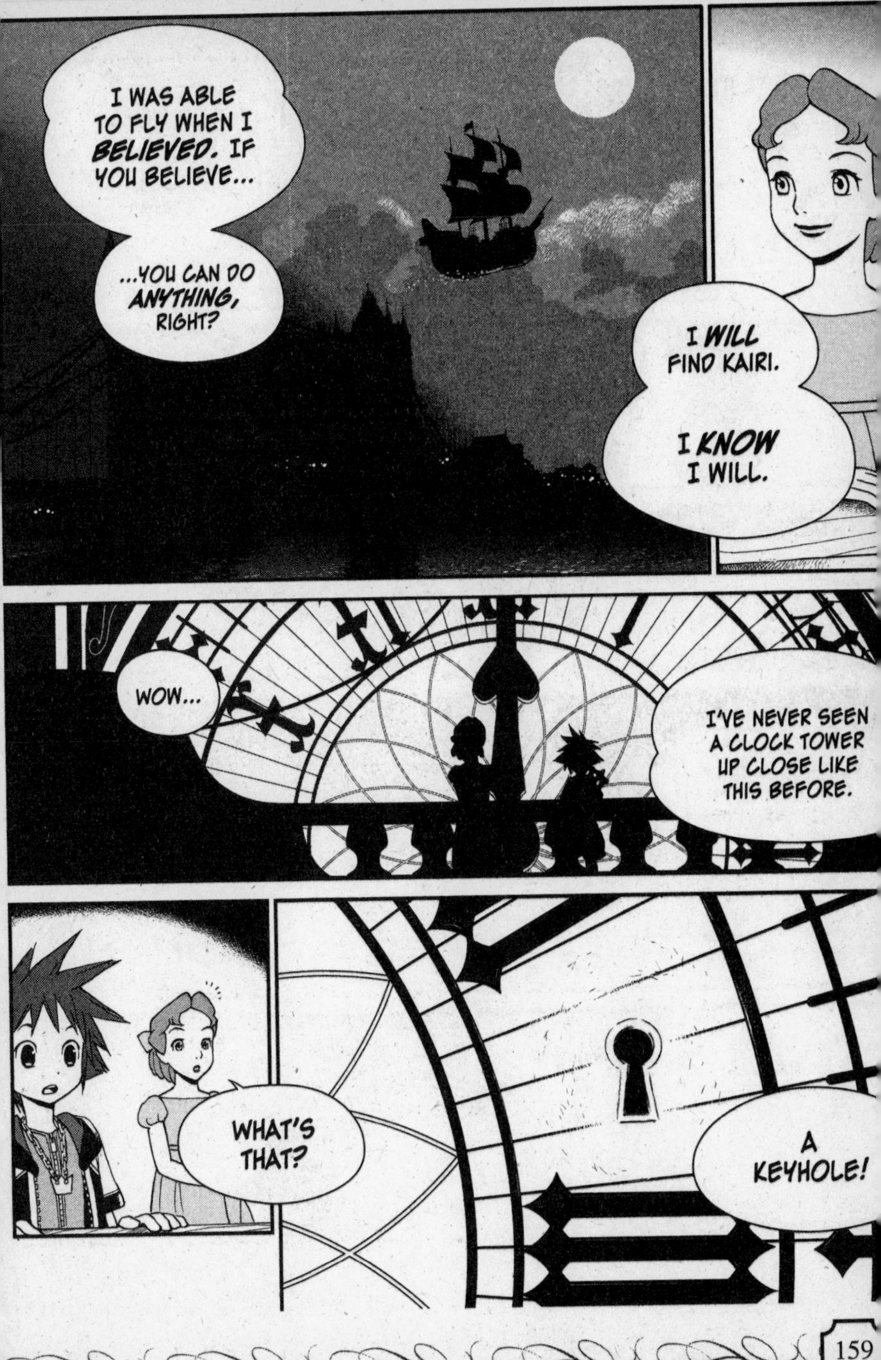
I WAS ABLE TO FLY WHEN I BELIEVED. IF YOU BELIEVE...
...YOU CAN DO ANYTHING, RIGHT?
I WILL FIND KAIRI.
I KNOW I WILL.
WOW...
I'VE NEVER SEEN A CLOCK TOWER UP CLOSE LIKE THIS BEFORE.
WHAT'S THAT?
A KEYHOLE!

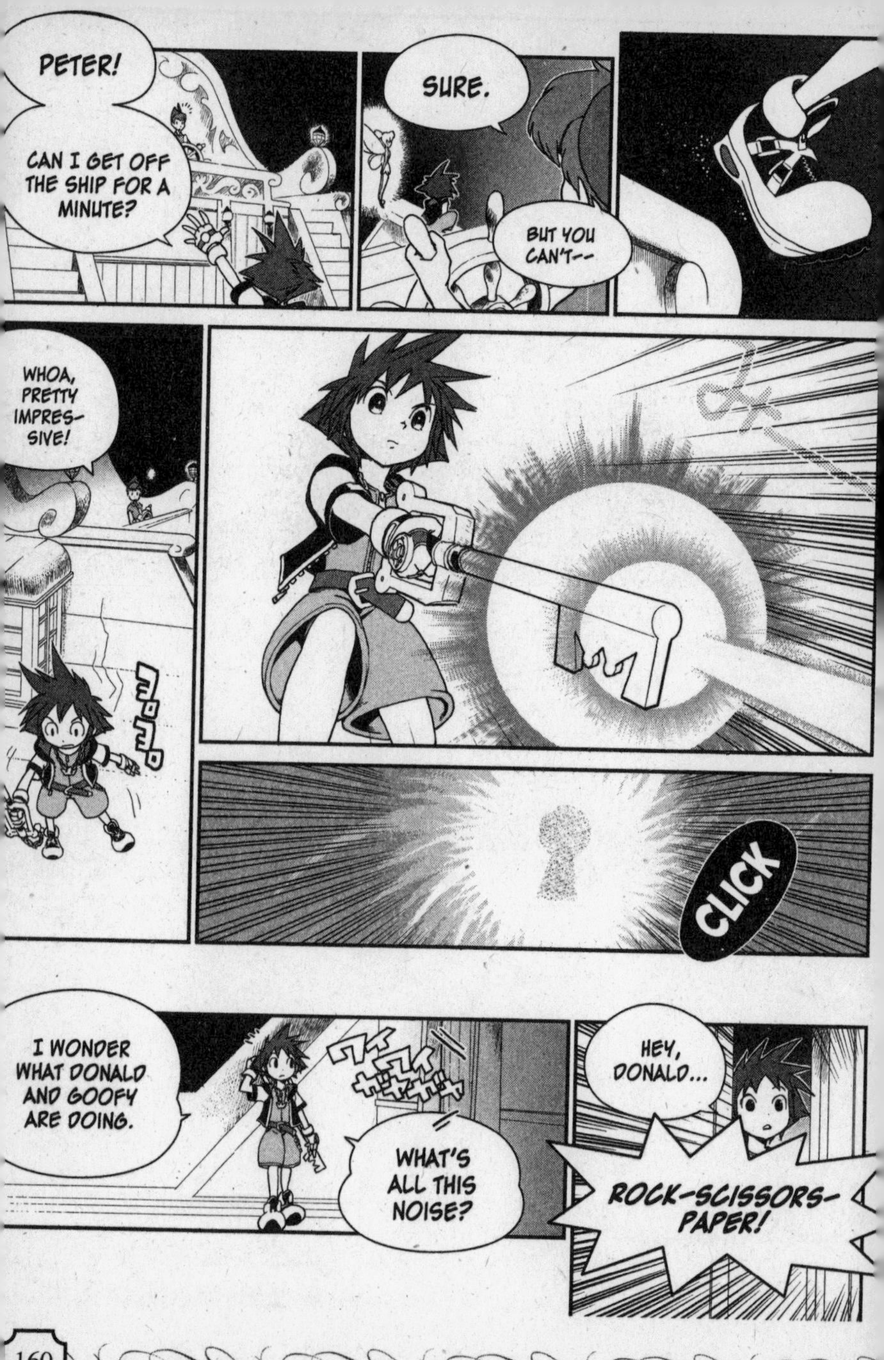
PETER!
CAN I GET OFF THE SHIP FOR A MINUTE?
SURE.
BUT YOU CAN'T--
WHOA, PRETTY IMPRES-SIVE!
CLICK
I WONDER WHAT DONALD AND GOOFY ARE DOING.
WHAT'S ALL THIS NOISE?
HEY, DONALD...
ROCK-SCISSORS-PAPER!

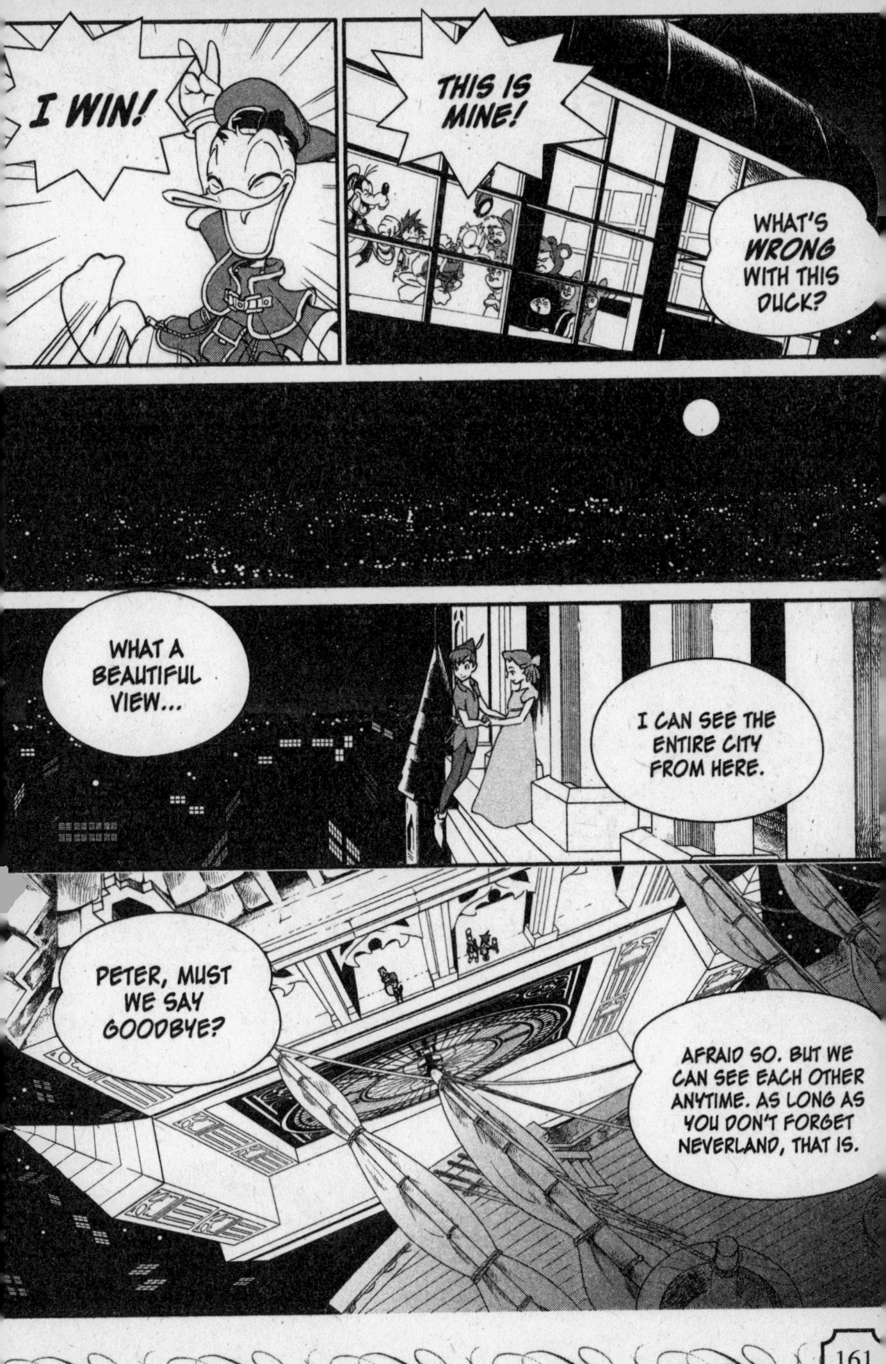
I WIN!
THIS IS MINE!
WHAT'S WRONG WITH THIS DUCK?
WHAT A BEAUTIFUL VIEW...
I CAN SEE THE ENTIRE CITY FROM HERE.
PETER, MUST WE SAY GOODBYE?
AFRAID SO. BUT WE CAN SEE EACH OTHER ANYTIME. AS LONG AS YOU DON'T FORGET NEVERLAND, THAT IS.

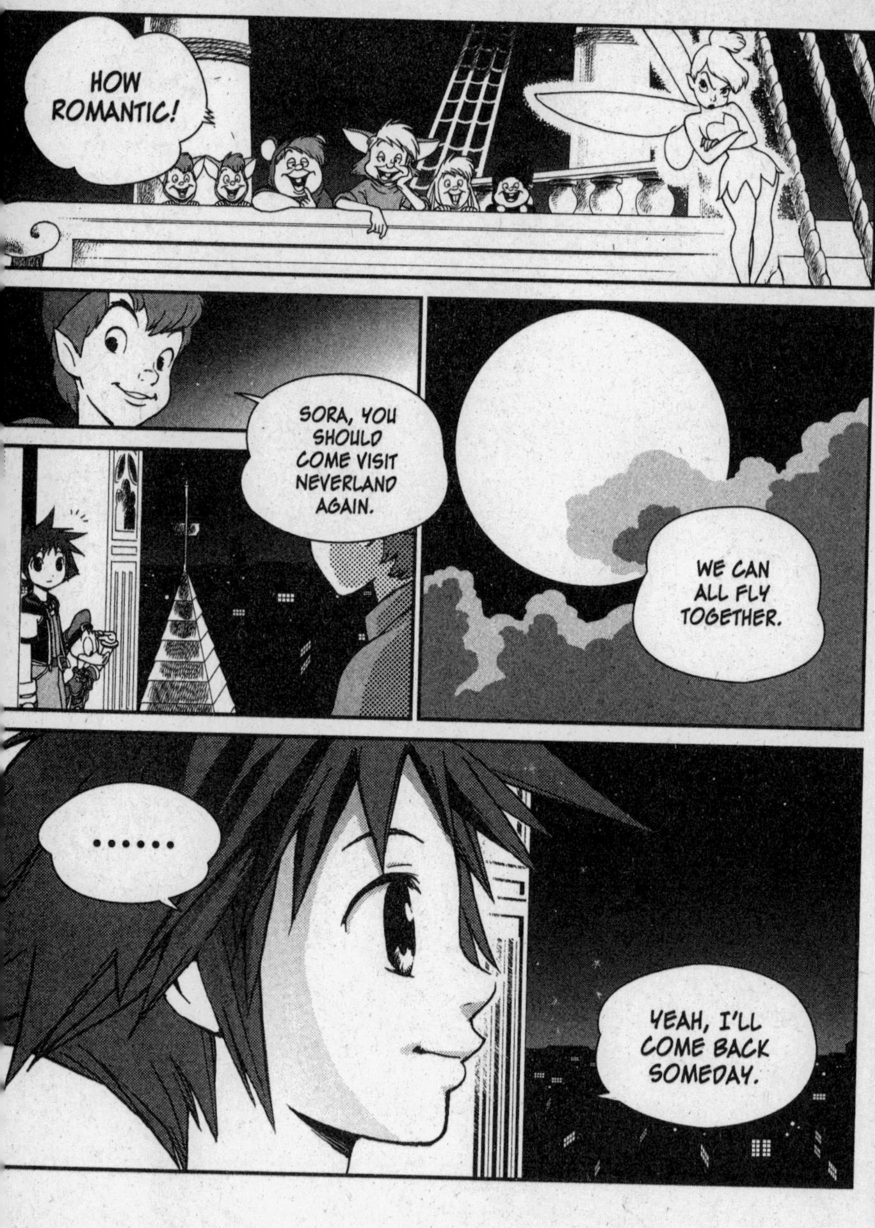
HOW ROMANTIC!
SORA, YOU SHOULD COME VISIT NEVERLAND AGAIN.
WE CAN ALL FLY TOGETHER.
......
YEAH, I'LL COME BACK SOMEDAY.

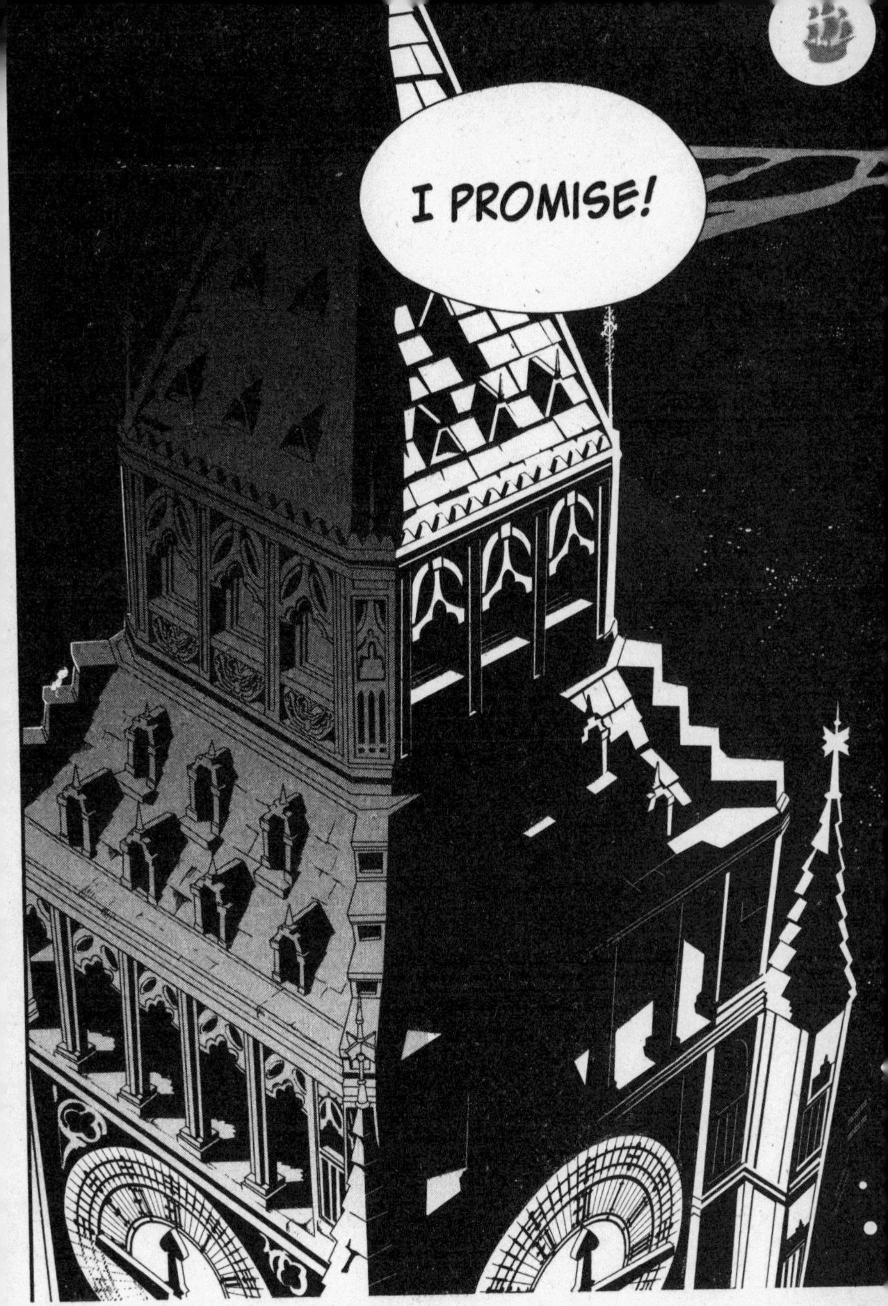
I PROMISE!

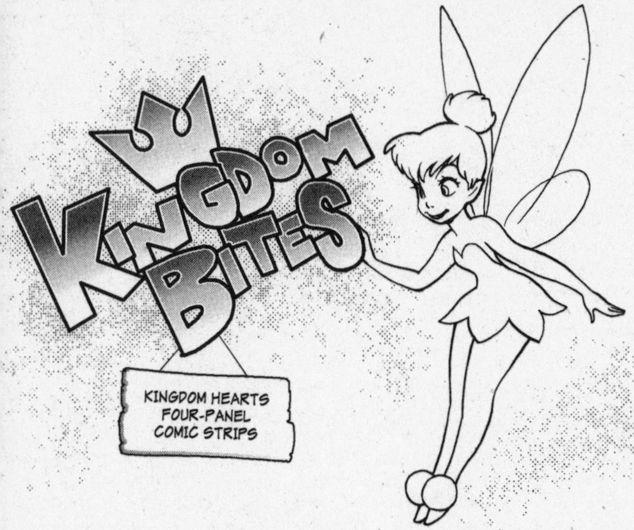

KINGDOM BITES
KINGDOM HEARTS FOUR-PANEL COMIC STRIPS


A Day in the Life of Captain Hook

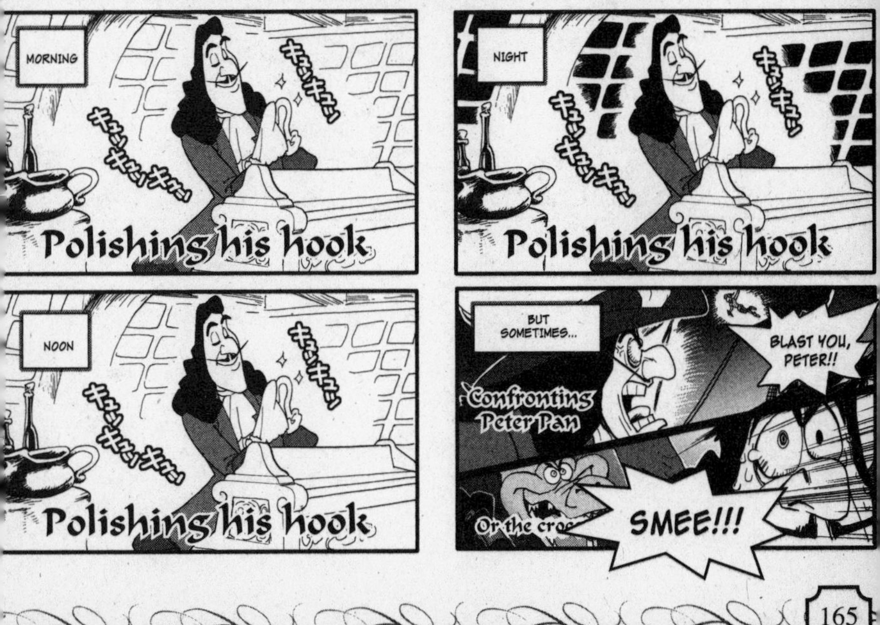

MORNING
キュッキュッ
キュッキュッキュッ
Polishing his hook
NOON
キュッキュッ
キュッキュッキュッ
Polishing his hook
NIGHT
キュッキュッ
キュッキュッキュッ
Polishing his hook
BUT SOMETIMES...
Confronting Peter Pan
BLAST YOU, PETER!!
Or the cro
SMEE!!!

## Farewell Gift

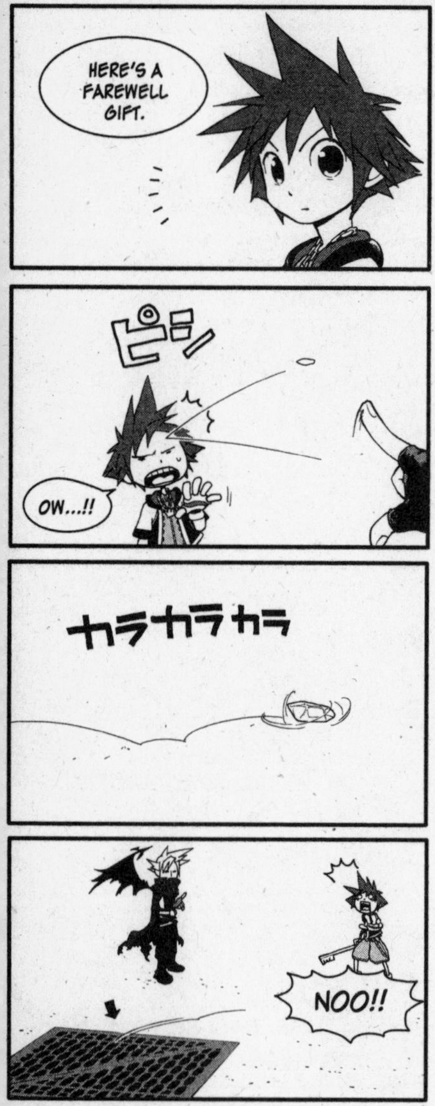
HERE'S A FAREWELL GIFT.
ピシ
OW...!!
カラカラカラ
NOO!!

## Dinner

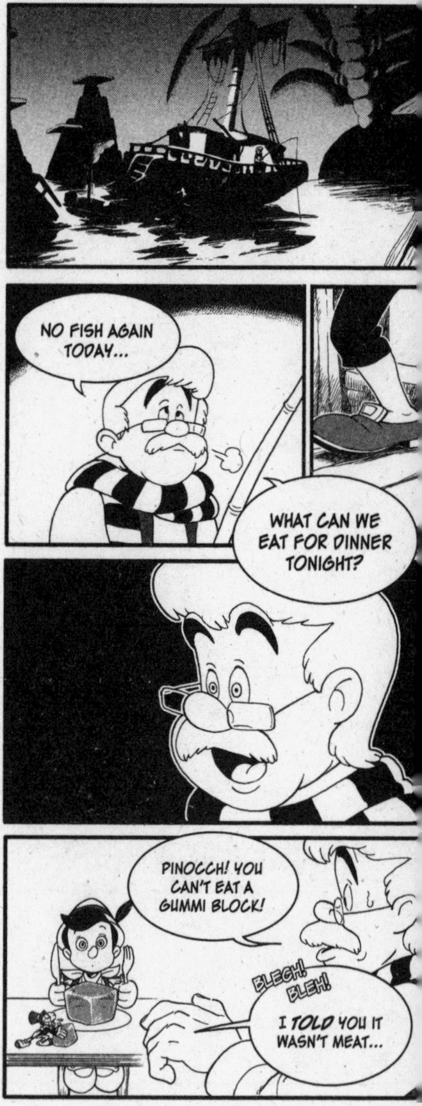
NO FISH AGAIN TODAY...
WHAT CAN WE EAT FOR DINNER TONIGHT?
PINOCCH! YOU CAN'T EAT A GUMMI BLOCK!
BLEGH! BLEH!
I TOLD YOU IT WASN'T MEAT...

## Present

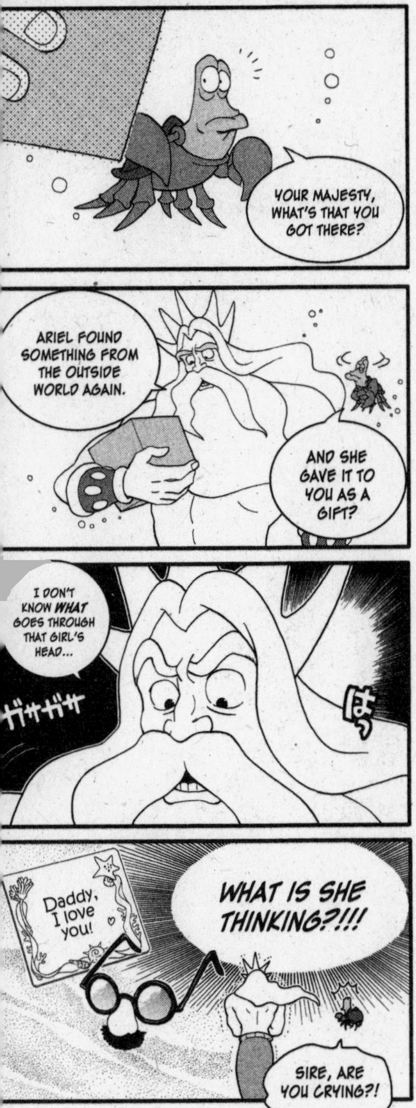
YOUR MAJESTY, WHAT'S THAT YOU GOT THERE?
ARIEL FOUND SOMETHING FROM THE OUTSIDE WORLD AGAIN.
AND SHE GAVE IT TO YOU AS A GIFT?
I DON'T KNOW *WHAT* GOES THROUGH THAT GIRL'S HEAD...
ガサガサ
はっ
Daddy, I love you!
WHAT IS SHE THINKING?!!!
SIRE, ARE YOU CRYING?!

## Ansem Memo

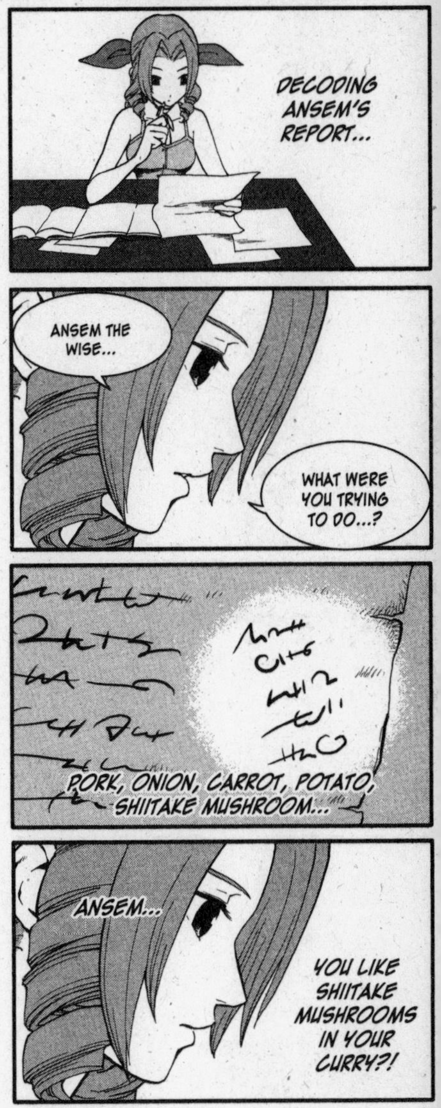
DECODING ANSEM'S REPORT...
ANSEM THE WISE...
WHAT WERE YOU TRYING TO DO...?
PORK, ONION, CARROT, POTATO, SHIITAKE MUSHROOM...
ANSEM...
YOU LIKE SHIITAKE MUSHROOMS IN YOUR CURRY?!

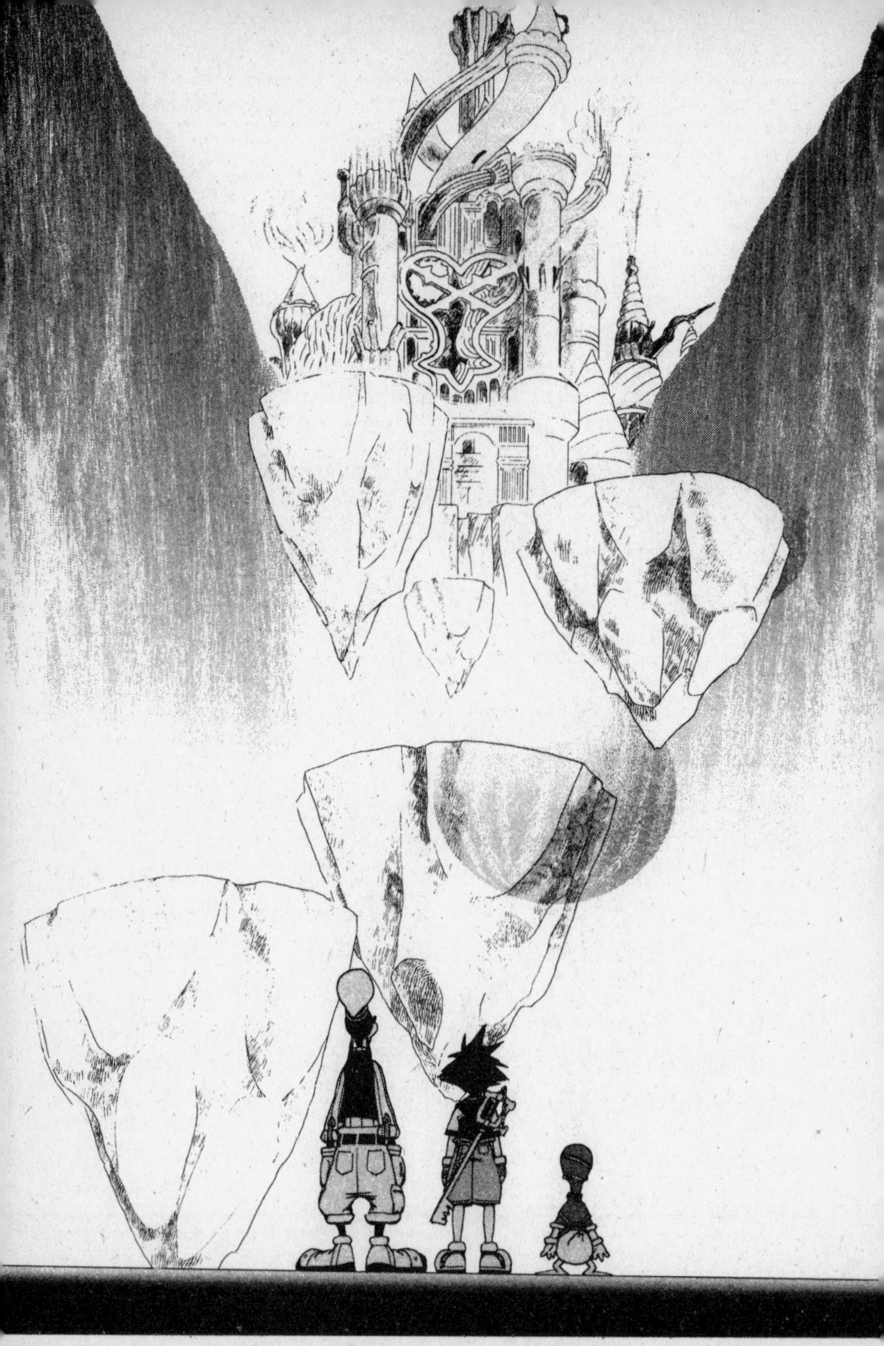

# IN THE NEXT VOLUME OF

DISNEY SQUARESOFT

# KINGDOM HEARTS

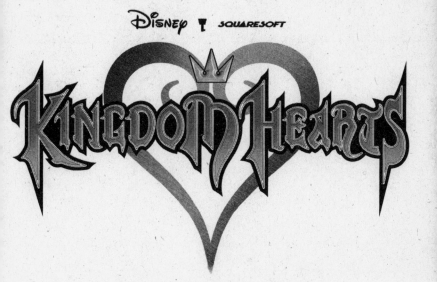

The saga comes to a close as Sora, Donald and Goofy are forced to choose between their duty and their friendship to each other. The evil truth becomes apparent as our heroes discover who is really behind the Heartless and the Darkness. Each must follow their own heart if they are to succeed and defeat the growing Heartless menace. But the choice will not be an easy one!

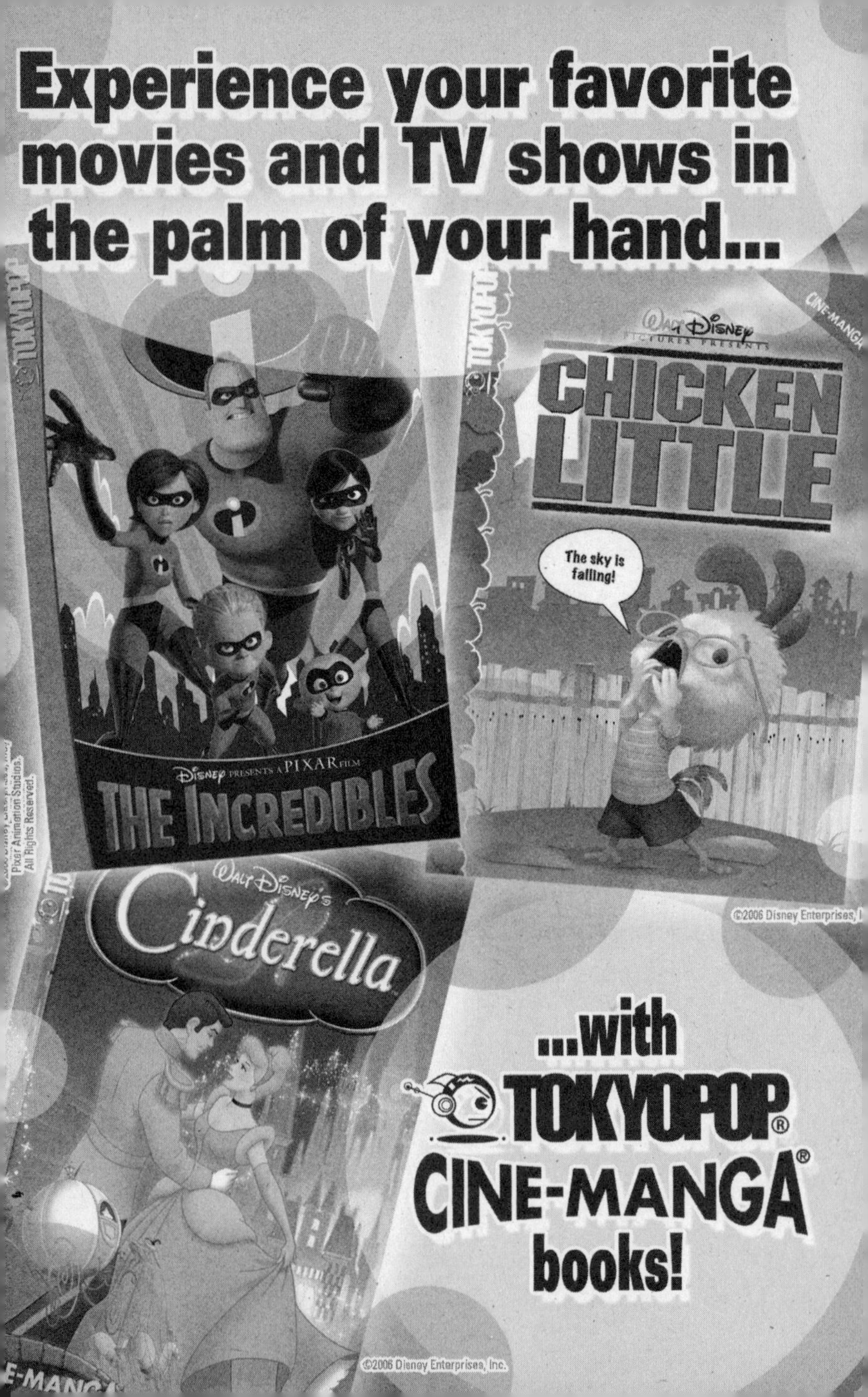
Experience your favorite movies and TV shows in the palm of your hand...
TOKYOPOP
DISNEY PRESENTS A PIXAR FILM
THE INCREDIBLES
Pixar Animation Studios.
All Rights Reserved.
TOKYOPOP
CINE-MANGA
WALT DISNEY PICTURES PRESENTS
CHICKEN LITTLE
The sky is falling!
©2006 Disney Enterprises, I
WALT DISNEY'S
Cinderella
©2006 Disney Enterprises, Inc.
...with
TOKYOPOP®
CINE-MANGA®
books!

Bonus Lab Experiment

# Kat & mouse™

**1** teacher torture

Story: Alex de Campi
Art: Federica Manfredi

SPECIAL LOW MANGA PRICE: $5.99

When Kat moves to a posh private school, things seem perfect--that is, until a clique of rich, popular kids frame Kat's science teacher dad for stealing school property. Can Kat and her new friend, rebellious computer nerd Mouse, prove who the real culprits are before Kat's dad loses his job?

Y YOUTH AGE 10+

PREVIEW THE MANGA FOR FREE: WWW.TOKYOPOP.COM/MANGAONLINE

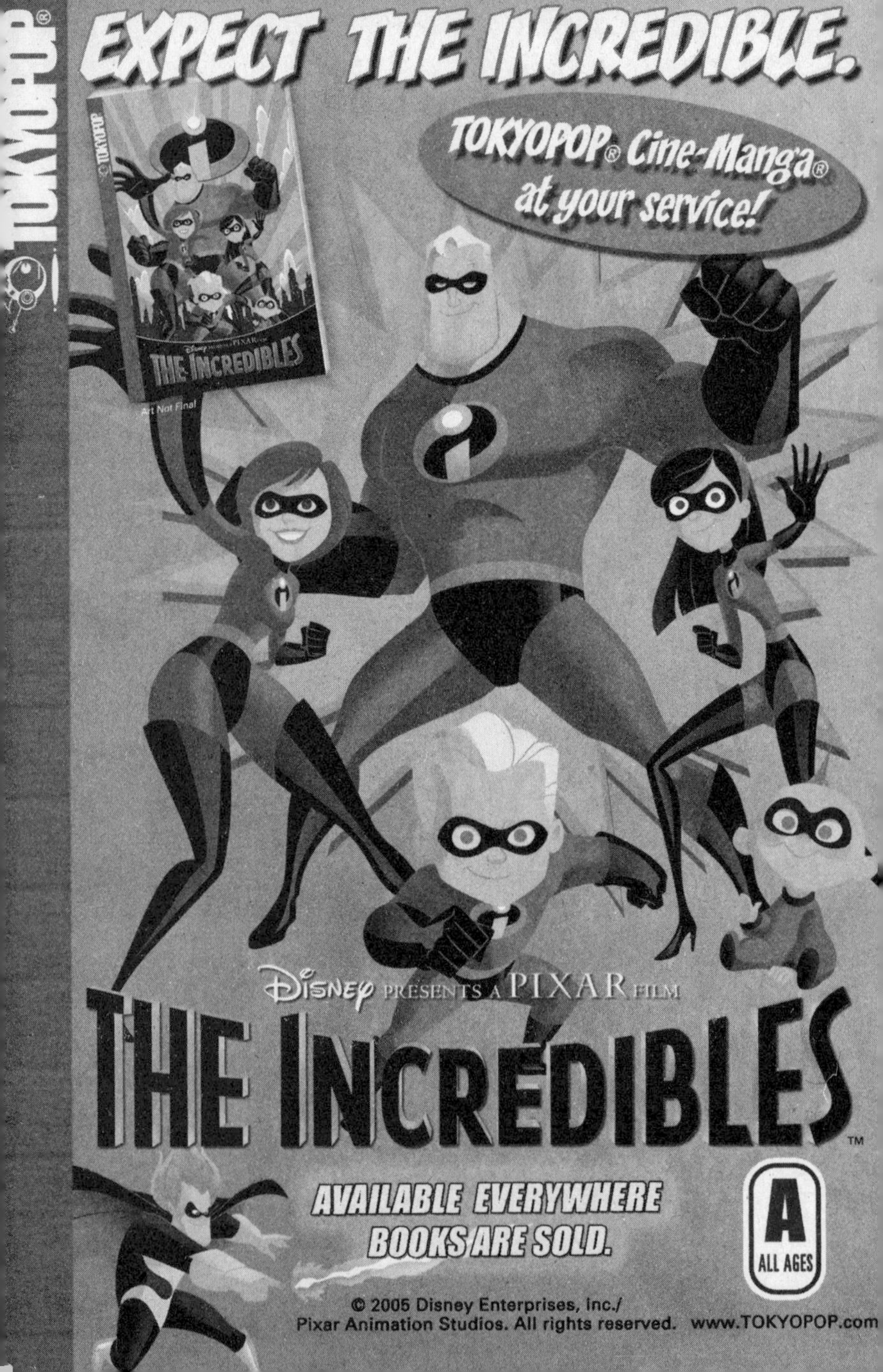
TOKYOPOP®
EXPECT THE INCREDIBLE.
TOKYOPOP® Cine-Manga®
at your service!
Art Not Final
DISNEY PRESENTS A PIXAR FILM
THE INCREDIBLES™
AVAILABLE EVERYWHERE
BOOKS ARE SOLD.
A
ALL AGES
© 2005 Disney Enterprises, Inc./
Pixar Animation Studios. All rights reserved.
www.TOKYOPOP.com

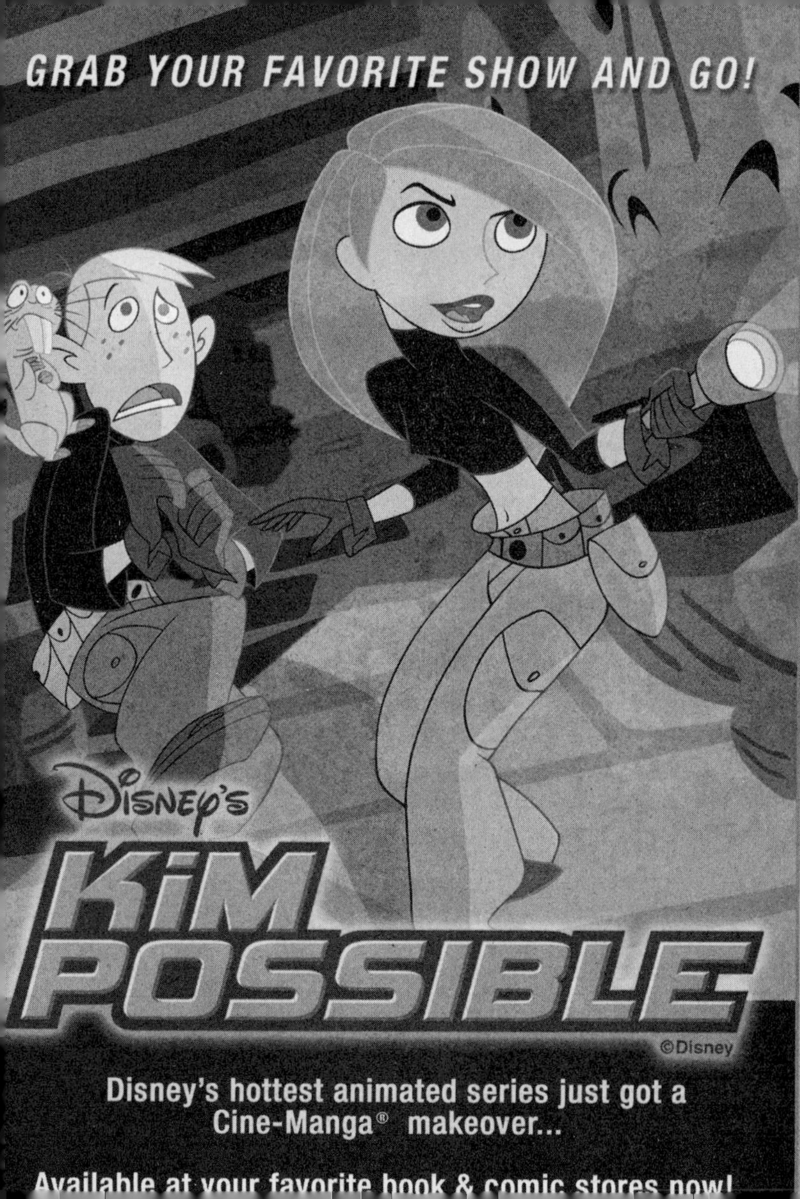
GRAB YOUR FAVORITE SHOW AND GO!
TOKYOPOP®
DISNEY'S
KIM POSSIBLE
©Disney
Disney's hottest animated series just got a Cine-Manga® makeover...
Available at your favorite book & comic stores now!

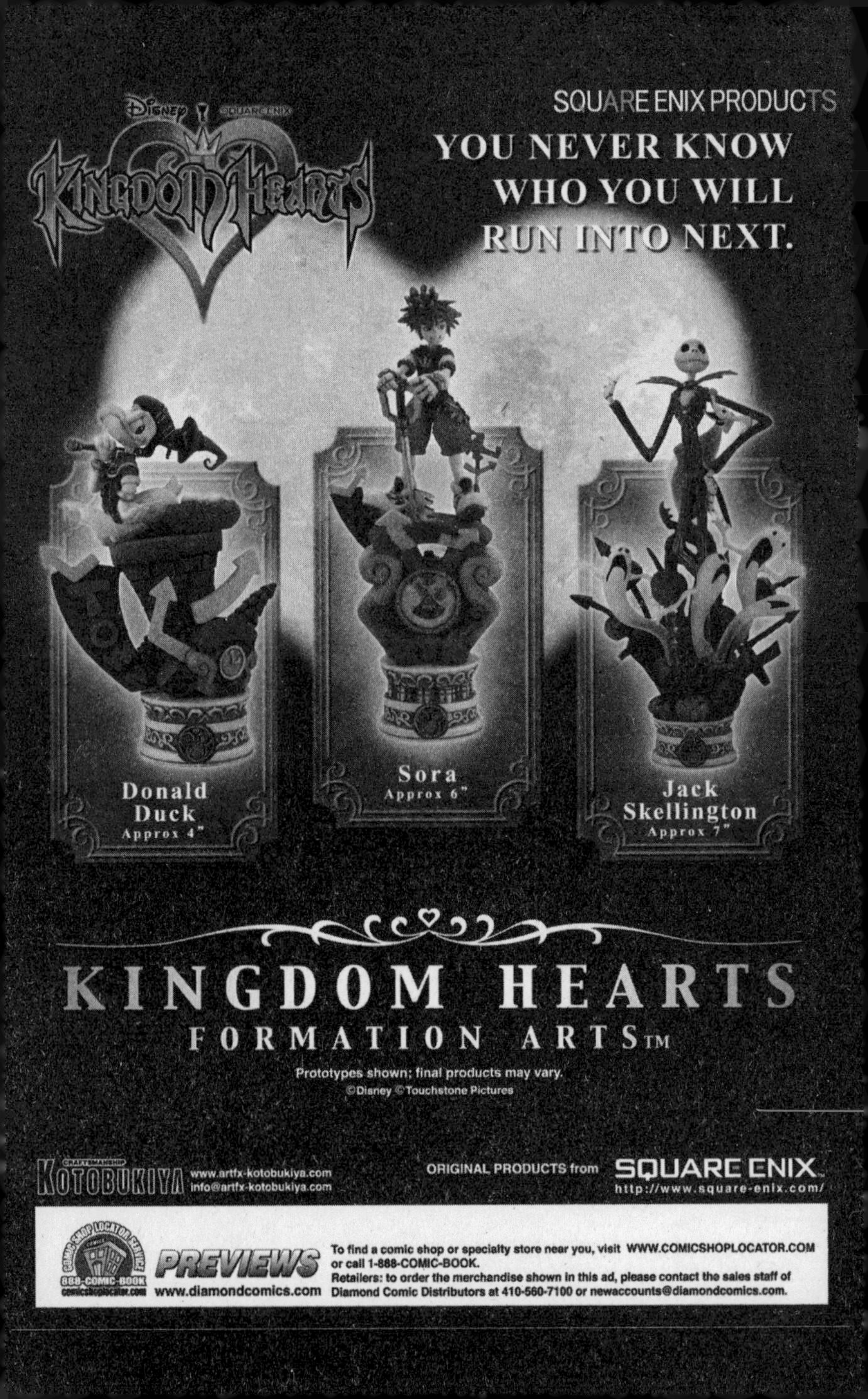